M. E Ducas

WRONGLY HANGED?

BY

WILLIAM BEADLE

First Published 1995

Copyright © William Beadle

ISBN 0952448920

Typeset by: In-House Typesetting
P.O. Box 227
Brighton
Sussex
BN2 3GL

Printed & Bound by:
Redwood Books
Trowbridge
Wiltshire

Published by: Wat Tyler Books
P.O. Box 17
Dagenham
Essex
RM10 8XF

IN MEMORIAM, MY MOTHER,

ALICE ELIZABETH BEADLE 1908–1991

SHE WAS THE MOST HONEST PERSON I HAVE
EVER KNOWN AND HATED LIES AND INJUSTICE.

"SHE NOTHING MEAN OR COMMON DID"

By The Same Author:

Jack the Ripper: Anatomy of a Myth
The Killing of Leon Beron

My first acknowledgement goes to the late Basil Donne Smith, owner of a Crime bookshop in Crewkerne, Somerset. Shortly before his death "The Donne" did me an act of personal kindness without which this book could not have been written.

Acknowledgements and thanks also to:
Peters, Fraser & Dunlop & Arthur for permission to quote from 'Reflections on Hanging'
William Heinemann for permission to quote from 'Cases in Court' by Sir Patrick Hastings Q.C.
Poolbeg Press & Sean O'Brien for permission to quote from 'Bloody Ambassadors'
Other sources could not be contacted.
Finally my thanks to Chris who typed my manuscript with great speed & efficiency.

CONTENTS

LIST OF ILLUSTRATIONS

AUTHOR'S PREFACE

The thought of innocent people being hanged for crimes which they did not commit rightly appalls us.

Until the case of Timothy Evans, which was swiftly followed by Derek Bentley and later, James Hanratty, there was a widely held view that this could not happen under the modern judicial system. This belief was positively encouraged by contemporary crime historians and so called criminologists. Indeed, to read most works published before the 1970s is to gain the impression that the Defence case did not exist. There is in fact still a view held in some quarters that prior to Evans nobody had been wrongly executed this century.

This is an illusion. Doubts appertain to some sixteen cases. This book is about two of them; — and the system which put them to death.

Introduction

This is a book which analyses a system at work. The system is the British Judicial system, maintained by some to be the best in the world.

In March, 1910 John Alexander Dickman, a Newcastle man, was arrested for the murder of a Wages Clerk. Dickman, was described at the time as a Bookmaker, although in reality he was a professional gambler. Ostensibly middle class, and with the trappings of that life-style to maintain, Dickman appeared to be in need of money at the time of the murder, the motive for which was undoubtedly robbery. At the beginning of July that year Dickman was tried and convicted. An appeal failed and the following month he was executed. But today, over eighty years later, we still do not know for sure whether John Dickman was guilty.

Walter Graham Rowland holds a unique place in our history. He is the only man to have occupied the same death cell twice. On the first occasion he had murdered his small daughter but the Home Secretary decided to reprieve him. Twelve years later Rowland found himself back in that same cell again, this time convicted of the murder of a Manchester prostitute. On this occasion he was not so lucky and on the 27th of February, 1947, he was hanged. But was he guilty? Read the evidence and judge for yourselves.

Capital punishment ended in Britain in 1965. Today, it is a bitterly contentious issue with an estimated 80% of the population demanding its return. Judicial execution seems to strike a deep chord in the Anglo Saxon psyche. Why is a psychological question and beyond the scope of this work. But we can examine the surface arguments.

On moral grounds there can be no doubt that capital punishment is perfectly justified. Nobody can sensibly argue that the Moors murderers, Brady and Hindley, did not deserve to hang, or serial killers and child murderers in general. Nor can there be any argument that armed criminals prepared to kill to gain their objectives, and violent political extremists, should not suffer the same fate as their victims. The problems begin when we try to establish moral criteria. 75% of all murders are domestic tragedies and few would be in favour of putting domestic killers to death. But, and it is an important but, is the brutal husband who batters his wife to death during an argument any less culpable than the armed robber who pulls the trigger during a moment of panic? How do we arrive at moral decisions over who should or should not shake hands with the executioner? Lord Birkett once asked during a famous murder trial: 'What is the co-efficient of the expansion of brass?' To that question there is logical, scientific answer. But what is the co-efficient of morality? Here there is no simple answer, only a mire of complexity. And whose moral values decide the issue? Mine? Yours? The Home Secretary's? Forty years ago Sir David Maxwell-Fyfe decided that Derek Bentley should die. In 1993 the then Home Secretary, Kenneth Clarke, turned down demands for a posthumous free pardon for Bentley on the grounds that he considered his conviction safe and satisfactory. But Clarke also placed on record his view that Bentley should have been reprieved.

The decision to hang Bentley justifiably outraged public opinion. His role in the murder of a Police Officer was less than that of his co-defendant who could not be hanged. But public opinion — our joint morality — can also be highly fickle. A year after Bentley was hanged Styllou Christofi was executed for the murder of her daughter-in-law without any discernible public outcry. Mrs Christofi was almost certainly insane. The following year Ruth Ellis became the last woman to be hanged in Britain. Put very simply Ellis murdered an ex- boyfriend who had tired of her and on the facts of the case the decision to hang her was morally justifiable. Yet it provoked a storm of outrage missing from the Christofi case. Ruth Ellis was young and attractive; Styllou Christofi was old and ugly and nobody cared about her. What the experience of these three cases shows us is that the public mood is at best inconsistent and at times strikingly at odds with the judgement of its paid officials which in turn can also be described as variable. That is what happens when we try to make moral decisions about issues of life and death.

The deterrent argument is much more straightforward. Does hanging deter others from killing? There is not a shred of proof that it does and plenty of evidence that it does not. Of the many studies of the issue only one, a controversial American report, concluded that capital punishment was a deterrent. In the U.S.A. some states have capital punishment and some do not. There is no appreciable difference in the murder rate between those that do and those that don't. Nor has there been any ostensible increase in the murder rate in other European Countries which have abandoned the death sentence. In Britain the murder rate has increased but there has been an upward trend in all levels of violence. Why is difficult to judge. The probability is that there are many factors at work.

Arthur Koestler in his book "Reflections on Hanging" asked rhetorically who the death sentence was meant to deter:

> *'It is certainly not a deterrent to murderers who commit suicide—and one third of all murderers do. It is not a deterrent to the insane and mentally deranged; nor to those who have killed in a quarrel, in drunkenness, in a sudden surge of passion—and this type of murder amounts to 80% to 90% of all murders that are committed. It is not a deterrent to the type of person who commits murder because he desires to be hanged; ... it is not a deterrent to the person who firmly believes in his own perfect method ... Thus the range of hypothetical deterrents ... is narrowed down to the professional criminal class'*[*]

To Koestler's professional criminal class we can add two other categories

---

*   "Reflections on Hanging" p54

which the pro-execution lobby claims hanging will deter; serial killers and terrorists. They are wrong on all three counts. Where the rewards of crime are high enough the professional criminal will always be prepared to risk execution, a point very graphically illustrated by the American experience. Serial killers are not deterrable. Brady and Hindley are a prime example. Although their trial took place several months after the death penalty was shelved their murders were committed whilst it was still in force. The I.R.A. has never been deterred by capital punishment. Execution has in fact created Martyrs, the most notable example, Dublin 1916. After the failure of the Easter rebellion the I.R.A. rank and file was marched off through the streets to British Gaols. Huge, hostile crowds lined the route, jeering and bombarding them with fruit and eggs. But when, twenty-four hours later, the Authorities executed the I.R.A. leaders the mood changed abruptly and irrevocably to one of sympathy.

Koestler also advances the thesis that in some instances judicial executions actually inspired others to imitate the crimes:

> *'Fauntleroy confessed that the idea of committing forgery came to him while he watched a forger being hanged. A juryman, who found Dr Dodd guilty of forgery, committed soon afterwards the same crime and was hanged from the same gallows. Cumming was hanged in Edinburgh in 1854 for sexual assault, which immediately led to a wave of similar assaults in the region. In 1855, Heywood was hanged in Liverpool for cutting the throat of a woman; three weeks later Ferguson was arrested in the same town for the same crime. The list could be continued indefinitely!*[*]

There was also clear evidence that pickpockets, then a capital offence, enjoyed their richest pickings from the crowds watching executions. Parliament's response was to ban public executions, a move which so far as deterrence was concerned had all the hallmarks of rearranging the deck chairs on the Titanic. Koestler again:

> *'...if watching with one's own eyes the agony of a person being strangled on the gallows does not deter, it seems logical to assume that unseen execution ...would deter even less. One may further argue that if the penalty of hanging does not frighten even a pickpocket, it would not frighten a potential murderer, ...they (the authorities) assumed that while watching an execution from a few yards did not act as a deterrent, reading a Home Office communique about it did.'*[**]

Slipping neatly into this context is the case of Francis "Flossie" Forsyth, who was hanged in 1960 for kicking a young man to death. Three hours after the execution Forsyth's friend, Victor Terry, held up a Bank and murdered a Cashier. Whether Forsyth's crime and execution actually spurred Terry on we do not know. It is possible: — Terry believed himself to be the reincarnation of the American gangster, "Legs" Diamond. What we can say for certain however is that hanging

---

**   "Reflections on Hanging" p58
*** "Reflections on Hanging" p59

Forsyth did not deter Terry, and if it could not deter that close to home then what merit is there in the deterrence argument?

The supreme argument against the death penalty is the fallibility of the judicial system. The modern judicial system basically dates from legislation enacted in 1898, which allowed the accused to speak in his own defence, and 1907, the setting up of the Court of Criminal Appeal. It is this system, which is still with us today, which put John Dickman and Walter Rowland to death.

Prior to Timothy Evans, who was executed in 1950 and granted a posthumous free pardon in 1966, defenders of capital punishment believed that the modern judicial system made it impossible for an innocent person to be hanged. Their view was very forcibly expressed in the House of Commons in 1948 by Sir David Maxwell-Fyfe who argued that for the capital sentence to be carried out on the wrong person the Judge, Jury, Appeal Court and Home Secretary would all have to be stricken mad. In fact, in the forty-three years between the creation of the Appeal Court and Evans' execution, it is possible that as many as fifteen innocent men and women may have been hanged. That number includes Dickman and Rowland, but it would have been very possible to write this book using other very disturbing cases, William Podmore and Robert Hoolhouse for instance.

Since the abolition of capital punishment the situation has become markedly worse. We no longer talk in terms of individuals but numbers, the Birmingham six, the Guildford four, the Luton and Cardiff threes and so on. Provable miscarriages of justice have reached epidemic proportions. Defenders of our system of justice may argue that in a perverse way the number of errors now acknowledged shows that the system is working but this is untrue. That system convicted them in the first place and the Appeal Court only acted later with extreme reluctance. The Birmingham six spent eighteen years in prison, the Guildford four sixteen and two members of the Luton three were only freed after the Appeal Court had rejected their applications on a record five occasions. Technically their convictions remain in force. It is a sobering fact that of the thirteen people mentioned above twelve would have been hanged had the death penalty still existed, and twelve is probably only half the overall total of what would have been a massacre of the innocents.

The reaction of pro-hangers to this rash of miscarriages has been to argue that the capital sentence should only be carried out when there is no possible doubt about guilt. Doubt is the key word. John Dickman was convicted mainly on eyewitness identification. After his trial the Police admitted that the witnesses had been tampered with. Rowland was found guilty and had his conviction rubber stamped by the Appeal Court despite an alibi partially corroborated by the Police themselves and a credible confession by another man who later carried out an identical assault on another woman. William Podmore was only charged after a statement by a witness so dubious that the Prosecution never called upon him to give evidence at the trial. Robert Hoolhouse was convicted despite the opinion of the Junior prosecution Counsel that the case against him was so flimsy that the Crown should not proceed with it. (The D.P.P. later admitted: 'The evidence was never strong'.) All were hanged. Evidence which one juror finds convincing may be totally unconvincing to another. The Peasenhall case in 1902 provides a classic example. William Gardiner was tried twice for murder, both trials ending in a hung jury. In the first the jurors voted 11 to 1 for conviction, in the second 11 to 1 for acquittal, which meant that 24 jurors hearing the same evidence had split evenly down the middle. Even when there seems no possible area of doubt the accused may still be innocent. In the appendix to this book I describe the execution of Timothy Evans as an act of capricious fate. On the evidence before them the jury could not have reached any verdict other than guilty and there were no plausible grounds for a reprieve. Despite the fact that he was innocent the Evans case was not really a sound argument against capital punishment. It is however a sound argument against those who argue that the system can be made foolproof and brings us back to where we started. No system is infallible. Those who believe that it can be made so have never put forward any sensible ideas to accomplish this objective. We can, by abolishing the adversarial system in favour of the inquisitorial, greatly improve the administration of justice in this country but infallibility is, to paraphrase Maxwell-Fyfe, moving in the realms of fantasy.

Decay begins at the top. Whatever our judicial system the final say in who lives and who dies rests with a Government department whether it be a Ministry of the Interior (in Britain the Home Office) or a Ministry of Justice. In theory the Home Office reprieved whenever it found an extenuating circumstance; in practice it did not and constantly ignored its own guidelines. Derek Bentley was hanged for political reasons, as a warning to wayward youth. In refusing to reprieve him the Home Office closed its eyes to no less than six points which should have brought him a reprieve. These were, sub-normal intelligence, epilepsy, widespread public opinion against the execution, Bentley was the lesser partner in the crime, the Jury had attached a recommendation of mercy to its verdict and there was a vestige of doubt about his guilt. Bentley had a mental age of eleven, was epileptic, the public were opposed to hanging him and the murder had been committed by his accomplice fifteen minutes after Bentley's arrest. In the latter context we can quote the case of Thomas Ley and John Smith who were convicted of the murder of a Barman in 1947. Ley, the prime mover in the affair, was subsequently found to be insane and reprieved. In view of this Smith was also reprieved even though, unlike Bentley, he had physically taken part in the crime.

Another ground for reprieve was where there were serious doubts about the person's sanity, Ley once again being an example. He was lucky. Styllou Christofi, as we have seen, was not even though she made a habit of setting fire to her in-laws. Nor were Frederick Holt, hanged in 1922 for murdering his fiancee, and Miles Giffard, executed in 1953 for killing his parents. Like Christofi there were the gravest possible doubts about Giffard and Holts' sanity. Many also believe that George Joseph Smith, the "Bride in the Bath" murderer, was demonstrably insane.

Doubt about guilt itself was obviously the strongest ground for a reprieve. Allegedly the death sentence was always commuted when a scintilla of doubt remained. Unfortunately not. This was brushed aside in seventeen[*] cases during the first half of this century and then a further eight (Bentley included) between 1950 and 1962. Podmore and Hoolhouse have already been mentioned and Dickman and Rowland are the subject of this book. Any one of the other twenty five could be quoted but for the sake of brevity I will comment on just three, Edward Rowlands, who was executed in 1923 after a Rugby player had been kicked to death during a brawl, Norman Thorne, hanged for the murder of his girlfriend in 1925, and James Hanratty. In Rowlands case the victim made a dying declaration stating that Rowlands was not one of his attackers. Thorne was hanged despite the evidence of no less than five pathologists that his fiancee could have committed suicide (as Thorne contended). Hanratty's is arguably the most disturbing case of all. He was executed in 1962 for the murder of a research chemist. No sound motive was offered, the Crown's evidence contradicted itself and Hanratty's alibi was well supported. The trial judge summed up in his favour and following his conviction several more credible witnesses came forward to support the alibi. 'Scintilla' means an atom or spark: in Hanratty's case doubt was a river in full flood. Later his family attempted to take out a private prosecution against the Home Secretary only to discover that ministerial decisions are apparently above the law, a prerogative which the British people have certainly never been consulted about. Even Parliament itself has proved powerless to force the Home Office to adhere to its own guidelines; in Bentley's case it was ruled that a debate on whether he should hang could only proceed after his execution!

At the beginning of this introduction I wrote that this book was about a system at work. For this reason I have excluded any in-depth biographies of Dickman and Rowland and the personalities of those involved in their trials sticking only to the relevant facts. To have done otherwise would have meant writing separate books about the cases and that would have defeated the purpose of the exercise. What I have sought to do is to first put the reader in the position of a juror, and then later an assessor at their Appeal Court hearings and the so-called inquiry into Rowland's guilt. My own views are made very clear but it is for the reader — come juror — come assessor — to agree with them or reject them as he or she feels fit. What is actually on trial here is not so much John Dickman and Walter Rowland but the system which put them to death. Decide for yourselves.

---

[*]   one before the setting up of the Appeal Court

JOHN ALEXANDER DICKMAN

"I can only repeat that I am entirely innocent of this cruel deed. I have no complicity in this crime, and I have spoken the truth in my evidence and in everything I have said."

WALTER GRAHAM ROWLAND

"I die for another's crime. I tell you mother and dad that before my maker I swear that I am completely innocent of the death of that poor woman."

PART ONE

JOHN ALEXANDER DICKMAN:
THE 10:27 TO DISASTER

'Before you say he is guilty you must be convinced that the evidence can only be explained upon the assumption that he is guilty. If upon any part of it which is necessary to the deciding of his guilt or his innocence you have a reasonable doubt, you must decide it in his favour'

(Lord Justice Darling at the trial of Stinie Morrison)

John Alexander Dickman:

THE 10:27 TO DISASTER

(1)

Credit for pioneering the railways is often wrongly given to George Stephenson. It belongs instead to Richard Trevethick who patented the first Steam Locomotive in 1804. Nine years later William Hedley invented an engine for use in the Tyneside Coalfields. Stephenson improved on this the following year, and in 1825 produced his "Locomotion No 1", forerunner of the famous "Rocket" and running between Stockton & Darlington.

By 1910, the year in which the story of John Dickman takes place, the Railways had become a vast system of sprawling networks which had revolutionised passenger and commercial travel. They had, at that time, a superb safety record eulogised by "Cassell's Book of Knowledge" in the following terms:—

> 'Not the least remarkable thing about railway travelling in Great Britain is the astonishing immunity from serious accidents...'[*]

William Huskisson would not altogether have endorsed this sentiment. President of the Board of Trade in the Duke of Wellington's Government, Huskisson holds the strictly dubious distinction of being the first fatal victim of a railway accident; — an engine ploughed into him at the opening of the Liverpool–Manchester line in 1830. A few years later a passenger, whose name has not come down to us (presumably because he was not a leading politician), froze to death in an open carriage. At least railway mishaps were democratic!

It was inevitable that murder would find its compartment in railway history. It took its time. Almost forty years after the opening of the Stockton–Darlington line, a Mister Thomas Briggs was robbed and murdered between Bow and Hackney Wick in London. A German immigrant named Franz Muller was convicted of the crime. Muller owed his capture to a piece of remarkable stupidity: he left his hat behind at the scene of the murder. As it was he protested his innocence until quite literally the last minute. Then, as the noose was about to be slipped over his head, he turned to the Priest in attendance and whispered, 'I have done it'.

Muller's crime led to a short lived panic about the safety of railway compartments. Not without justification. Two of the next four railway murders went unsolved. The victims were a Miss Camp and a Miss Money which suggested that women were particularly at risk, a conclusion that subsequent

* "Cassell's Book of Knowledge" p3037

criminal history has done nothing to offset. It also meant that the would-be railway killer had a 40% likelihood of avoiding capture; 60% if he remembered to keep his hat on!

However the sixth British railway murder did not involve a woman and whether it is unsolved is a matter for you to decide.

We return to Tyneside and the Coalfields, where almost a century before William Hedley's little locomotive had shunted its way between the mines.

John Innes Nisbet was a book-keeper for the Stobswood Colliery Company of Widdrington. He was a creature of habit, an admirable trait in a book-keeper but potentially disastrous for one of the functions which his job entailed. On alternate Fridays he collected the Colliery's wages from Lloyd's Bank, Newcastle and travelled, unescorted, to Widdrington with them.

There was no inkling that Friday, March 18th, 1910 would be any different. Nisbet had breakfast with his wife, Cicely, at their home in Heaton. The weekend beckoned, Spring was just around the corner and as he closed the front door that morning Nisbet could not possibly have imagined that it would be for the last time. Doubtless his thoughts were with Cicely with whom he would later snatch a few minutes conversation when the train passed through Heaton on the way to Widdrington. It was a little ritual which they performed (probably to assuage her fears about his safety) whenever he collected the wages. Neither could have dreamed that it would be their last meeting on earth.

At around 10 a.m. Nisbet presented himself at the Lloyd's Branch where Stobswood had their Account. John Wilson, a Lloyd's Clerk, made the payroll up for him, £231.00 in Sovereigns, £103.00 in half Sovereigns, £35-45 in silver and £1.02½ coppers, a total, in decimal money, of £370.41½. It was only a third of the normal wage bill because Stobswood was one of the collieries involved in a miner's strike in the region. Remember this. Although unperceived at the time, and since, it is an important point in the case.

These coins Wilson placed in three canvas bags and some small paper bags, and Nisbet put them into a large black leather bag he was carrying. He then made his way to Newcastle Central Station to catch his train.

John Nisbet never varied his routine, always caught the same train. No thief needed to attack him in the busy streets of Newcastle. A quiet compartment of the 10:27 was much easier and safer.

The 10:27 that morning[*] consisted of the engine and four carriages, each consisting of three individual compartments. There were no corridors. After leaving Newcastle Central from Platform 5, it was due to call at (outer) Newcastle, Heaton, Forest Hall, Killingworth, Annitsford, Cramlington, Plessy, Stannington, Morpeth, Pegswood, Longhurst, Widdrington, Chevington, Acklington and Warkworth before terminating at Alnmouth shortly after midday. It was due at Widdrington at 11:40. The train arrived, John Nisbet didn't, at least not alive.

[*]   The next train was at 12:38

Nobody encountered Nisbet between Lloyd's Bank and Newcastle Central. But he was seen several times at the Station. The first sighting was by John Alexander Dickman, a forty three year old professional gambler (he described himself as a free lance bookmaker) who had once held the important position of a colliery secretary. According to Dickman, he knew Nisbet and that morning noticed him at the booking hall. Like Nisbet, Dickman also travelled on the 10:27, but if he was telling the truth then he did not see Nisbet again after exchanging a polite 'good morning' with him at the booking hall.

If that was the truth then five months later the State hanged an innocent man.

Nisbet was next seen on Platform 4 by a commercial traveller named Charles Raven who had known him for five or six years. Platform 5 was reached by traversing the length of Platform 4 and then turning right at the gate. As Raven watched, Nisbet passed through the gate in the direction of Platform 5. He was in the company of a second man whom Raven would later claim was John Dickman.

Wilson Hepple was an elderly artist who had known John Dickman for over twenty years and had once roomed with him. Hepple was travelling by the 10:27 that morning. On Platform 5 he claimed to have seen Dickman in the company of another man. Whilst Hepple watched they came to a halt outside a compartment in the first carriage at the front of the train.

Percival Hall was a Wages Clerk who was engaged on the same business as Nisbet that morning. Unlike Nisbet's tight fisted employers*, Hall's Colliery provided him with an escort, his fellow Clerk, John Spink. That poor Nisbet was an obvious target for robbery should have been apparent even to the meanest intellect. He was not only alone but was a small, slightly built man and at forty-four no longer in the first flush of youth. Hall and Spink knew Nisbet and that morning Hall saw him walking up Platform 5 in the Company of a second man. Hall and Spink were in the second compartment of the front carriage. Nisbet and his companion got into the third compartment, immediately behind Hall and Spink's. The latters' destination was Stannington. On passing Nisbet's compartment there both men glanced in and saw him. Spink — but not Hall — noticed a second man in the compartment.

At Heaton Cicely Nisbet kept her routine appointment with her husband. But today was slightly out of the ordinary because he was travelling in the front carriage and not the rear as he usually did. A second man was also in the compartment his face obscured by the darkness from a nearby tunnel.

Morpeth was the ninth station along the line, immediately after Stannington where Hall and Spink had seen Nisbet alive and well. A railway platelayer named John Grant peered into Nisbet's compartment and saw nobody; ditto John Cosher, a station porter at Longhurst.

---

*   Cicely Nisbet later successfully sued them for compensation.

Widdrington was the next station. John Nisbet did not alight from the train and the Stobswood Colliery did not receive its wages. John Nisbet was very, very dead.

The body was discovered when the train terminated at Alnmouth. It had been stuffed under a seat. Nisbet had been shot five times in the head and face from close range. Even though he had been dead for over thirty minutes blood was still streaming out from two of the wounds. The wages bag was of course long gone. A policeman was summoned: by garish coincidence his name too was Nisbet. On the floor of the compartment was found a return ticket to Widdrington and one of Nisbet's gloves, heavily bloodstained. The other glove was on his hand. And nobody perceived how interesting these little details were.

Eighty minutes after John Nisbet's body was found, John Dickman had a chance encounter with two acquaintances, a Mr Elliot and Mr Saunderson, in Morpeth. In view of what was to follow, this casual meeting is of the utmost importance. Three days later Dickman was charged with the murder of John Nisbet. Four months later he was convicted of it. A month after that he paid the supreme penalty of the Law. But on that cold March afternoon neither Elliot or Saunderson noticed anything untoward about Dickman; no hint of nervousness, no sign of strain, no tell tale bloodstains on his clothes. On the contrary, he talked perfectly rationally and normally about the Grand National, which was to be run that afternoon, precisely the sort of topic a bookmaker would discuss.

The trio did not tarry long. Dickman bade Elliot and Saunderson goodbye and then made his way back to Newcastle by the 1:40 train from Morpeth.

(2)

Responsibility for tracking down the murderer — or murderers — of John Nisbet rested with the Northumberland County Police and the investigation was placed in the hands of its most senior Detective, Superintendent John Weddell.

Within hours of the crime Percival Hall and John Spink contacted the Police and made statements. They provided a description of Nisbet's companion which ran:—

> *'About 35 to 40, about 5' 6" high, about eleven stone, medium build, heavy dark moustache, pale or sallow complexion; wore a light overcoat down to his knees; black hard felt hat; well dressed and appeared to be fairly well to do.'*

If only murderers did not look like normal human beings then the Police's job would be much easier and society a lot safer! Unfortunately that is not the case and this description could have fitted half the men in Britain. Of more importance to the investigation was that Hall and Spink's evidence placed the murder between Stannington and Widdrington and suggested that the killer had travelled with Nisbet from Newcastle. A corner-stone had been placed, the foundation of a theory starting to be laid. Cicely Nisbet added some cement when she told the Police about the man in the compartment at Heaton. Exactly when Charles Raven came forward is unclear but it appears to have been on Friday evening, as he was later to say that his attention had been drawn by an account of the tragedy in the afternoon papers. His evidence extended the foundations. Finally there were John Grant and John Cosher (there are an astonishing number of 'Johns' in this case) with their stories of nobody apparent in the compartment at Morpeth and Longhurst. Foundation complete.

So the Police now built their theory. It was neat and simple. Nisbet had been killed by a man who fell in with him at Newcastle Central and travelled with him as far as Morpeth, slaying him just before the train reached that station. For good measure, at six minutes running time, Stannington–Morpeth was the longest stretch between stations along the entire route. The murderer was very probably known to Nisbet, who had no reason to be apprehensive of him, and he in turn knew Nisbet's routine and what he was carrying.

Well, that was the theory. There is no evidence that the Police ever considered another. If they did then all sight of it disappeared when John Dickman came into view because, as we shall see, his self-confessed movements that morning fitted the Police's theory exactly. Any snippet of evidence which did not fit snugly into their scenario was either ignored or brushed aside.

Sunday, March 20th. So far the only hint of a suspect had come from London, a drunk who claimed that he was in possession of the stolen money. He was swiftly traced and just as swiftly eliminated. But now everything changed.

The Police never actually said who their informant was. According to Detective Inspector Andrew Tait of the Newcastle City Police:—

> '...*We got a telephone message on the Sunday that a man named Dickman had been seen with Nisbet in the Central Station. We were not told in what part or anything.*'

There can be no doubt that the informant was Dickman's artist friend, Wilson Hepple, as Superintendent Weddell made clear at the trial:—

> *Q. ...he (Dickman) told you that he had gone into the hinder part of the train...?*

> *A. That was directly contrary to the information I had at that time.*

On Sunday, March 20th, only Wilson Hepple could have provided the information that Dickman had allegedly gone up to the front of the train.

Proceeding at Weddell's request, Tait spent the rest of Sunday and the following morning making inquiries about Dickman. Again in Tait's words:

> *'All my inquiries amongst people who knew him said that he was very hard up.'*

On Monday afternoon, the 21st, Tait telephoned Weddell at his Office in Gosforth with the results of his investigations. Weddell asked Tait to bring Dickman in for questioning and went himself to Newcastle Central Police Station to await their arrival. Dickman lived with his wife and two children at No 1, Lily Avenue, in the middle class Jesmond suburb of Newcastle. Tait arrived there at 4:35. He was not, however, the only person making inquiries in Jesmond that afternoon. Also in the area was a reporter from the "Newcastle Daily Chronicle" and he had been sent to investigate an intriguing little story from a commercial traveller named Brocklehurst.

According to Brocklehurst, about two weeks previously he had been travelling on the Newcastle–Morpeth express. Between Annitsford and Stannington he and his fellow passengers had been startled by gunshots fired, in Brocklehurst's opinion, from another compartment. Later they had discovered that the window frame of their compartment had been splintered by bullets.

A report appeared in the "Chronicle" the following day after which Mr Brocklehurst disappears from the story. We do not know what, if any, investigations were made into it by the Police. It is possible that Brocklehurst simply wanted to get his name in the papers, but it does not sound like a made up story. The train is different, also the carriage in which he said he travelled; there were other passengers in it and the incident took place between Annitsford and Stannington, not Stannington–Morpeth. What it suggests is that the killer was experimenting with the possibility of shooting Nisbet from another compartment and found it impractical.

Dickman, as we shall see, had travelled to Stannington on March 4th and the Prosecution at his trial were to suggest that this was a "dry run" for carrying out the crime two weeks later. One would therefore have thought that Brocklehurst's story, assuming it was reliable, strengthened their case. But in one material sense it did not. If Nisbet's murderer was experimenting with shooting him from another compartment then it suggested that he was a stranger to him, not an acquaintance with whom Nisbet would trustingly share a compartment.

None of this of course was in Andrew Tait's mind as he knocked on Dickman's front door. It was answered by Dickman himself. The conversation which following is reproduced from the evidence given at the trial. The language is formal, rather stilted, but there is no dispute about its veracity.

Tait (having introduced himself):—

> *'The Northumberland County Police have been informed that you were in the company of the murdered man Nisbet on Friday morning last. I have since learnt that you are an acquaintance of his. If that is so, the*

County Police would like to know if you could throw any light on the affair.'

Dickman:—

'I knew Nisbet for many years. I saw him that morning. I booked at the ticket window with him and went by the same train, but I did not see him after the train left. I would have told the Police if I had thought it would have done any good.'

Tait then asked Dickman if he would accompany him to Newcastle Central Police Station and make a statement. Dickman went willingly. Pausing only to put on his overcoat and change his shoes, he stepped out into the gathering dusk of a March evening on a journey from which he would never return.

At the Police Station Dickman was introduced to Superintendent Weddell. Weddell's greeting was polite and formal: there was no hint of what was to come. Confident that he would soon be home and having tea, Dickman made the following statement:—

'On Friday morning last I went to the Central Station and took a ticket, return from Stannington. Nisbet, the deceased man, whom I knew, was at the ticket office before me, and, so far as I know, had left the hall by the time I got round. I went to the bookstall and got a paper, the "Manchester Sporting Chronicle"; then to the refreshment room, and had a pie and a glass of ale. I then went on to the platform and took my seat in the third class carriage nearer the hinder end than the front end. My recollection is, although I am not clear on the matter, that people entered and left the compartment at different stations on the journey. The train passed Stannington Station without my noticing it, and I got out at Morpeth and handed my ticket with excess fare, 2½ pence (old money)* to the collector. I left Morpeth and walked to Stannington by the main road. I took ill of diarrhoea on the way, and had to return to Morpeth to catch the 1:12 p.m. train, but missed it, and got the 1:40 slow to Morpeth (sic). After missing the 1:12 p.m. I came out of the Station at the east side, and turned towards town. I met a man named Elliot, and spoke to him. I did not get into the town but turned and went back to the Station, and got the 1:40 slow to Newcastle. I got a single ticket for Stannington and did not give it up. I gave up the return portion at the Manors. I have been very unwell since, but was out on Saturday after-noon and evening. I went on this journey to see a Mr Hogg, at Dovecot, in connection with a new sinking operation there.'

It was a somewhat perfunctory effort; the sort of statement which a man might well give if he genuinely believed that he had little of consequence to

---

*   inserted by the Author.

9

impart. Even when one makes allowances for the fact that it was undoubtedly in the form of a question and answer session, there is still a hint of shrugged shoulders at a rather pointless exercise.

Dickman was to adhere to this story throughout adding only a few particulars. He later claimed to have visited a lavatory on Platform Eight before boarding the train, and he also enlarged on his illness stating that he had suffered an attack of piles and had laid down in a field to rest.

Having made his statement Dickman no doubt imagined that he would be thanked for his trouble and allowed to leave. But instead he was ordered to turn out his pockets. At this point it must have dawned on him that this was not simply a routine inquiry. A few seconds later he found himself looking on helplessly whilst Weddell and Tait rummaged through his possessions. Two items particularly drew their attention; £15 in gold sovereigns in a Lloyds Bank bag[*] and a money lender's card.

These seemed to clinch the matter in Weddell's mind for his next action was to arrest John Dickman for the murder of John Innes Nisbet. With shocking suddenness the Newcastle Bookmaker's world had disintegrated into a hellish nightmare. Turning to Weddell he replied:—

> '*I do not understand the proceedings; it is absurd for me to deny the charge because it is absurd to make it. I only say I absolutely deny it.*'

But his arrest was only a foretaste of the agonies to come.

Once Dickman had been charged, Weddell visited his home, the first of two visits[**], and after a thorough search of the premises took away the following items; a batch of letters, two bank books, two pawn tickets, a pair of suede gloves, and a pair of trousers. Later the overcoat which Dickman was wearing at the time of his arrest, a fawn coloured burberry, was also taken from him. The importance of these articles and the evidence which they yielded will be dealt with presently.

Later that same evening Dickman was placed on an identity parade attended by John Spink and Percival Hall. Spink was unable to make an identification, but, after some hesitation and an extremely curious remark to the Officer conducting the parade, Hall picked Dickman out as the man who had boarded the train with Nisbet.

✳✳✳✳✳

John Dickman was formally arraigned before the Magistrates, seven of them no less, on April 14th. Here another piece of identification evidence emerged against him. At the close of her testimony Mrs Nisbet fainted. The hearing was then adjourned. When it reconvened on the 22nd she returned to the witness box and identified Dickman as her late husband's travelling companion.

---

[*]   He had on him, in total, £17.50.
[**]   The second took place on March 26th.

Despite this, Dickman's solicitor, Edward Clark, appealed to the Magistrates to set his client free. In ringing tones he declared:—

> *'I do not ask you to give my client the benefit of the doubt. I ask you to give Dickman what every Englishman is entitled to until there is something against him — his liberty.'*

But his words fell on deaf ears. Dickman was formally committed for trial at the Newcastle Summer Assizes.

Worse followed. On April 28th a Coroner's Jury, sitting at Nisbet's inquest, returned a verdict of wilful murder against John Alexander Dickman. They had heard only the Prosecution's evidence.

In 1910 Inquests were often *pro forma* trials, rather like mock G.C.E.'s, only harmful to the accused's interests. Such verdicts meant that a jury had publicly decided guilt in advance of the trial proper. Almost twenty years after the Dickman case one such Inquest-cum-trial pilloried an American Actor named Philip Yale Drew who had been charged with a murder in Reading.[*] After a two week hearing the Jury declined to indict Drew and he was released. Public opinion, which I earlier described as our fickle morality and which had been deaf to the plight of John Dickman and many others, now underwent a metamorphosis and demanded that the Law be changed to prohibit indictments by a Coroner's jury pending the trial. Unfortunately this was all much too late for John Dickman, who having been tried at the inquest and found guilty was now tried in the Press and found guilty. Here again the safeguards which are imposed today — or rather should be — on what the Press can publish about an accused, did not exist.

The trial was calendared to begin on Monday, July 4th. Three weeks before it opened an important discovery was made at the Barr Moor East Colliery, Morpeth. On June 9th the Colliery Manager, Peter Spooner, went down to a pit called the "Isabella" to inspect the air shaft. What he found is best described in his own words:—

> *'I saw a leather bag lying on the bottom of No 2 air shaft... There were some coppers in it and also a considerable amount of coppers lying all around the place where I found it.'*

Spooner handed the bag over to the Police. Papers in it firmly identified it as John Nisbet's wages bag. But there was more to come from Spooner.

> *'I know Dickman,— he was a fellow worker of mine years ago. At certain times I have talked about the difficulties on my mine... I could not say that he knew where the pit was, although I had discussed the difficulty with him... The grate [covering the air shaft] could be quite easily lifted by hand... Anything the size of the bag could be put down between the [bars of the] grates.'*

---

[*] For a definitive account of the case see "The Ordeal of Philip Yale Drew" by Richard Whittington-Egan.

At the time this discovery seemed a devastating blow to Dickman's protestations of innocence.

A strong body of circumstantial evidence *appeared* to have built up against John Dickman. But as the trial judge, Lord Coleridge, was to tell the Jury circumstantial evidence may be:—

> '*A mere gossamer thread, as light and unsubstantial as the very air itself. It may varnish at a touch. It may be that, strong as it is in part, it leaves great gaps and rents through which the accused is entitled to pass in safety.*'

Circumstances explicable by guilt may be equally explainable by innocence. Not one suspicion nor a thousand suspicions are adequate to prove a person guilty of murder. That must be done through evidence and evidence alone. Otherwise there is reasonable doubt and reasonable doubt is all that is required to acquit. In some instances evidence may be adduced pointing to outright innocence, but the accused, at least in theory, is not required to provide this. Let us now try to turn the theory into practice, examine the trial of John Dickman, and see whether there is, at the end of it, reasonable doubt.

(3)

In theory, the way in which the Criminal Justice System works is that the State is represented by a Barrister who presents the case against the accused, the accused is represented by a Barrister who answers the charge on his behalf, a strictly impartial Judge oversees the proceedings and a Jury of twelve ordinary citizens — in those days all men — decides whether or not the case has been proved.

The reality is very different. The State has unlimited resources at its disposal and in important trials is represented by an advocate of the highest calibre, in Dickman's case Edward Tindal Atkinson, K.C. In his early sixties, Tindal Atkinson was celebrating forty years at the Bar in 1910. Many prestigious appointments had come his way during that time and he had sat on the Bench as a Crown recorder. His junior for the trial was Charles Lowenthal, Junior Counsel to the Commissioners of Works.

By contrast John Dickman's resources were very limited. One of the Crown's strongest points against him was to be his need of money at the time of the murder. A defence fund had been gotten up by the gambling fraternity but its limits did not run beyond Edward Mitchell-Innes, K.C. Mitchell-Innes was some twenty years Tindal Atkinson's junior. He had built up a thriving local practice and "taken silk" as a King's Counsel in 1908, but the case really called for an advocate of Edward Marshall-Hall's stamp. Fenton Bresler Q.C., describes Mitchell-Innes as 'dandified' and 'blind and insensitive' and he writes that, 'he hardly seems to have had a very close grip on this case.'[1] He was all this and more. Despite the local prejudice against Dickman, Mitchell-Innes failed to apply for a Change of Venue. The result was that a trial which should have ended up at London's Old Bailey was held amidst a hostile atmosphere at Newcastle's Moot Hall, in which Moot became mute as far as justice was concerned.

Mitchell-Innes' Junior was Lord William Percy, a former pupil of his.

The choice of Judge was also to prove unfortunate for John Dickman. The Right Honourable Bernard John Seymour, Lord, Coleridge, K.C., was the son of a Lord Chief Justice and had enjoyed a meteoric career in the Legal profession. An outstanding Barrister, he had become a Judge in 1894, whilst still in his early forties and only seventeen years after being called to the Bar. Sydney Rowan-Hamilton, Editor of "The Trial of J A Dickman", states that, 'his success was such that no surprise was occasioned by his elevation to the Bench.'[2] Like Tindal Atkinson, Coleridge was also a Commissioner of Assize to the Midland Circuit. From the half way point of the trial Coleridge was to lean blatantly towards the prosecution.

We do not know the composition of the Jury. We can be sure that their minds were fettered by local prejudice. John Dickman had already been found "guilty" by both the Coroner's Jury and the Press. The case was the major talking point in Newcastle that summer and there was enormous sympathy for the murdered man. Such a vast throng had turned up for Nisbet's funeral that the cemetery gates had been closed before the cortege arrived. Rowan-Hamilton describes in very graphic terms the extent of the prejudice against Dickman on the morning the trial opened:—

> '...*thousands lined the road, booing and vociferating as he passed, hidden from view in the prison van; while even old women, old enough to have acquired some silent pity for others, gathered up their petticoats, and joining in the crowd, ran as far as they could behind the van shouting their execrations.*
>
> '*Have such scenes as these no effect on a jury, however much they may be determined to find their verdict according to the evidence produced before them?'*[3]

Clearly they did. Public opinion was to swing dramatically Dickman's way after the trial, and no less than five of the Jurors who convicted him later signed

---

1   "Scales of Justice"
2   "Trial of J A Dickman" p210
3   "Trial of J A Dickman" p3

the petition for his reprieve. But by then it was too late. Pre-trial prejudice had worked only too well its ugly machinations.

(4)

Scene setting occupied the opening period of the trial. There was evidence of the composition of the 10:27, its route, and the lay-out of Newcastle Central railway station. Mitchell-Innes established that there was a public urinal on Platform Eight, which was reached by by-passing Platform Five. Dickman contended that he had first visited the urinal before making his way back to Platform Five.

John Wilson testified to the money that Nisbet had drawn on March 18th, money placed largely in three Lloyds canvas bags similar to that in Dickman's possession on the 21st. Mitchell-Innes held the bags up to Wilson:—

Q. These bags seem to have seen some wear?

A. Yes.

Q. They look oldish?

A. Yes.

Dickman had maintained a Lloyds account for many years and as Wilson confirmed it was common practice for customers to receive their money in them.

Aware that the Defence had made an important point, Tindal Atkinson tried to negate it in re-examination. He did not succeed.

Q. I see on the bag is written 'please return this bag'?

A. Yes, but it is not carried out.

On finding one such bag on him, Police suspicion hardened against Dickman and he was arrested. Wilson's evidence showed that the matter was without substance.

Charles Raven was the next witness. His stay in the witness box was not long; unfortunately the confusion which it engendered was, stretching all the way up to the Appeal Court.

Raven's evidence seemed straightforward. He knew Nisbet; he had seen Nisbet and Dickman walking alongside each other on Platform Four and then they had gone in the direction of Platform Five. *They were not in conversation.*

Raven seems to have known Dickman only by sight (possibly as a Bookmaker). Dickman was emphatic that he did not know Raven.

The problem here lay with Mitchell-Innes. His answer to Raven's evidence was that Dickman, engrossed in the Grand National, had fallen into step alongside Nisbet, without noticing him, on Platform Four and then gone to the urinal on Platform Eight. This would have been fine had Raven's evidence stood alone. But it didn't; it was the first link in a chain of connected sightings which placed a man, allegedly Dickman, in Nisbet's company at least as far as Heaton. It was certainly not improbable that a man who could be mistaken for Dickman had walked alongside Nisbet and boarded the train with him; what was unlikely was that Dickman first had walked side by side with Nisbet and had then been replaced by a man who resembled him. This rather strains credulity, as Dickman himself made clear during cross-examination.

Q. If the deceased had been walking by your side you must have seen him?

A. Yes, I think I would have seen him.

The second link in the chain was forged by Wilson Hepple. He told the Court that on the morning of the 18th he had seen Dickman standing in the queue for the ticket office. Although they had been friends for a long time they did not speak.

After leaving the booking hall Hepple stopped for several minutes in front of the train indicator board waiting for it to post the information about which platform the 10:27 would depart from. On eventually reaching the train he selected the middle compartment of the third carriage from the engine and stowed his luggage inside it. There were still nine or ten minutes to go before the train pulled out so he wiled them away by pacing up and down outside his compartment. Whilst he was thus engaged he saw Dickman again, only by now the latter had acquired a companion, a slightly built man whom Hepple did not know. The two men strolled past him on the other side of the platform, a distance of some eighteen feet. Their faces were turned towards each other but no sounds of conversation drifted back across the platform to him. Having passed Hepple they walked on to the head of the train and came to a halt. Then one of them put his hand on the door of a compartment — which of the two Hepple could not say — and that was the last he saw of them because he turned and retraced his steps back to his own compartment. When he looked again they had both disappeared from view. Hepple then got into the train and it pulled out about a minute later.

The Artist continued his testimony by telling the Court about a visit to Newcastle Central railway station on the morning of April 3rd. There he took part in an experiment devised by the Police. First he identified his own compartment by a photograph on the wall. Then, Superintendent Weddell walked slowly backwards along the Platform until Hepple's shouted command brought him to a halt beside the compartment the two men had entered. It was the third compartment of the first carriage behind the engine, the compartment in which John Nisbet had travelled, the compartment in which he had died.

Sydney Rowan-Hamilton dismisses Hepple's evidence with the comment: 'He saw Dickman on the Platform with somebody but his evidence carries the case no further on this point.'[1] But in fact Hepple's testimony was very formidable, especially when taken in conjunction with Raven's. Raven claimed to have seen Dickman and Nisbet together on Platform Four, and then according to Hepple they had gone to the head of the train together shortly afterwards. Hepple was unable to actually identify Nisbet as Dickman's companion but this was negated by the fact that Nisbet had indeed boarded the train with a man, and, if Hepple's evidence could be relied upon, Dickman and his companion had gotten into the same compartment as Nisbet and his companion. It did not require any great feat of consecutive thought to reach the perfectly logical conclusion that Nisbet's companion was John Dickman and *vice versa*.

Having failed to challenge Raven's identification of Dickman, Mitchell-Innes now found it difficult to make any tangible in-roads into Hepple's. There was no ostensible reason for him to want to hurt Dickman. Reading his testimony one has the impression of a faint air of regret; certainly no hint of animosity emerges. Dickman himself was to merely say that Hepple was now elderly and 'very failed', but the Artist belied this and his advancing years with a convincing performance during cross-examination. He could not be shaken on a single point.

But that does not mean that his recollections were accurate.

British Legal history is replete with bizarre errors of identification. At this point I shall quote one, the Drew case which I mentioned earlier. It is of some relevance to the Dickman case.

Philip Yale Drew was accused of murdering a Reading Shopkeeper in 1929. Eight witnesses identified him as a drunk seen loitering outside the shop around the time of the murder. But at the Inquest a Local Butcher came forward to say that Drew was *not* the man. He knew Drew and had also spoken to the loiterer, who resembled him but was not him. For good measure Drew also had a strong alibi for the time of the murder. But Drew had been drinking in that locale earlier on which illustrates the role coincidence plays in crime.

During the Inquest Drew's Counsel put this question to a Police Sergeant named Harris:—

> *Q. Of your general knowledge and experience as a Detective and as a man, have you ever gone into the street and seen a man whom you could have sworn was a friend of yours, and on closer investigation found he was a perfect stranger?*
>
> *A. I have seen people, certainly, I thought might have been friends of mine from a distance, but on getting closer to them I have found that they were not.*

---

1   "Trial of J A Dickman" p8

It was, as Harris went on to say, a common occurrence, and is particularly relevant to Hepple and Raven's identifications. Bear in mind too that Raven did not know Dickman well and Hepple was an old man with an old man's eyesight. He was not, for example, able to determine which of the two men had put his hand on the carriage door.

The next witness was Percival Hall.

Hall repeated his story of seeing Nisbet board the train with a man. He had gotten a 'fairly good look at him for two or three seconds'. He made no mention of the two men being in conversation. On leaving the train at Stannington he had seen Nisbet sitting in the compartment and had nodded to him. He had not noticed anybody else in the compartment.

On the evening of March 21st Hall and John Spink had attended an identity parade at Newcastle Central Police Station. There Hall had made a rather tentative identification of John Dickman as Nisbet's companion.

In cross-examination Mitchell-Innes worried away at Hall's identification like a dog with a bone and he fared rather better than he had done with Hepple.

Was it not a fact that Hall had walked up and down the line three times without picking anybody out? No, only once, said Hall, a reply which failed to satisfy the Defence Counsel.

Q. I put it to you that you walked more than once.

A. I think not.

But would Hall swear to that. And here he hesitated a long time before qualifying his earlier answers; certainty underwent an amendment and re-emerged as 'to the best of my knowledge'.

So he would not swear to it after all? — 'now be careful' Mitchell-Innes warned him.

'No I will not swear that.'

With this in the bag Mitchell-Innes moved on. Had Hall then approached the Officer in charge of the parade and asked what he should do next? Affirmative, and after some more hesitancy Hall went on to say that the Officer had instructed him to point out the man whom he thought might have been Nisbet's companion.

Q. What did you say in answer to his direction, 'point him out'?

A. I think — well, I must not say that — I said I would not swear that the man I was going to point out was the companion of Nisbet, but that if I was assured that the murderer was there I would have no hesitation pointing out that man, and I pointed to the Prisoner.

But this was not what Hall had said at the Magistrates Court as Mitchell-Innes was quick to remind him.

Q. You said 'I will not swear that the man I pointed out was the man I saw get in with Mr Nisbet but if I could be assured that the murderer was there' — whatever that means — 'I would have no hesitation in pointing the prisoner out'?

'Yes,' answered the now thoroughly unhappy Mr Hall.

So had he pointed Dickman out before or after making this curious statement? The reply was a classic attempt at sitting on the fence. 'I said it as I did it', which a little while later became 'I was just going to point him out.'

Hall ended up by opting for his original answer; that he had made the remark before pointing to Dickman. But by this time he had so repeatedly stumbled from one contradiction to another that it was plain that no reliance could be placed on him.

Mitchell-Innes also revealed that Hall's testimony was tainted with prejudice. He had, according to one of his statements, referred to Dickman not as Nisbet's companion but as 'the murderer'. Had he then, asked Mitchell-Innes, already formed some conclusion about the case? 'No, not at all,' came the too hasty reply.

'It was merely a pleasant way of referring to the prisoner?' Mitchell-Innes voice dripped with sarcasm.

No doubt wishing that the ground would open up and swallow him, Hall merely stared into space.

Then there was the question of the overcoat. At the identity parade Dickman had worn a light fawn overcoat. In court Hall testified that Nisbet's companion had worn a light fawn overcoat. But his original description of the man merely referred to a light overcoat and made no mention of 'fawn'.

Mitchell-Innes clearly demonstrated Hall's unreliability. But had he been more venturesome then he might have achieved a spectacular coup which could have altered the whole course of the trial.

'Whatever that means.' Earlier Mitchell-Innes had interjected his own terse comment on Hall's statement to the Magistrates. It is a pity that he did not follow through on the line of his interjection. According to Rowan-Hamilton, he felt at the time that there might be more to Hall's remark than met the eye.

Indeed there was. Hall and Spink had in fact been afforded a sneak preview of Dickman prior to the identity parade! A Detective — who was never named — had encouraged them to peek through the window of the interview room. At this point they could see only the back of Dickman's head so the obliging Detective opened the door in order that they could have a better look!

This unfortunately only came to light after the trial. Both Hall and the Police claimed that he and Spink had still only seen Dickman from the rear. But if Hall's statement to the Magistrates is the accurate version of what he said at the parade then he knew exactly who the suspect was:—

'...*if I could be assured the murderer was there I would have no hesitation in pointing the prisoner out.*'

'Pointing the *prisoner* out!'

Any further comment might seem superfluous but for one crucial point.

Hall had originally doubted that Dickman was the man he had seen with Nisbet!

Outlining Hall's subsequent testimony at the Appeal Court, Rowan-Hamilton writes:—

> '*The impression the witness got in his view through the doorway almost led him to make up his mind that the man was not the man he had seen in the train because the man at the police station seemed from a back view so much more massive. Spink and the witness had both discussed that at tea [Author's note: prior to the parade] and came to that conclusion.*'[1]

Had this emerged at the trial then it would have had two effects, one direct, the other indirect. Directly, it would have killed Hall's identification of Dickman stone dead. Indirectly it would have dented Raven and Hepple's identifications. Raven said that he saw Dickman and Nisbet walking side by side on Platform Four. Hepple inferred that they were together on Platform Five. But if Hall, who got a closer glimpse of Nisbet's companion than either of them, originally thought that he was not Dickman — and Spink likewise — then this made out a clear case for Raven and Hepple having been mistaken.

The shaken Percival Hall retreated from the witness box to be succeeded by John Spink.

On the whole his testimony was more useful to the defence than the prosecution.

Spink occupied the witness box for only a short time. The main point of his evidence was the fleeting glimpse he had caught of Nisbet's companion at Stannington. He recalled that the man had worn a black felt hat, and had a moustache. Pressed by Tindal Atkinson he somewhat reluctantly said that Dickman resembled Nisbet's companion, but he refused to put it any higher than that. At the identity parade he had failed to pick Dickman out.

The crucial point here is that Spink failed to recognise Dickman as the man who had sat opposite Nisbet. This assumes even greater importance when one recalls that Spink, like Hall, accepted the Police's invitation to an advance preview of Dickman before the identity parade. Yet in spite of this he could not reconcile him with the man on the train.

---

1   "Trial of J A Dickman" p196

The next witness was Mrs Cicely Nisbet. Her evidence was to be every bit as controversial as Hall's. The Nisbet's home was close to Heaton station, the second stop out from Newcastle Central. Whenever her husband travelled to Widdrington, Cicely Nisbet walked the short distance to Heaton Station in order to have a few moments conversation with him. Whilst they were talking on the 18th she had noticed a man sitting opposite her husband. He had had his overcoat collar pulled up and only a small part of his face, in profile, was visible. Even this was obscured by a shadow cast by a nearby tunnel.

Mrs Nisbet made a deposition before the Magistrates on April 14th. During her evidence she fainted. Revived, she carried on only to pass out again at the finish. Eight days later she was allowed to return to the witness box and identify Dickman as the man who had sat opposite her husband.

Sydney Rowan-Hamilton has this to say of Cicely Nisbet's identification:—

> '*It would have been better if she had returned into court on the 14th and made her statement then, rather than postpone it for days — till the 22nd — when she must have had every opportunity of talking it over with the police and others. One would have thought she would have returned to the Court and then and there denounced Dickman. Her excuse for delay is that she "was not called upon to do so". Surely after such a startling incident this would have suggested itself even to the lay mind.*'[1]

Quite!

Cicely Nisbet did not fare well during cross examination. Mitchell-Innes swiftly drew her attention to what she had actually told the Magistrates — 'All I can say is that he resembled the man', which at its highest was somewhat inconclusive. But by the time the trial had opened her convictions had undergone a drastic stengthening. Now it was:—

> '*...the man I saw in that carriage is the man I now see in the dock, the man Dickman. I am perfectly certain of this.*'

Having made this point, Mitchell-Innes followed it up by establishing that Mrs Nisbet had only had an extremely dim view of the man's features because of the turned up collar and the tunnel shadow which was, 'right on him' — her words. Moreover she had not had very long to have a view of him. Normally her husband travelled in a rear compartment and it was at that end of the platform that she had waited for him. She had had to make her way up to the front of the train in order to speak to him.

It was a neat piece of cross-examination but unfortunately Mitchell-Innes ruined it with a macabre faux-pas. One moment he was exclaiming triumphantly:

1   "Trial of J A Dickman" p10

'I accept that answer Mrs Dickman', and the next he was squirming inside his gown, the words turning to ashes in his mouth as Cicely Nisbet's anguished response cut through the tense air of the court room:—

> *'Please will you not call me Mrs Dickman. You have called me Mrs Dickman all through.'*

There stood the widow her loss beseeching the Court's silent pity as she lamented the insensitivity of Counsel's error. It clearly struck a chord in the hearts of the jurors.

It did not deserve to.

Somewhere along the line Cicely Nisbet lost sight of the fact that she had known John Dickman for as long as eighteen years. Perhaps amidst her fainting fits and her lamentations it slipped her mind.

Mrs Nisbet's slight lapse of memory was later examined by the Appeal Court. There she deposed:—

> *'...the view in profile I got of my husband's companion did not enable me to identify him as anyone I knew.'*

But what then of her identification of Dickman at the Magistrates Court?

> *'He was in the same position, and I had the same view of his profile as I had in the train, and I then recognised him as being the same man.'*

What we are being asked to swallow here is that although she was unable to recognise a man she had known for many years on the morning of the murder — or for four weeks afterwards — she was able to identify him in Court.

This is not credible. The man she saw had his collar pulled up, was shrouded in darkness, and in her own words to the Police: 'I only had a momentary glance at him.' She never attended an identity parade saying: 'I can give no description whatsoever', and when she saw Dickman in Court he was in the dock. Nowadays dock identifications are considered wholly unsafe.

And there is another factor. Her husband knew Dickman; she knew Dickman. *But Nisbet never made reference to him, never drew her attention to him.*

Why? Was it because the man was in fact a stranger?

Now apply the same reasoning in reverse. Whoever killed John Nisbet had studied his routine; knew his habits, was aware that Cicely would be at Heaton. A stranger would travel through the Station with him, his coat collar pulled up. But a man who knew them both? Does this make sense? Particularly when all an acquaintance had to do was note Nisbet's compartment at Newcastle and then change compartments to join him after Heaton.

Unhappily these points were never made by Mitchell-Innes. Although Dickman's acquaintance with Cicely Nisbet came to light during Dickman's evidence, Mitchell-Innes never recalled her, never made a comment about it.

The issue lay mute at his feet and he failed to pick it up.

Eyewitness identification. It has been described by one of our Lord Chief Justices as: 'the most serious chink in our legal armour'. Today we are much less readily inclined to accept it, and rightly so. Probably the most infamous case of wrongful identification evidence occurred almost a Century ago. Adolph Beck, a roving Norwegian, was convicted of fraud in 1896 based on eyewitness identification by eleven women. In 1904 he was similarly convicted after identification by four women. In fact Beck was innocent and on both occasions had been mistaken for a man named William Wyatt, a.k.a. "John Smith". Beck was pardoned and compensated. This appalling miscarriage of justice was primarily responsible for the setting up of the Court of Criminal Appeal in 1907.

The Beck case does not merely refute the value of eyewitness identification; it is also highly relevant to John Dickman. All of the women knew the man who defrauded them yet they each made a mistake about him. Eric Watson, Editor of "The Trials of Adolph Beck" comments as follows:—

> *'What would be the position of a Beck today, tried on the evidence of 1896... can anyone doubt that he would be convicted, and that the Court of Criminal Appeal would sustain the verdict...?*
>
> *'The evidence as to identity was stronger than in any of the cases just glanced at...*
>
> *'About twenty-two occasions were spoken to by the eleven women, and on not one of these...could Beck render...[an] alibi or other evidence that he was elsewhere... He was poor, pawn tickets relating to female jewellery, brooches, and rings were found in his possession... and all he could prove... was that twenty years before... he had mixed with decent people.'[1]*

That is astonishingly similar to the situation which John Dickman found himself in. He was identified in part by people who *thought* they recognised him. Eric Watson's comment, that the Appeal Court would have upheld Beck's wrongful conviction is prescient to the point of prophecy[*]; as though Dickman had been selected to prove him right.

Watson's remarks about Beck's lack of alibi, his finances and his past respectability also correlate with the Dickman case, as we shall see. Adolph Beck was not believed and was convicted. Then it was found that not one but two mistakes, had been made. Dickman was his twin in circumstances; was he also his twin in a miscarriage of justice?

---

1   "Trials of Adolph Beck" p102

*   Although actually written fourteen years after Dickman's trial.

(5)

If the identification evidence falls, or at least is not reliably proved, then the case against John Dickman does not exist. What is left is ill assorted ballast; theory built not on foundation but quicksand. There is nothing of substance left. But let us sift it anyway.

The Crown said that Nisbet's murderer had travelled with him from Newcastle to Morpeth. What in fact do we actually know? Just this. A man boarded the train with him, a man was with him at Heaton and there was a man in the compartment at Stannington. There were seven stops between Newcastle and Stannington.

John Grant and John Cosher gave evidence that Nisbet's compartment appeared vacant at Morpeth and Longhurst. Grant was standing at the head of the platform waiting for the train to come in. That was confirmed by a passenger in the first compartment who knew Grant and saw him there. Grant said the third compartment was empty. But if the Crown's theory was right then there is a very serious omission in Grant's evidence.

He did not see anybody get out of the compartment!

John Dickman indisputably left the train at Morpeth. He said that he travelled in a compartment towards the rear of the train. John Grant's mute testimony does in fact indirectly support this.

Dickman said that he was visiting a mine at Dovecot, situated near Stannington Village. He bought a return ticket to Stannington, missed the stop because he was studying the Grand National, and got out at Morpeth paying an excess fare of 2½ pence. Asked why he had not caught the train back to Stannington, he gave the perfectly logical answer:

> '*If I had got out at Stannington I should have gone to Dovecot Pit, and then I should have walked from the Dovecot Pit to Morpeth, so that by walking back from Morpeth to the Dovecot Pit I should pass this drift, so I was merely stopping, as it were, at the wrong end of the journey.*'

The 'drift' he was referring to was a coal drift alongside the Morpeth–Stannington Road. Dickman claimed that he had intended to assess the quality of the coal for a Newcastle Coal Merchant named Houldsworth.

At no point did the Crown attempt to explain why a man who intended to commit murder at Morpeth should only buy a ticket as far as Stannington, or why he made no attempt to catch the train back to Newcastle *which reached Morpeth only eight minutes after the train from Newcastle arrived.* Instead they said that he strolled through the barrier drawing attention to himself by paying an excess fare. Now does this make sense?

Yet another John, John Athey, the ticket collector at Morpeth, was called to give evidence. He confirmed Dickman's story: the excess fare was the only one collected by him that day.

Under the adversarial system of justice any action by the accused, no matter how innocuous, how routine, even if it is a point claimed in his favour, can be turned against him if the Prosecution feels that some sort of damaging inference can be drawn from it.

According to the Crown, Dickman had the excess fare 'suspiciously ready'.* How that, by itself, can possibly be suspicious is beyond my comprehension. Dickman disputed it anyway. He said that he had had to get the ticket and the money out of his waistcoat pocket. This was not the only dispute between Athey and himself. Athey said that Dickman had been wearing an overcoat which meant that a bag might conceivably have been concealed under it if it was the fawn burberry which had slits in the sides. According to Athey the overcoat was hanging slightly forwards. But as Dickman recalled it he had his coat over his arm or shoulder, and it was his brown burberry.

It was Dickman who unhesitatingly volunteered the information that he had travelled to Morpeth that morning — the Police had no way of knowing about it until he told them. It was Dickman who mentioned the excess fare. Here again the Police knew nothing of it and Athey could neither identify Dickman or say what colour coat he was allegedly wearing. Yet the details which he, Dickman, provided were then turned against him. But where there was a significant point in his favour the Prosecution did not mention it. They were later to offer in evidence Dickman's left glove and left trouser pocket. The thumb, and forefinger of the glove were bloodstained, and there were specks of blood on the lining of the trouser pocket. Dickman had handed over the ticket and the money with his left hand. The outward half of the ticket was produced in Court; *there was no blood on it.*

The same manipulation is evident in the Crown's explanation of why Dickman was travelling back and forth between Newcastle and Stannington that winter. He explained it when he gave his evidence. Unfortunately he explained it very badly. This is what he said:—

> *'Mr Christie (a coal merchant and business acquaintance of Dickman's) was interested in these sinking operations at Dovecot... I wished to have some private information, and I also wished to give Mr Hogg (a Contractor with interests in the Dovecot mine) information of a private nature...'*

In other words Christie, Hogg and Dickman were each trying to make money out of the Dovecot operation. Dickman seems to have been scuttling between Christie and Hogg to his own advantage. Nefarious possibly, but it has

---

* Lord Coleridge's description.

no relevance to the crime Dickman was being tried for. Yet it was made to count against him, first in terms of character and then, more importantly, to suggest that Dickman had no real interests in Dovecot and was merely using the trips to plan the robbery and murder of John Nisbet. Hogg and Christie both gave evidence for the prosecution.

Hogg:—

> *'He [Dickman] had nothing to do with the work I had on hand... He did not ask me [about] that [Christie's involvement in the Company], nor did he mention it...he had nothing to do with it.'*

Christie:—

> *'He [Dickman] had nothing to do with this sinking operation at Dovecot... He had no authority from me to go to Dovecot or to discuss any matters in connection with the sinking.'*

Which was all very satisfactory for the Prosecution in that they were able to use the fact that Hogg and Christie did not want their affairs scrutinised too closely as a point against Dickman. It had a lot to do with winning the case; very little to do with arriving at the truth.

Hogg and Christie were, at best, being economical with the truth. Mitchell-Innes, for the most part of this trial pallid in logic and energy, for once roused himself to a performance. He hammered away at Hogg until he admitted that Dickman had indeed discussed affairs at Dovecot with him.

> *Q. Did he not mention Christie to you because Christie was interested in the sinking operations?*
>
> *A. If he mentioned Christie that was the reason he mentioned it.*

This was not what Tindal Atkinson wanted to hear so he re-examined.

> *Q. ...have you any distinct recollections at all?*

For once his subtlety did not get past Mitchell-Innes:—

> *'I submit this witness has clearly said he did mention it.'*

Hogg confirmed it:—

> *'I would say he has done it'*

Coleridge:—

> *'He (Hogg) said to me...that he (Dickman) may have mentioned Christie's name and if he did it may have been with reference to the sinking operations.'*

Hogg underlined this with a simple, 'yes'.
Christie was even more difficult to pin down.

Q. I suggest to you that the prisoner...had in fact mentioned the Dovecot sinking to you from time to time?

*A. He may have done, but I have no recollection. **I have no doubt it was discussed.***

Q. I suggest to you that on one occasion, or perhaps more, you suggested to Dickman he should accompany you, not on business, out to Morpeth and Dovecot?

A. I may have done so, but I have no recollection of it.

I think we can dispense with Mr Christie's convenient lack of recollection and take it as confirmed that Dickman was in some way expecting to benefit from what was going on at Dovecot.

That having been established, we can now point to other flaws in the Crown's case.

The 10:27 reached Morpeth at 11:16. Dickman left the station. The next time he was seen (by Elliot and Saunderson) was in Morpeth at 1:20. He later claimed to have spent the intervening two hours on an abortive journey to Dovecot which was abandoned because of an attack of piles.

The Prosecution said that he spent those two hours disposing of the bag at the Barr Moor East Colliery, although nobody saw him there.

In order for the reader to fully understand these matters I have reproduced a map of the Morpeth-Stannington-Dovecot locale on the next page.

As can be seen from the map, the Barr Moor East Colliery was located on the Blythe Road, nearly mid-way between Morpeth and Stannington Stations. The distance from Morpeth was 1.6 miles. The normal walking time per mile for a 43 year old man would be no greater than twenty minutes at the most, which means that Dickman should have accomplished the journey by 11:45. Allow a few minutes to dispose of the bag and then around 30 minutes for the return journey and Dickman should have been back at Morpeth by 12:20, certainly not much later, enabling him to catch the express train to Newcastle at 1:12. But he missed that train and had to take the 1:40 slow train. The timings here support Dickman's account; they most decidedly do not support the Crown's.

Nor is this the only problem with their thesis. If Dickman was lying then why did he not travel on to Dovecot to give credence to his story?

Look at the map again. The Morpeth to Stannington Road is 3 miles long. It then turns off towards Dovecot, another mile. Assume for the moment that Dickman was telling the truth then without the piles he would have been at the Colliery by 1 p.m., allowing for time to inspect the coal drift en-route.

Now let us assume that he was not telling the truth. He firstly travels to the Barr Moor East Colliery arriving at 11:45 and leaving at say 11:50. The distance then to Stannington Station is 2 miles. Dovecot is a further 1.6 miles on from Stannington Station. Dickman would have reached Dovecot Colliery at almost

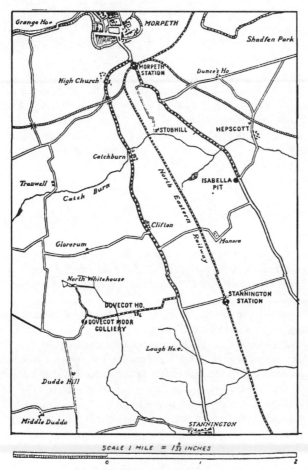

Map of Morpeth District.

exactly 1 p.m., i.e. the same time as if he was telling the truth. Had anybody mentioned that it had taken about 25 minutes longer than such a journey should take, the coal drift story was there to fall back on.

What we have here is the straightforward story of a man going about his business, supported by common sense and timings; also by evidence, even though it had to be dragged out of two un-co-operative witnesses. On the other hand there is the Crown's account. It is a monument to illogicality, inconsistency and timings which do not hang together. Was this not one of Coleridge's 'rents which a man may pass through in safety'? Judge for yourselves.

The next two witnesses were Inspector Andrew Tait and Superintendent John Weddell. There was, by admission, Police misconduct in the case, but nobody has ever suggested that Tait and Weddell were parties to it. They were models of veracity. From Weddell, Mitchell-Innes summoned up Elliot and Saunderson to speak for Dickman. From this, the Police testimony, he drew one of his strongest cards — the fact that Dickman had, without qualm, provided much of the evidence that was now being used against him.

Then he went and ruined it with another horrendous gaffe (it was not to be the last).

> *'You have not traced a half penny of this money except the £17 to Dickman?'*

And although he tried to make amends by putting the question again — this time prefixed by 'unless it is the £17' — the damage had been done. Dickman's own Counsel appeared to be conceding that he was in possession of some of the stolen money.

The last witness on day one of the trial was Dr Charles Burnham, the Police Surgeon who had examined Nisbet's body.

Burnham's evidence makes gruesome reading. Nisbet had died instantly when a bullet had entered his head two inches below the left ear. There were four other wounds: one directly behind the left ear, another immediately behind the right ear, and two separate wounds above and below the left eye. Of these only the latter was a serious injury. Burnham had extracted three bullets from the body and later recovered a fourth from the floor of the compartment. The fifth bullet was never traced.

The Doctor was cross-examined by Mitchell-Innes.

> *Q. ...you found blood on the neck and the front of the overcoat and other articles of clothing?*
>
> *A. Certainly.*
>
> *Q. It had flowed back and down?*
>
> *A. It was all over the hand which was not covered with the glove and also it covered the glove. It covered his clothing where he had been lying.*

Q. As well as the upholstery and the floor?

A. Yes. They had covered the floor with sawdust when I saw it, but there had been a considerable quantity of blood about.

Q. As a matter of fact, blood was still flowing when you examined the body?

A. Yes, especially from the pistol wound in the skull.

At which point Mitchell-Innes disengaged the question having successfully created the impression of a carriage awash with blood.

Realising that his opponent would lay a great deal of emphasis in his closing speech on the killer's clothes being covered with blood, Tindal Atkinson tried hard during re-examination to quell the effect of Dr Burnham's testimony. He did not succeed.

Q. Would there necessarily be a large quantity of blood at the moment after this man met his death?

A. The blood which flowed from his nose would be very considerable. The wound at the back of the head opened large vessels which would bleed considerably.

This was not quite the answer which the Prosecutor was looking for. A simple "yes" and he would later have claimed that the killer's clothes would not necessarily have been heavily bloodstained; that most of the blood had been disgorged at the moment of death. But instead Burnham's answer had only reinforced the extensive nature of the bleeding. So Tindal-Atkinson altered his tack slightly.

Q. Would it commence at once?

A. Yes.

Q. Where would the blood be flowing from?

A. In whatever position he was in the haemorrhage would take place where the face had been injured, particularly the posterior wound, or the wound in the nose.

And earlier on Burnham had said:—

'The blood would continue to flow from the wound which had traversed the nose bones.'

Re-examination continued:—

Q. He would continue to bleed after death?

A. Yes, it would run especially from the posterior wound...especially if he lay on his back.

Q. That is the wound behind the ear?

A. Yes.

Based on this highly selective piece of examination, Tindal-Atkinson was to suggest during his closing speech that although blood had continued to flow from one wound, it did not necessarily follow that the killer's clothes would be extensively stained with blood. This is what he told the Jury:—

> *'It was said there would have been more blood upon the prisoner had he murdered Nisbet. But, with one exception, the wounds would not bleed very much until afterwards.'*

This was both a subtle piece of evasion and an adroit attempt to link some minuscule specks of blood on Dickman's clothing with the amount of blood which the killer might have gotten on his clothes. But it was certainly not a correct interpretation of Dr Burnham's evidence. He had said nothing about the bleeding not becoming extensive until afterwards. Quite the reverse. He had said that there would have been a considerable quantity of blood at the time of death and that blood had then continued to flow from two, not one, wounds afterwards.

Here, the prosecution found itself in real difficulties. Burnham's testimony was about a man shot five times, two ghastly wounds which bled for more than thirty minutes after death, and a compartment more reminiscent of a slaughterhouse than a railway carriage. The only conclusion to be drawn was that the killer's clothes would have been drenched in blood. Yet Dickman had calmly left the train, strolled through the ticket barrier drawing attention to himself with an excess fare, and two hours later was mooching around Morpeth discussing horse racing with an acquaintance. But nobody noticed even the faintest trace of blood on him. It is worth recalling that whoever shot John Nisbet blasted him five times from close range and then wrestled his lifeless corpse under the seat of the compartment. Blood had spurted and flowed and it seems inconceivable that it did not permeate the killer(s) clothes to a considerable extent. But John Dickman was virtually untarnished.

(6)

On the morning of day two, the Prosecution attempted to prove four things: that Dickman had bought a gun, that he was contaminated by Nisbet's blood, that he had deposited the wages bag down the air shaft and, lastly that he was in dire financial straits at the time of the crime.

Miss Henrietta Hymen was summoned to the witness box. She managed a Newsagent's where Dickman received mail under the alias "Fred Black". In October, 1909 a parcel had arrived for him; shortly afterwards a card requesting the return of a gun, sent in error. Dickman had collected the parcel in January and asked Miss Hymen for a label so that he could return it. On that occasion he had told her his real name.

There was no suggestion that Dickman had kept the gun. He testified that he had returned it to the senders, Bell Brothers of Glasgow. This was not disputed, either by the prosecution or by Bell Brothers.

The next witness ought not to have appeared. His name was Andrew Kirkwood and he was employed by a Newcastle Gunsmith, Pope's. Kirkwood turned out to be the witness who never was:— his testimony was ruled to be inadmissible.

Tindal Atkinson had seemingly decided to exclude Kirkwood altogether. However, when the prosecutor sought to pass him by Coleridge intervened and asked why.

Tindal Atkinson:—

> *'...Both I and my learned friend [Mitchell-Innes] agree that there are circumstances...which would prevent it [Kirkwood's evidence] capable of being proved, but I will put the witness in the box if your Lordship thinks the question should be investigated.'*

Initially Coleridge appeared to bow to Tindal Atkinson's judgement. But then, with a sharp *volte face*, the prosecutor argued Kirkwood into the box after all.

> *'...I think that would be more satisfactory, perhaps, to see how far the proof legitimately can go.'*

Having previously acquiesced with Tindal Atkinson's decision, Coleridge now allowed himself to be persuaded that it was only right and proper to go along with the Crown's second thoughts on the matter:—

> *'As I have mentioned it, I think that would be the best course to take.'*

Mitchell-Innes was apparently not very good at spotting inadmissible evidence which might unfairly damage his client because he made no objection.

Kirkwood was duly sworn and told the Court:—

> *'...I kept a register of pistols sold, which I produce. There is an entry on the fourth line from the bottom of the page in my handwriting. It is in this book that I enter whenever a revolver is sold, either by myself or by someone else in the shop in my employ. By looking at this entry I could not say that I had sold a particular revolver to the person whose name appears there, because I make the entry myself, whereas the fact is that sometimes it has been sold by an employee. I cannot say whether I sold this one or not.'*

That, said Tindal Atkinson, was the difficulty, the evidence was inconclusive. And with much grave noddings of be-wigged heads and pats on the back to the fairness of British Justice, the matter was dropped and Mr Kirkwood was excused further testimony. However it is worth recounting Mitchell-Innes comment on the matter:—

> *'Needless to say, I very much appreciate the absolutely fair spirit in which this is conducted, as one would expect in such a case as this.'*

Oh really?

The Jury had heard what the prosecution wanted them to hear without the possibility of the evidence being destroyed in cross examination. Indeed, they had heard the accused's own Counsel describe the proceedings as 'absolutely fair'.

There are times during this case when one feels that with Mitchell-Innes leading the defence a prosecuting Counsel was not really needed.

Revolvers were far easier to obtain in 1910 than they are now. Dickman, as a free lance bookmaker, not operating from any premises, would have had a good reason to carry one, particularly in October, 1909. As we shall see, he had arranged to borrow a large amount of money at that time.

But no gun was in fact ever traced to John Dickman. The Police had combed the Stannington–Morpeth district but failed to find anything, as Superintendent Weddell confirmed. They had ransacked Dickman's home, 'cut it into mincemeat' said Dickman, dug up his garden, searched the drains and examined the neighbourhood with a fine toothcomb. The outcome was described by Weddell: 'we found no pistol anywhere.'

The prosecution then resorted to sheer desperation tactics, Henrietta Hymen and Andrew Kirkwood. But the revolver sent in error to Dickman had been returned and Kirkwood's 'evidence' was not viable. In my view it was abysmally unfair that any of this should have been led against him.

Thomas Simpson also worked for Pope's. He was in the witness box for only a few minutes; the stunning effect of his testimony lasted considerably longer.

Simpson had examined the four bullets extracted from Nisbet's body. Two were nickel capped .250 calibre which would have been fired from an automatic pistol. The others were lead, .350, and would have been fired from a heavier calibre pistol. Simpson concluded:—

> *'These four bullets must of necessity have been fired from different pistols.'*

Two guns suggested of course two killers. Once again, Tindal Atkinson fell back in desperation:—

> *'Whoever committed the murder must have thought it necessary to have two pistols...he must have thought it was necessary to... use two of them... to secure the death of the man he intended to rob.'*

Why?

Two-gun walking-arsenals do not really exist outside the fictional world of the Hollywood Western. But Tindal Atkinson did have another theory, one so ridiculous that he did not dare to raise it in Court. It later succeeded in convincing one person however: *Mitchell-Innes*.

Sydney Rowan-Hamilton takes up the story:—

> *'Although I have treated... the evidence as pointing to two pistols being used... there is little doubt that only one was employed. The murderer had endeavoured to make the smaller bullets fit the barrel by wrapping paper round the cartridge... one such piece of paper was found in the carriage, but it was not realised to what use it had been put. The prosecution, having to account for the bullets of different calibre, naturally formed the conclusion that two revolvers had been employed. There is now no doubt that only one was used. My authority for this statement is Mr Mitchell-Innes, K.C.'* [1]

John Nisbet was slain on March 18th. Thomas Simpson gave his evidence on July 5th, a gap of nearly four months. Inclusive of the two dates, it amounts to 110 days. Yet we are asked to believe that given all this time, and with the infinite resources of the State at their disposal, the prosecution was unable to produce this answer until after the trial had closed. Does this not stretch belief just a little too far?

When it did surface it was at a time when many people were profoundly disturbed that a miscarriage of justice had occurred!

It was not put to Thomas Simpson because he would undoubtedly have ridiculed it, particularly as, in his words, ammunition was 'quite easily' obtained. It was not placed before the Jury because they would have seen just how frail the Crown's case really was. It relied on a piece of paper on a carriage floor without any provable link to the case. And only one. There should have been two and probably three, because three of Nisbet's wounds were superficial and two of these had definitely been inflicted by the smaller calibre bullets.

As for Mitchell-Innes' acceptance of this ludicrous idea, his performance in the trial suggests that he was not much given to thinking, or that he had much to think with.

The most rational explanation of Simpson's evidence is that there were two guns and two killers.

The 'evidence' now shifts to the blood stains found on Dickman's glove and trousers and an oil stain discovered on his fawn burberry coat.

---

1   "Trial of J A Dickman" p11

Dr Robert Boland, Professor of Jurisprudence at Durham University, had made a minute examination of these articles. His findings were as follows:—

The glove: On the tips of the thumb and forefinger of a left hand suede glove were dark red stains ¾" by ¼". They were

of recent origin having been acquired between March 12th and March 26th (the date of his examination), and they were certainly bloodstains although he could not say whether the blood was human or animal.

The overcoat: There was a large, darkened stain on the left front of Dickman's burberry overcoat which had been partially treated with paraffin.

The trousers: In the left pocket were nine minuscule bloodstains, the largest being about the size of the head of a small shawl pin. The stains were clustered together in an area 2" by 1" halfway down the eleven inch deep pocket.

In cross-examination Mitchell-Innes revealed how pitifully weak this all was.

Q. Could you find any evidence of blood whatever on the burberry coat?

A. None.

Q. With a glove of that size, is it true to say that the little pin points... of blood in the pocket, were in such a position as might have been caused by the thumb of the glove being put into the pocket?

A. Yes.

Q. I am right in suggesting that you will admit that these stains might well have been caused by that?

A. Very probably.

This was all very satisfactory but now came yet another blunder.

'I take it the stain on the coat might have been a stain contracted by a man walking in a Colliery with oil and coal dust around?'

Mitchell-Innes was presumably referring to Dovecot, but the next witness the Jury were to hear was Peter Spooner, Manager of the Barr Moor East Colliery where the wages bag had been found!

Mitchell-Innes had unwittingly scored a bonus point for the prosecution.

Dickman's explanation was that it was bicycle oil and that is the question his Counsel should have asked.

Two minor bloodstains on a glove, some minute spots in a trouser pocket. We are asked to accept that there were the entire residue of bloody murder. Read Dr Burnham's Testimony. It was of a man shot from only a few inches away:

of a large quantity of spurting blood at the moment of death; of a compartment and corpse drenched in blood.

Tiny pin pricks on a glove and trouser pocket. This is desperation evidence, in every sense of the word.

Dickman said he had not worn the gloves or coat on the 18th. He quarrelled with Dr Boland's opinion that the blood on the gloves was recent, hardly the behaviour of a guilty man who has heard his defence Counsel advance a perfectly logical explanation for it.

The specks in the trouser pocket Dickman thought were from a nosebleed, facial cut or cutting his corns. That fits the evidence; the abattoir on the 10:27 does not.

Peter Spooner then gave evidence of finding the bag. The Crown were contending that Dickman had disposed of it on the morning of the 18th. Eleven weeks had elapsed between then and Spooner's discovery.

In cross examination Mitchell-Innes knocked the prosecution's theory into a cocked hat.

> *Q. It is your duty, no doubt, under the coal mines regulation acts to constantly inspect the air shaft?*
>
> *A. Yes.*
>
> *Q. How often in a week do you inspect it?*
>
> *A. We are not tied to once a week in roads like that... just occasionally, once in a month, one in five weeks.*
>
> *Q. But you do carry out your duties?*
>
> *A. Yes.*

It is not strictly necessary to prove motive, but not to attempt it leaves a very large hole in a case. In this particular one there were already as many as in the "Titanic", two years later. Showing that Dickman was in need of money on March 18th was therefore a necessity for Tindal Atkinson. To a certain extent he succeeded.

One Robert Sweeney recounted how in October, 1909 Dickman had tried to borrow £10 from him. A Jeweller named Kettering gave evidence that in February, 1910 he had lent Dickman £5 for betting purposes against the security of a gold scarf ring and a set of gold studs. 'I have still these articles in my possession... I have not yet been paid back the money,' he complained. Two pawntickets against pledges by Dickman under the alias of "John Wilkinson" told a sad story. Both related to the pawning of binoculars in March, 1910; the second pair on the day before Nisbet's murder.

But these witnesses and items were merely potboilers. The main bulk of this part of the case against Dickman was delivered by a moneylender named

Samuel Cohen, Dickman's friend Frank Christie, two Bank Clerks... John Babcock and Robert Sedcole, Thomas Paisley the Treasurer of the local Co-op Society, and William Christie, a Post Office Savings Bank Clerk.

William Christie first: Dickman's wife Annie had, between 1907 and 1910 deposited some £20 in her Post Office Savings Account. On January 1st, 1910 her account had stood at £15.04* but following a series of withdrawals between January 5th and March 14th it was reduced to 54 pence.

Thomas Paisley: On October 30th 1907, Annie Dickman's account stood at £73.86. By March 17th, 1910 it had been reduced to £4. The withdrawals had been 'pretty frequent' during 1909 although in fairness Mrs Dickman had made a deposit of £3 in July of that year.

John Babcock: On June 30th, 1909 Dickman had had in his National Provincial Bank Account the princely sum of three pence. On September 13th he had deposited the sum of £4.53 but three days later withdrew £4.37 leaving 19 pence. Then on October 18th he had banked a cheque for £20 made out by Samuel Cohen. Three days later Dickman had drawn out £20.05 leaving a mere 14 pence, but on November 14th another cheque, this time for £200 and written by Frank Christie was paid in. Dickman had subsequently debited the account by £160 on November 26th and had completed the withdrawal by taking out the balance of £40 on November 29th. A bank charge of 29 pence had then put the account into the red by 15 pence on December 31st.

Robert Sedcole: The last important deposit into Dickman's Lloyds Bank Account had been £10 on May 13th, 1909. The account was then steadily run down until it stood at a nil balance on October 16th. The account was closed on December 14th.

Samuel Cohen: On October 18th 1909, Dickman had visited him at his Company, the Cash Accommodation and Investment Company, and arranged to borrow £20 at a rate of interest of £1 per month, the principal sum to be repaid in three months. Dickman had met the monthly interest payments but when the three months were up he had announced that he could not possibly repay the loan. Cohen had agreed to extend it by a further three months at the same rate of interest. The last interest payment had been made on March 17th, 1910. On May 9th, Mrs Dickman had paid back to Cohen the original loan of £20.

In November, 1909, Dickman had introduced Cohen to Frank Christie who had subsequently borrowed £200 from him.

Frank Christie: From time to time he had placed money with Dickman for betting purposes. In November, 1909 Dickman had introduced him to Samuel Cohen from whom he had borrowed £200. This money he had passed on to Dickman who had first banked it and then returned £100 to him for what Christie described as his 'own private affairs'. The other £100 Dickman had retained for placing bets on his, Christie's behalf. 'He (Dickman) was not to receive anything

---

*   Decimalised money.

out of it for himself, but if they were successful he would undoubtedly have received something.' Dickman had told him that none of the bets had been successful.

Dickman's answer to the question of being hard pressed for money was a very simple one... he denied it.

> *'In February of this year I had £120 of my own. I had given my wife £50 of it, that left £70 and some went in different ways. At the time the Waterloo Cup was run* I would have about £40 of my own. I had £17 odd over of my own, with which I intended to go to the Waterloo Cup [Author's note: he decided not to attend it after all]. I gave my wife £15 or £20 out of the £40. I was keeping the rest of the money to start my season with.'*

Which very neatly explained the £17 he had on him when he was arrested.

Unfortunately Dickman's finances were neither neat nor simple. It was a story of depleted bank accounts, visits to pawnbrokers, and, most damaging of all, a loan from a moneylender which he was unable to repay. And later Tindal Atkinson was able to time to perfection the introduction of a letter from Mrs Dickman which strongly implied that the Dickman family was in less than affluent circumstances.

Dickman's finances were his achilles heel. Objectivity insists that the Crown had demonstrated a motive. This having been said, three specific points need to be made on Dickman's behalf. He may, as he said, have allowed his wife to think he had less than what he did have; it is not uncommon. A professional gambler might be inclined to bet with other people's money, such as a money-lender's, working on the premise that the winnings will outweigh the interest. Similarly a professional gambler can be strapped for cash one day and rolling in it the next. Remember, that was what Dickman was, a professional gambler.

But even if we concede that there was a motive, that by itself cannot prove a case; motive is a corollary to other evidence, not a substitute for it. What other evidence was there? Identification? It was in the highest degree unsatisfactory, and in part actually pointed away from Dickman, to some other man. The rest of the prosecution's case was worthless. There were huge holes in their theory of Dickman's movements that morning, movements consistent with innocence, inexplicable with guilt. There was no real forensic evidence, they had not tied him to possession of a gun, and the two guns implied two killers.

You are now the Jury. Would you hang a man on this evidence?

---

* February.

(7)

Thomas Paisley, the co-op treasurer, put the final touches to the prosecution's case. As he descended from the witness box Tindal Atkinson rose to announce that that completed the case for the Crown. Now it was the defence's turn. But in fact the most brutal and tormenting part of John Dickman's ordeal was only just beginning.

Thirteen years earlier Dickman would not have been permitted to set foot in the witness box. Prior to 1898 no accused person was allowed to give evidence on their own behalf in a serious criminal trial. Throughout the 19th Century pressure to change the law on this fundamental point built up inexorably. There were any number of cases where the verdict might have been different had the accused been allowed to give evidence. Those given most prominence include William Kirwan,[*] Thomas Scampton[**] and Serafino Pelizzioni[***]. But perhaps the trial which epitomised the situation more than any other was that of Arthur Orton, the Tichborne Claimant. Orton, a butcher from Wapping in East London, laid claim to being Sir Roger Tichborne, long lost heir to the Tichborne estates[****]. Orton's claims fell apart during a civil action in which he was able to give evidence. He was then tried for perjury which being a criminal offence meant that he could not go into the witness box. Douglas Woodruff, in his book "The Tichborne Claimant" sums up the resultant farce very neatly:—

> *'The Claimant was seated opposite the Judges, unable to speak or to be questioned, while Judges and Counsel went on speculating what he had meant by answers given in the civil action.'*[1]

Such cases amply demonstrated the need for a change in the law and it came in the shape of the Criminal Law Amendment Act of 1898. But any major alteration involves overriding valid objections, as in war an option of difficulties. Although on balance the reformers were right, dissenters nevertheless had some valid points. One was that juries would be suspicious of an accused who chose not to give evidence. Two years after the Law was changed Herbert Bennett was tried for the murder of his wife. He elected against going into the witness box, an action which undoubtedly weighed against him in the minds

---

1   "The Tichborne Claimant" p259

*   Convicted of murdering his wife: her death may have been accidental.
**   Wrongly convicted of arson.
***   Wrongly convicted of murder.
****   Tichborne almost certainly perished at sea.

of the Jury. Bennett was convicted and hanged. Many believe he was innocent[*].

A second objection, closely tied in with the first, is that an accused might feel compelled to give evidence when it was against his or her interests, particularly somebody who would not make a good witness on their own behalf. Unhappily, John Dickman is a case in point. Rowan-Hamilton has this to say:—

> *'...many, I feel sure, will contend that, if it had been possible to keep Dickman out of the witness-box, the probability is that the Jury would have acquitted him, on the ground that the prosecution had failed to satisfy them entirely as to his guilt.'*[1]

Mitchell-Innes had three options; call no evidence whatsoever and stand on the Crown not having proved its case, call Dickman only, or call Dickman and any other available witnesses. Number three was correctly discarded. There were few, if any, witnesses of consequence who could aid the defence, and if he called them Mitchell-Innes lost the right to speak after Tindal Atkinson.

The decision lay between one and two. In retrospect one would have been the best choice although it involved a fearful risk. Robert Hoolhouse, whose case I referred to in the introduction, lost his life when his advocate adopted this course. Mitchell-Innes veered away from it and pumped for number two. We do not know what persuaded him but he seems to have had little contact with his client, and, judging by the way he handled the case, he appears neither to have mastered his brief or liaised very closely with Dickman's solicitor, Edward Clark.

Dickman took the witness box shortly after lunch on July 5th. He was conducted through his evidence in chief by Lord William Percy. It was of course a perfectly innocuous examination aimed at showing the accused man, and the vexed question of his finances, in the best possible light. We need only summarise it very briefly.

Up to 1906 Dickman had been the Secretary of the Morpeth Moor Colliery. That year the Colliery had been sold. Dickman had negotiated its sale through Frank Christie and had received a commission of between £500-£550[**]. At around the same time he had been the beneficiary of a legacy amounting to another £220. Armed with these resources he had gone to work for himself as a freelance bookmaker.

His interest in the Dovecot Colliery resulted from his having introduced Hogg to Christie. He had visited Hogg on several occasions, the last being on March 4th, to discuss matters of a private nature involving both Hogg and

---

1   "Trial of J A Dickman" Preface

---

[*]   Although he may have been guilty of treason, also a capital offence.
[**]   Around £30,000 on today's values.

Christie. Lord Percy skated nimbly over this path of thin ice; the enigma of Dickman's relationship with the two witnesses was never resolved in court. What remained was the impression of something a little dubious.

Talk of Hogg and Christie led directly on to the events of March 18th. A full account of Dickman's movements has already been given. This naturally formed the bulk of his direct evidence. The remainder consisted of his confirmation that he had returned the gun to its senders, a survey of his financial position, the essential points of which have already been examined, and an accusation that the police had intimidated Hall into identifying him. Dickman concluded his direct examination by repeating what he had said to the police when they had arrested him:—

> '*I said in answer to the charge... I do not understand the proceedings. It is absurd for me to deny the charge, because it is absurd to make it. I can only say that I absolutely deny it... with the stress on the word absurd, because I thought then it was a most absurd charge to be made against me, and I still think so.*'

This resounding declaration brought Dickman's direct examination to a close on a high note. But cross examination was to be a very different story. It would not be true to say that he stumbled badly; a more accurate description would be that he fell flat on his face at the outset and remained there throughout Tindal Atkinson's scorching barrage of questions. It might not have been so bad had the onslaught come only from one quarter, but Lord Coleridge repeatedly interrupted with questions of his own, questions which in many instances were duplicates of those the Prosecutor had just asked. An eminent Judge has said that it is the duty of the Judge to hold his tongue until the last possible moment. It seems that this was not Coleridge's view, at least not on this occasion. Reading through the transcript it is impossible to make a provable accusation that any of his questions were improper. They are open to the legitimate interpretation of being designed to clarify Dickman's answers. But taken in conjunction with Coleridge's summing up later, they are also open to the inference that the bench was expressing dissatisfaction with Dickman's answers. Much of the proceedings can be described as a legal hunting season with Tindal Atkinson and Coleridge in full cry after their hapless prey in the box.

Dickman's ordeal began with Tindal Atkinson — and Coleridge — asking him about his relationship with the murdered man:—

> *Q. You say you knew the deceased man?*
>
> *A. I knew the deceased man; but if I had been asked off-hand what his name was I could not have told you.*
>
> *Q. Did you not know his name?*
>
> *A. No, if anyone had said to me — do you know Nisbet? — after a*

description, I would have known the man.

This seems to me to be a perfectly reasonable answer, but it failed to satisfy either the Judge or Counsel.

Q. I do not understand you. Did you know his name or did you not?

A. Yes, but if I had been asked off-hand I would not have been able to call that man Nisbet.

Q. But you knew his name was Nisbet?

A. Yes.

Q. (Coleridge) You knew him and you knew his name?

A. Yes, if it had been mentioned to me.

Taking his cue from his colleague on the bench, Tindal Atkinson, who knew a dray horse when he saw one, complained:—

Q. I do not quite understand that. Did you know his name independently at that time of anybody telling it to you?

A. No, he was not an individual who was on my mind at all.

Q. I did not ask you that. It is a very plain question?

I submit that earlier Dickman had given a very plain answer, but let us resume again with Mr Tindal Atkinson:—

Q. Did you know this man by name?

A. Yes, I did know him by name.

Q. On the 18th March did you know this man by name?

A. I did.

One of the Barrister's little tricks of the trade is to try to unsettle the witness at the very outset of cross-examination. Tindal Atkinson had managed this splendidly. It is fair to say that Dickman never recovered from this first disastrous brush with the prosecution. Tindal Atkinson, on the other hand, was to sail blithely on, drowning Dickman in a welter of confusion at almost every turn.

Returning to his relationship with Nisbet, Dickman appeared on the surface to be rather contradicting himself, but a closer examination of his replies suggests that he was saying something quite simple; — that he knew Nisbet by sight and had heard his name, but that to the casual inquirer he would not have been able to fit the face to the name without a description. There is an important point here, a subtle one which clearly flew over the heads of the jurors; if Dickman was guilty then surely he would have refused to admit anything beyond knowing Nisbet by sight.

He did deny knowing Nisbet's occupation, which in turn led on to the obvious question of whether he was himself familiar with the routine for collecting colliery wages. Having been a colliery secretary he could hardly have said no, but he did make the useful statement that his own colliery's wages had been collected from Morpeth, not Newcastle. Unfortunately, he then succeeded in obscuring this point by adding, quite gratuitously: 'I have done the same business myself.' He was doing the prosecution's work for them, but once again the question arises of whether a guilty man would have volunteered such a remark. Moreover, the plain truth is that if Dickman was not aware of Nisbet's occupation — and there was not the remotest shred of evidence to show that he was — then the fact of his knowing the general routine for colliery wages becomes entirely academic.

Tindal Atkinson shelved this particular line for the moment in order to concentrate on Dickman's March 4th visit to Dovecot. The prosecution's purpose here was to suggest that Dickman had no valid reason for his visit.

Dickman's replies were not particularly satisfactory. Tindal Atkinson traded deftly on his obvious reluctance to discuss his affairs involving Hogg and Christie. It would not be true to say that Dickman was evasive, although the Jury doubtless thought so. Instead there was a curious ambience about his answers. He seemed not so much to evade issues as to surround them with unnecessary mystery. One theme runs poignantly through his testimony: he had no real perception of the mortal danger in which he stood. He would not delve fully into the murky waters of his relationship with Hogg and Christie; he clearly thought it was his business and nobody else's, and that the Jury would inevitably free him in order to pursue it. He could not have been more wrong.

But was this the attitude of a guilty man?

A period of desultory questioning about Dickman's reading habits on trains, and his knowledge of the local collieries, led back to the subject of wage routines. This ended with Dickman denying knowledge of the workings of any particular colliery. But the prosecution still succeeded in showing him up in a bad light. At one point Tindal Atkinson demanded: 'I want an answer'. In fact Dickman had attempted an answer, not a very articulate one, but an answer nonetheless, and a more responsible comeback by the Prosecutor would have been to ask him to clarify it. But then perhaps Tindal Atkinson was rather more interested in suggesting to the Jury that Dickman was being deliberately vague.

Next Tindal Atkinson returned to the subject of whether Dickman knew what Nisbet's occupation was.

Q. You knew he was in the employment of a colliery company?

A. I did not.

Q. Did you know what his business was?

A. No.

Q. Did you know what his business was?

A. I just knew he was a clerk somewhere on the quay.

Would Dickman have noticed Nisbet had he found himself walking beside him that morning? He thought so, but he had known himself to pass people by without realising it. Tindal Atkinson pressed hard on this point and got Dickman to say that his mind was occupied at the time. Which was just what the Prosecutor wanted.

Q. There were few people about. I think that is what you said just now?

A. I did not notice a crowd anywhere.

Q. (Coleridge) Were there few people about?

A. So far as I know, there were very few people about.

These questions had two edges both culminating in a chopping blade directed at Dickman's neck. If there were few people about then how could he fail to notice Nisbet? If on the other hand he was that preoccupied then how did he know there were so few people about? Or, put more simply, heads I win, tails you lose. It was however an unpleasant distortion of what Dickman had actually said.

'There was nobody with me that I know, although there might have been people about.'

Nothing about there being few people about. Entirely what you might expect from a man whose mind was occupied. Where was the defence? How was it that they sat there and allowed the Prosecution to put words in Dickman's mouth that he had never uttered?

The next part of the evidence dealt with Raven and Hepple's identifications. We have already seen what Dickman had to say about them. Unfortunately he did not deny their evidence with any great firmness or clarity, and he simply played into the Prosecution's hands. But the point has to be made — it cannot be restated too often — that a guilty man would surely have been more positive; more emphatic. Instead Dickman's replies were a further illustration that his mind had been elsewhere that morning. We can perhaps peer into that mind as it ticked away in the witness box that day — 'Could I have walked alongside Nisbet without knowing it? — Are Raven and Hepple right?'. The answer which should have come to him — and his instinct seemed to tell him what it was — was no, because he could hardly have strolled alongside Nisbet, made his detour to the lavatory, and then picked him up again on Platform Five. If Dickman was innocent then Hepple was certainly wrong and in my view Raven as well. But if Dickman was prey to such thoughts in the witness box then they can fairly be construed as the perplexities of an innocent man. Conversely, prevarication may have been rooted in guilty deliberations — 'how can I get round this one — what did Hepple say exactly?' — and so on. But surely he is entitled to the benefit of the doubt.

Whatever the truth, uncertainty and vagueness were Dickman's lot in the witness box. Tindal Atkinson turned them against him with damning effect. Viewed in the cold print of the transcript the Prosecutor appears to be merely scoring petty debating points, but there in the courtroom it was devastating. And worse, much worse, was now about to befall Dickman. He was on the threshold of turning uncertainty into a bizarre art form.

Q. What was the compartment that you say you got into?

That was the first of no less than seventeen questions put to Dickman by both Tindal Atkinson and Coleridge before the hopelessly confused witness staggered into the middle compartment of the third carriage. If this was true then he had actually gotten into the compartment immediately in front of Hepple's. This brought forth a tart reminder from Tindal Atkinson.

'If your story is true you must have passed just around him and got into a compartment just ahead of where he was standing?'

Dickman could only reply very lamely that he did not know — he had never seen Hepple that day. But the damage had been done. The prosecution had dealt him a heavy blow. But this does not mean that he was lying. His testimony suggests that he was guessing at the compartment. If so, then it was symptomatic of his performance as a whole, stumbling blindly from one pitfall to the next, trying to be helpful. He was; — but not to himself.

I submit that Dickman really did not know which compartment he had travelled in. This seems to me to make two points in his favour. The first is that a guilty man would surely have worked out in advance a compartment in which to place himself in. The second is that it strengthens his claim that his mind was occupied that morning.

Surprisingly, during the next part of the cross-examination, Dickman provided the Court with his one really intelligent response to Tindal Atkinson's barbs. Here he was being questioned about the coat he had worn on March 18th.

Q. If Hall says you were wearing that fawn coat is he mistaken?

A. Well, I do not think he referred to me at all as wearing a fawn coat. He referred to some individual wearing a fawn coat.

If only all his answers had been in the same vein.

After some discussion about the colour of his coat that morning — Dickman claimed to have worn a brown burberry and not the fawn coat — Tindal Atkinson moved on to his travelling companions that morning.

Q. Did anybody travel with you in your compartment?

And Dickman was back again floundering in his own private sea of indecision. He thought so, he could not say; he thought so, there would be people sitting in the corners; somebody else might have gotten in and out; — or so he thought. Finally it came down to: 'they both got in and out.'

Taken at its face value — which is precisely what the Jury did — then it was all pitifully weak. But peer beneath the surface again. Is there not, once again, a subtle truth in this mish mash. Surely a guilty man would have attempted to be more definite. There were no witnesses to support Dickman, but equally there were none to gainsay him.

A guilty man might well have felt emboldened to invent a few people for the Jury's appetite. But not John Dickman. Instead, he wandered around the corridors of his mind seemingly trying, to be of assistance. And yet again it strengthens the belief that his mind was at Aintree that March morning. Take it forward another step and you have the clear possibility that he genuinely missed his stop as he claimed.

But why then had he not caught the 11:24 back to Stannington. This was Tindal Atkinson's next sally. As we have already seen this was very much a point in the Defence's favour, but regrettably they had not appreciated its strength, and so it was left to the Prosecution to put an interpretation on it in their favour.

Next Tindal Atkinson dealt with the contradiction between Dickman's story of passing through the Morpeth ticket barrier with his coat over his arm and Athey's recollection that he had been wearing it. We need not travel over this old ground again. Doubtless the Jury decided it in Athey's favour.

John Athey receded from Tindal Atkinson's mind to be replaced by Dickman's account of how he had sought relief from an attack of piles by laying down in a field. Here the prosecuting Counsel launched his most sustained attack yet. He knew that it was a story which was entirely without corroboration and he made the most of his opportunity. No less then 116 questions were directed at the hapless Dickman, 14 of them by Coleridge who, as the cross-examination wore on, seemed to become more and more an auxiliary arm of the Crown. Such behaviour cannot have helped Dickman, either in regaining his lost composure or in the eyes of the Jury. In strict legal terms there was perhaps nothing to object to, but Dickman must have felt as though he was being simultaneously interrogated by two Prosecutors.

Even so, he stuck doggedly to his story. Well he might for he had not other. Part of the questioning revolved around whether he had entered the field through a gap in a hedge or a fence. He declined to make a commitment to one or the other; he did not remember and that was that. Nor could he reasonably have been expected to. Piles is a painful and debilitating illness. The sufferer is hardly likely to be concerned with landscape impedimenta. No doubt Tindal Atkinson had something in mind when he raised the issue. Presumably that stretch of road was bordered by either a hedge or a fence. But it does not really matter because Dickman refused to be pinned down on it.

However, the Prosecution did score a point when Dickman admitted going out for a drink on the evening of the 18th. Would a man with an attack of piles be well enough to go out drinking? But then piles do not necessarily last all day, and Dickman said that he had felt better as the afternoon wore on. Would a guilty man inventing a bout of piles admit being well enough to go out that evening? Would it be in his interests? I think not, but under Tindal Atkinson's relentless hammering this point, like so many others, eluded the jury.

Perhaps the main problem connected with Dickman's illness was his extreme reluctance in admitting that he suffered from it at all. It was as though piles had some sort of social stigma attached to it. Possibly, in Dickman's mind it did. There was never any dispute as to the fact that he did suffer from piles. But there in the witness box on trial for his life, he found himself unable to refer to the malady by name, carefully skirting round it by referring to 'bad feelings' and 'lumps'. Finally, during re-examination, Mitchell-Innes snapped at him:—

'It is no use mincing matters. You had a bad attack of piles.'

Dickman then reluctantly conceded the matter and confirmed that he had treatment for it whilst on remand.

Has Dickman's story the ring of truth? Firstly, it seems odd that if he was guilty he did not try to invent a more plausible yarn. We know that he suffered from piles and we also know that he was not the sort of man who would want to be seen *'in extremis'* on the public highway. The trial reveals him as the last man who would to display illness in public. So it makes sense that he crept into an adjoining field where he could lay down until the worst of the attack was over. He said that the attack commenced at about 11:45 a.m., just after he had passed the village of Catchburn. This was about 1¾ miles from Morpeth Station along the road to Stannington. The time of 11:45 aptly fits the distance; thirty minutes walking time would be about right for 1¾ miles. He paid no real heed to the time he spent in the field. Asked to estimate it, he thought that it would be in the region of thirty minutes. If correct, this brings us to 12:15. He then walked back to Morpeth arriving there at 1:20, which means that the return leg of the journey took 65 minutes, twice as long as the outward half. But then he would be sore and tired and walking very slowly. On this basis it is certainly not inconceivable that the return to Morpeth took twice as long. It was certainly a more credible timetable than the Crown's.

With John Dickman's illness adroitly buried beneath a legal rubbish dump of hedges, fences and night-time carousings, Tindal Atkinson then switched his attention to the forensic evidence. Here, the Prosecution must have felt that they were skating on woefully thin ice, but amazingly Dickman succeeded in strengthening the evidence slightly in their favour. He dealt neatly with the coat; the stain was probably some bicycle oil. But when it came to the bloodstains on the glove Dickman's fatal penchant for self-inflicted wounds re-asserted itself.

Q. How do you account for the blood on these suede gloves?

A. I cannot account for it at all. I know I discarded the use of those particular gloves a good long period.

Q. How long?

A. Before Christmas.

Q. (Coleridge) (quoting Dickman's replies in the form of a question) I had discarded them three months before?

A. Yes.

This whole exchange was most unfortunate. First, Tindal Atkinson's question was unfair; there was blood on only one of the gloves. Secondly was it right that these everyday spots of domestic trivia be brought against him for such dreadful carnage? The murder of John Nisbet was a blood saturnalia.

What was this? A judicial inquiry or a contest geared to winning?

Things now went from bad to worse. On the subject of Dickman's finances Tindal Atkinson knew that even if the accused man acquitted himself well during the rest of his cross-examination he could still be dented on this point. On the other hand, if he performed badly then it would be the *coup de grâce*.

And so it proved.

Seventy-eight questions were put to Dickman, seventy-eight piercing inquiries or damning innuendoes. It might have been better had the defence admitted that he had had some lean times that winter; — an occupational hazard. A disarming answer such as, 'I had enough to live on, but from time to time needed money to help out with my racing activities' would have sounded so much more convincing than Dickman's blanket denial. And it would have strengthened the impression that he had nothing to hide.

Instead, he appeared to be evading the truth. He had borrowed from Cohen as an experiment; the moneylender had told him to keep the principal sum as long as he liked (which was not as absurd at it sounds); the £10 loaned from Sweeney was for somebody else; he had asked Hogg for £2 because he had gone out without sufficient money; the links and studs had been deposited with Kettering because there had been a spate of burglaries in the neighbourhood; true, he had pawned the binoculars using a false name and address, but he had intended using the money to buy another pair. In fact Dickman had also told the Police:—

> '*I pawned then... so that if any of the boys [gambling fraternity] asked me for money I could pull out the pawntickets and say, "look here, this is what I am down to", and they may think you are hard up.'*[*]

He had decided to use a phoney name on the spur of the moment; the wrong address was an error. His two accounts were not closed; — just lying dormant. He had not been aware that his wife's post office savings had been so gravely

---

[*] This may explain why Inspector Tait was told that Dickman was very hard up.

depleted; he was aware that she had reduced her Co-op account but not by how much; he thought that she often had money in reserve which he knew nothing about. Dealing with the money in Dickman's possession at the time of his arrest, Tindal Atkinson asked:—

> *Q. Except your account that this was the balance of your winnings after racing, is there any other source which you can suggest from which this money came?*
>
> *A. None whatsoever.*

This was undoubtedly the most plausible explanation which John Dickman could put forward. It may well have been the correct one. If he was the murderer then where did the rest of the money go? Those who believe that Dickman was guilty would be well advised to ponder that question. The answer which Dickman had given Tindal Atkinson was the best he had, but unfortunately it was given at the end of a sequence of thoroughly inadequate responses which must have tainted it by association with them.

All of which supports the idea that Dickman might have been better served had he admitted that he was in some degree of difficulty. At least he would have partially blunted the cutting edge of Tindal Atkinson's withering cross examination, and the devastating effect which it must have had on the jury.

Tindal Atkinson brought his interrogation to an end on a seemingly inoffensive note by alleging that Dickman had been hard pressed to pay his rates, a suggestion which was promptly and firmly denied. No evidence had so far been led to show that this was the case, but, as we shall see, Tindal Atkinson may have been laying a trap for an unwary defence.

Mitchell-Innes tried hard to repair the damage, in re-examination, but he was not auspiciously successful. Dealing with the question of the rates, he asked:—

> *Q. ...if you could not pay your rates, a distress would be put in?*
>
> *A. I can explain this.*

But Mitchell-Innes had had quite enough of Dickman's febrile explanations and he snapped back:—

> *'Will you answer the question? I suppose, if you do not pay your rates... a distress would be put into your house?'*
>
> *A. Of course, it would be, but there has never been any occasion like that with me. I have never been in such a position, or in such a condition. I might have allowed my wife to think I was short of money, merely to cause her to keep expenses down.*
>
> *Q. As to money matters, did your wife, as a matter of fact, ever complain to you that she was in want of money?*

A. No; she has never complained — not in a complaining way.

If Tindal Atkinson's final questions were indeed a trap then this particular question and answer had just sprung it. Came there now the ominous sound of papers being rustled on the Prosecution ledge and within a short time Tindal Atkinson was on his feet to introduce an item which virtually killed the defence stone dead.

> *'There are some documents that I could not use in the first instance; documents written by the wife to her husband. My friend has chosen to ask the question whether the wife had ever complained about the want of money. Under these circumstances I am entitled to use these documents, I think.'*
>
> *(Coleridge) 'I think you are.'*
>
> *(Mitchell-Innes) 'I have no objection — none whatsoever — but I shall have a comment to make upon it at the bar.'*

Rather a case of complaining about the treatment after the funeral.

Tindal Atkinson now proceeded to read a letter from Annie Dickman to her husband. It was dated January 23rd, 1910, and ran:—

> *'Dear Jack — I received your card, and am very sorry that you have no money to send. I am needing some very badly. The weather here is past description. I had to get in a load of coals, which consumed the greater part of a sovereign. The final notice for rates has come in — in fact, came in last week, which means they must be paid before next Thursday. Also Harry's school account. With my dividend due this week and what is in the post office I dare say I can pay the most pressing things, but it is going to make the question of living a poser, unless you can give me some advice as to what to do.'*

Neat flows the evidence, devastating and damning. The letter showed that Dickman had been pressed for rates on at least one occasion. But this was really secondary. It was the overall tenor of the letter which bit so deeply into Dickman's cause. It certainly gave the clear impression that money had been hard to come by for the Dickman family. It kicked the props out from under Dickman's absolute denials. If Tindal Atkinson's closing questions during cross examination had been designed to inveigle the defence into raising the subject of Annie Dickman's fortunes, then the ploy had succeeded brilliantly.

The contents of the letter were put to Dickman. He lamely bleated that an outsider might put a different interpretation on it than what it really meant. Mitchell-Innes reminded the jury that Annie Dickman had had £32 in her two accounts at the time of the letter* but the reality remained that the defence had

---

* Actually £20.59. Mitchell-Innes was in error (again).

been struck a mortal blow.

On this sad note Dickman's ordeal in the witness box reached its merciful end. Putting him in there turned out to be a mistake. The prosecution had attacked every weakness in his story in masterly fashion, and Dickman had frittered away the points in his favour with miserable ineptitude. Tindal Atkinson was not able to directly contradict Dickman's story so he sought instead to show him in as poor a light as possible. And Dickman had helped in his own destruction.

Viewed retrospectively Dickman's very indecision, his seeming inability to perceive the terrible danger in which he stood, were points in his favour. But these were subtle truths, difficult to spot. Some may argue that this is a sort of Catch 22 argument in favour of the defence; i.e., if an accused performs creditably it is because he is innocent, but he is also innocent if he shows up badly because if he was guilty then he would have invented a more coherent story. But in fact there is no hard and fast rule or yardstick by which an accused's evidence can be judged. An innocent man may give his evidence well; so may a guilty man, and an innocent man may perform as badly as a jury expects a guilty man to perform.

John Dickman may have been the first person to have been wrongly hanged because he lacked the ability to make a good witness on his own behalf.

However we should also ask whether Tindal Atkinson overstepped the mark during cross-examination. His blistering bombardment of questions, many simply duplicates of earlier inquiries, constituted an extraordinary display of vehemence. Was there not an unhealthy desire to convict? Was he seeking the truth — or was he trying to win the jury by substituting implication for fact?

After Dickman left the witness box there was still sufficient time on that July day for both Counsels to make their closing speeches. Tindal Atkinson spoke for an hour. His presentation was excellent, but he went gravely out of bounds at one point by commenting on the fact that Annie Dickman had not given evidence. The 1898 Act specifically forbade him to use this fact against Dickman.

Mitchell-Innes closing speech lasted an hour and twenty minutes. He began well but finished lamely.

I will not belabour the point that he had not done this case effectively. That is there for all to see.

(8)

Lord Coleridge did not commence his summing up until the following day, which meant that he had the advantage of a whole evening in which to read his notes and form a clear perspective on the case. This makes his subsequent performance even more inexcusable for what followed was possibly the most biased summing-up in a capital case this century.

Photographs of Coleridge show a thin lipped Victorian patriarch. It is a forbidding countenance, frigid and harsh, set firm against the world of wrong-doers which his work daily brought him into contact with. No spark of warmth seems likely to be struck from this cold flint. Yet in his private life he was a man of considerable culture, greatly interested in politics, music and the stage. His memoirs are more a theatrical review than an autobiography. Astonishingly, he does not delve into his career on the bench at all, and he mentions only two cases in which he appeared as Counsel. Both of them are interesting in that they have a bearing on his performance in the Dickman trial. The first provides us with an insight into Lord Coleridge's character.

In 1888 Coleridge was briefed to defend a couple named Miller who were accused of the murder of their teenaged daughter. Before making his closing speech Coleridge asked his Junior to study the jury very closely while he was speaking. He then proceeded to attack the salient points in the Crown's case and once this was accomplished he bent down and whispered to his Junior 'Have I got them?' Back came the answer 'no', and so Coleridge then went on to build a hypothetical case against a neighbour of the Millers who had given evidence for the prosecution. Finally he turned and dramatically pointed at the man. Both the prosecuting Counsel and the Judge vehemently rebuked Coleridge for this tactic but it won the jury. They acquitted his clients.

Coleridge had not led any evidence against the neighbour; nor had he accused him of the crime during cross-examination. His conduct was therefore highly irregular. On the other hand he seems to have had a genuine belief that the neighbour was indeed the guilty party. If his actions saved the lives of two innocent people then all well and good, but there is another side to this particular coin. If Coleridge was prepared to go to such lengths to secure an acquittal when he believed his clients were innocent then might he not be prepared to go to the same lengths to obtain the conviction of a man whom he thought was guilty? In other words, was he prepared to bend the rules to suit his own personal opinion?

There can be no doubt that Coleridge was satisfied that John Dickman was guilty. Rowan-Hamilton describes his summing-up as:—

'not altogether in favour of the prisoner'[1]

which under the circumstances can only be termed as a masterpiece of under-statement. It was in fact almost frighteningly against him.

The first part of Coleridge's charge dealt with motive; Dickman's finances. Robert Sweeney's name was invoked: 'he asked Sweeney for a loan of £10', followed by Cohen the moneylender, Kettering the Jeweller, Frank Christie and

---

1   "Trial of J A Dickman" p22

the pawning of the field glasses. Except for Cohen, at no point did Coleridge reiterate Dickman's reasons for these transactions.

With Cohen, the Judge had a reason for putting the Defence's explanations;— he ridiculed it!

Dickman had borrowed £20 from Cohen at a rate of interest of £1 per month: 'exorbitant' commented Coleridge, and went on to say that the overall interest on the loan worked out at 60% per annum, a point made by Tindal Atkinson during Dickman's cross-examination. Arithmetically, this was correct; fair and accurate it was not. Dickman had made five interest payments amounting to 25% of the loan. He said that he had borrowed it for three months (rate of interest 15%) and extended it for a further three with Cohen's approval (rate of interest 30%). The loan was repaid in May by Annie Dickman.

Coleridge put none of this before the Jury. He only mentioned the loan extension in the context of Cohen's evidence that Dickman had been unable to repay it in January.

Instead the Judge unfairly inflated the rate of interest. As for Dickman's reason for borrowing it in the first place, this is what Coleridge told the Jury:—

> '...he entered into this obligation to decide for himself and I presume in the interests of the public, or the assumed interests of the Public, whether or not this particular moneylender would be ready and willing to perform the obligation which he set forth in some advertisement of his.'

'In the interests or assumed interests, of the Public...' This contemptuous sneer almost leaps from the pages of the transcript. In fact, based on Dickman's experiment Frank Christie had borrowed £200 from Cohen, at least half of which was for betting purposes. It was never suggested that Christie was hard up for money. Nobody mentioned — least of all Coleridge — that gamblers, like businessmen, borrow to finance their activities. Coleridge did comment on the Christie loan, but only to make the point that Dickman's bets on his behalf had been unsuccessful.

It was an unhappy augury of what was to come. The defence was either ignored or distorted to suit the Prosecution.

Coleridge then tackled John and Annie Dickman's personal finances.

How much had Mrs Dickman in her two accounts on March 18th? '£5, £6 or £7' thought the judge. And Dickman himself? Well now, Coleridge imagined that the accused had awarded himself 'something like £40', and later this was extended to '£40 or £50, or whatever the exact amount may be'.

It was of course for the jury, 'to trust or not to trust' the accuracy of Dickman's claims that his betting ventures towards the end of 1909 had been successful. He, Coleridge, was not saying that they ought not to believe it because Dickman could not prove that he had had £40 on March 18th. There might be other documentary evidence which could not be produced. The jury must not regard the lack of such evidence as conclusive. But nevertheless, possession of this '£40–£50 depended purely on his uncorroborated testimony'.

Dickman had never claimed possession of £40, or £40–£50, at the time of the murder. This was a piece of pure fiction on the Judge's part. Dickman had told the Court that he had not known that his wife's resources had been depleted by so much on March 18th. Coleridge did not mention this.

On this display Coleridge seems to have been quite incapable of even following the defence evidence, let alone placing it intact before the dozen men who were shortly to decide John Dickman's fate. It is worth repeating exactly what Dickman had given in evidence about his finances between November 1909 and March 1910. At the end of November he had had a reserve of £120. £50 of this he had given to Annie Dickman. By February, not March, £40 remained. At this time he had handed over another £15–£20 to his Wife. On March 21st he had had just over £17, the sum found on him.

Coleridge turned now to Annie Dickman's letter of January 25th. The defence had argued that this was simply a domestic dispute over who should pay some bills. This particular item had of course sounded their death knell. Because it had been so damaging, it was up to Coleridge, as an allegedly responsible Judge, to treat it with the greatest possible care, and to ensure that the jury was entirely conversant with Dickman's explanation. Instead it was turned aside with the dismissive comment:—

> *'The arguments may have put a different complexion on that if you think they are of weight.'*

The curtain now descended on this part of the summation. The Prosecution's side had been intonated beautifully. The defence's version had either not been put at all, or it had shown Dickman in the worst possible light.

'Who was the deceased?' asked his Lordship, and he went on to tell his captive audience about Nisbet's occupation and routine. And Dickman?

> *'...he does not dispute now that he knew that the deceased was going on that day, and he does not dispute that this was a practice with which he was familiar, a general practice.'*

Part one of this statement is completely untrue.

The second part is accurate only to a point. Dickman had collected wages himself, but denied knowing the routine of any other colliery.

In the interests of fairness — it is not necessary to be unfair to Coleridge to show how unfair *he* was — the Judge then did go on to neatly capsule the events leading up to the departure of the 10:27. Dickman's version was concisely put, and Coleridge delivered a stern edict to the jury that they must not conclude that he was lying because his testimony was uncorroborated. It was one of the few occasions on which Coleridge was fair to the man whose life he was now crumbling to pieces in the palms of his hands.

Coleridge then launched into an account of Raven's evidence. He summed up the main point of the salesman's testimony as follows:—

> '*He saw the deceased and the prisoner together, walking along together... not as strangers who happened to be walking alongside of each other, but in the way in which two persons who have some sort of intercourse, some sort of knowledge of each other, some sort of companionship, would walk...*'

This was completely untrue.
Now Hepple:—

> '*...a man who had known the prisoner for twenty years, and could not, if he was sober and had his wits about him, make a mistake with regard to the prisoner, unless the prisoner has a double.*'

It is not unfair to say that Coleridge fastened on to Hepple's testimony as though it was Holy Writ. The possibility that Dickman might be right, and Hepple wrong, was only broached at the end of a long sermon which virtually sanctified the old man's evidence. At no point did Coleridge warn the jury that Dickman might by coincidence have travelled by the same train as a man who resembled him.

Yet Coleridge knew all about coincidences.

The second case which he mentioned in his memoirs occurred in 1883. A young farmworker named Joseph Wedlake attacked and killed a labourer named Cox on a lonely country road at the dead of night, mistaking him for a man named Thatcher. Quite unbeknown to Joseph Wedlake, Cox had earlier that night had a blazing row with his brother, Thomas Wedlake, and Thomas had been heard to say to Cox: 'I will do for you'. Naturally suspicion fell on Thomas who was then obliged to reveal that Joseph was the real killer. It was an extraordinary coincidence.

But if this case came to Coleridge's mind — and we know that he always remembered it — then he spurned it. John Dickman was not to receive the benefit of any possibility of coincidence having played a role.

Next came Percival Hall. He too received the Bernard, Lord Coleridge seal of approval as a good witness. First there was a neat piece of embroidery:—

> '*The deceased and this other man were in conversation.*'

This was completely untrue.
He went on:

> '*If that other man got into that compartment as the deceased's companion, no one could doubt that he was the author of the deceased's death.*'

This was pure assumption.

The other man had on a light fawn overcoat; 'so says Hall' quoth the Judge. Say that he did, but only in Court. There was no mention of the crucial word 'fawn' in the description which Hall gave to the Police on the 18th.

Coleridge clearly thought it a pity that he had to slightly mar the testimony of this perfect witness by reminding the jury of his unsatisfactory performance at the identity parade. But little local difficulties can always be surmounted.

> *'...there are persons... who are so proud of their accuracy that in their very pride you may discover grounds for doubting it. There are other persons who are scrupulous, careful, conscientious, who do not want to be more sure than their mind and conviction justify, and will not go for any purpose beyond what they are satisfied they can swear to. My experience tells me that class of mind is more to be depended upon than the mind of a man with a cocksure mind. You may depend upon it that, if he is sound and sensible and is of very good memory, so far as he goes he is a person who ought probably to be trusted.'*

Thus did a thoroughly inadequate identification, which Northumberland's Chief Constable, Fullarton James, was shortly to describe to the Home Secretary as 'extremely weak' become 'scrupulous, careful and conscientious', adjectives which most emphatically do *not* apply to Percival Hall.

Coleridge went on to remind the jury that Hall knew that he was at the Police Station to perform the most responsible task imaginable — recognising a murderer. In fact Hall had been summoned forth to identify Nisbet's travelling companion, nothing more, nothing less.

Mitchell-Innes had raised this as a defence point. Coleridge never asked why.

Now came the witness's conversation with the Police Officer. Here Coleridge dreamt up his own version and put it to the jury:

> *'I said I was not sure enough to bind myself by pointing out anybody. I wanted to know whether by pointing the man out I was swearing that he was the man who was with the deceased.'*

This bore no resemblance whatsoever to what Hall had actually said.

Coleridge's fictional account rendered the real one harmless. Instead of a witness who was in effect asking the Police to reassure him that he was picking out their suspect, whom he had already sneaked a look at, we have the final anointment of Hall with the oils of responsibility, scrupulousness, and conscientiousness. The remark which was later to lead to Hall being stripped of these virtues and unmasked as a tainted witness, was distorted to the jury as the wholly innocuous comment of a thoroughly reliable person who only wanted to be fair!

The judicial train now moved on having left one passenger stranded. Dickman's claim that Hall had been intimidated by the Police was left high and dry on the platform, unheard, forgotten, consigned to oblivion.

Cicely Nisbet was next summoned forth. No one could doubt, said his Lordship, that the man she had seen in the compartment was still there when her husband was murdered.

Thus was the previous assumption extended: wholly in favour of the Prosecution of course.

The dramatic story of how Mrs Nisbet had identified this man whom she had known for eighteen years at the Magistrate's court was then recounted. According to Coleridge:—

> '*It [Dickman's profile] struck her absolutely as being the profile of the man whom she saw in the carriage.*'

A gross exaggeration: all she had said at the Magistrate's hearing was that Dickman's profile 'resembled' that of her husband's companion. The Judge passed by without comment the fact that eight days had elapsed between Mrs Nisbet's fainting fit and her tentative identification; that Dickman had stated during his evidence that he knew Cicely Nisbet; that if Dickman had known Nisbet's routine then he would have been unlikely to pass through Heaton with his intended victim and run the risk of being recognised; that Nisbet failed to draw Cicely's attention to him.

Stannington was now reached. Dickman's account was that he was engrossed in the betting for the 'Liverpool Handicap' said Coleridge. At this point Mitchell-Innes interrupted and reminded him that it was in fact the Grand National. Coleridge partially corrected himself; 'the Grand National had been run and Dickman was reading about it.' Mitchell-Innes rose again:

'I think it is of importance. The Grand National was to be run; and it was the calculation of the odds that was important.'

In fact, the race meeting itself was not of importance. Mitchell-Innes had sat mute whilst the Judge had inflated the financial evidence, placed in evidence things which had never happened and grossly distorted Hall and Cicely Nisbet's evidence. When he did finally get to his feet and object it was over something trivial. He then went back to sleep again while Coleridge raced through John Spink's evidence.

At Stannington, Spink had seen Nisbet with a companion *who was reading a newspaper; 'clearly the same man whom Mrs Nisbet had observed at Heaton.*'

The statement about the Newspaper is wholly untrue. Nor was it the first time Coleridge had added one — according to him, the man in the compartment at Heaton was reading a newspaper too! He then married these ugly inventions to his assumption that the man seen at Stannington was the same man in the compartment at Heaton, whom he had already branded as the murderer.

The offspring of this hybrid pairing was that Dickman's very justification for missing his stop was distorted into a deadly point against him.

Unlike Hall, Coleridge wasted little time on John Spink. Whether by accident or by design he omitted entirely to mention that Spink had failed to identify Dickman!

Next John Grant got out at Morpeth; or rather he got in, as Mr Lowenthal did not fail to remind Coleridge.

> '*You are quite right. He got in and returned the same day [incorrect], but*

whether he got out and got in really does not affect what I am saying.'

Having put Lowenthal in his place, the Judge then repeated Grant's testimony to the jury. He had looked into Nisbet's compartment and it had appeared to be empty. But just like everybody else, Coleridge failed to grasp the reverse logic of Grant's evidence; that he had not seen anybody alight from the compartment as he most certainly should have done if Dickman or anyone else had gotten out of it.

A suggestion had been made by Mitchell-Innes that the killer had jumped from the train between Stannington and Morpeth. Having placed this in the minds of the jury Coleridge left it and passed on to other matters.

Athey's evidence and his conflict with Dickman about the overcoat was recounted. The Judge made great play, inordinate play, with Athey's claim that Dickman had had the excess fare ready in his left hand. In a nutshell, the Prosecution's contention was that it was 'suspiciously ready' because Dickman was carrying Nisbet's bag in his right hand. Coleridge rounded things off with a neat little flourish:

> *'Of course, it is only a little fact, not a fact from which you should draw unmerited conclusions, but it is a fact which has been pointed out to you by the Prosecution.'*

True to form, Dickman's version of paying the fare was not put. But then this was not a court of justice. As the Judge's long speech wore on it looked more and more like a hangman's court.

There is no point in lingering further at the Morpeth Ticket Barrier. Instead we can follow Coleridge further along the line to Pegswood, Longhurst, Widdrington and Alnmouth. Cosher at Longhurst had scrutinised the train and Nisbet's compartment had seemingly been vacant. George Yeoman, the Station Master at Widdrington, had also failed to notice the deceased although he had examined the train. This gives some indication of how successfully Coleridge had followed the case as it had unfolded. Yeoman was the Station Master at Longhurst, not Widdrington, and in his own words:—

> *'I did not go up to the head of the train.'*

A little further on confusion and inaccuracy are again in the saddle. Two or three stations are conjured up out of nowhere to line the route between Pegswood and Widdrington. There was in fact only one, Longhurst, and it seems that the Judge was under the impression that Longhurst and not Pegswood was the next station up from Morpeth. Mitchell-Innes corrected him, a thankless task which only succeeded in muddying the waters even further because Alnmouth now became the next station along from Longhurst, and Widdrington, Chevington, Acklington, and Warkworth all disappeared from view. Whatever railway line Coleridge had in mind, it certainly was not the one constructed by the North Eastern Railway Company.

Back on the tracks again, the Judge proceeded to deal with William Hogg's evidence — or perhaps it would be more true to say that he shunted it out of the courtroom window in so far as Dickman's interests were concerned. Hogg, he interpolated, was unable to assign any reason for Dickman's visits to the Dovecot Colliery. In fact after a prolonged bout of questioning Hogg had admitted that Dickman and he had discussed Christie and the latter's interest in the sinking operations.

Coleridge supposed — his term — that the Prosecution was arguing that Dickman's visit on March 4th was either a trial run for devising his murder plan or an abortive attempt to carry out the crime. Correct, but what it really boiled down to was that routine activities had now acquired the stamp of diabolical cunning because a man had been whisked out of the role of ordinary citizen and transformed into a murder suspect. The Judge made no attempt to explain Dickman's previous visits to Dovecot. But then of course a reasonable juror might have drawn the reasonable inference that Dickman was travelling back and forth for a reasonable purpose.

Coleridge now summed up the evidence to date, laying great stress on the Prosecution case. The jury could only believe Dickman if they were prepared to throw the evidence of Raven, Hepple, Hall and Cicely Nisbet to the winds. The prisoner had said that he had no companion. Stated his Lordship:

> *'If he says he had no companion when we know that he had, who was that companion?'*

I do not wish to take the remark out of context. It was put to the jury as a question in the form of whether or not they believed Dickman. But it strains forbearance to the limit to say that it was anywhere near fairly weighted and balanced. The tenor and leaning were blatantly towards the Prosecution as was the summing up as a whole. it was a wretched performance.

The pitiless spotlight was now turned on Dickman's movements after leaving the train. Coleridge laid great emphasis on the fact that there was a train back to Stannington and yet Dickman had not caught it.

He then put — and very fairly put — Dickman's explanation that it did not really matter to him whether he got out at Morpeth or Stannington. But the Judge omitted to point out that the murderer might have chosen Morpeth because it was the best station to catch the return train to Newcastle. Why the omission? Because it did not fit the Prosecution's case?

Some other omissions. Why, if Dickman was the murderer, had it taken him so long to dispose of the bag? Why had he not gone on to Dovecot to add credence to his story? Why had he only purchased a ticket to Stannington? These were huge rents in the prosecution's fabric. They could not be patched up; so instead they were ignored.

Coleridge had been speaking for some considerable time but his summing up still had only just passed the halfway mark. It was at this point that Dickman is suddenly struck by what his Lordship described as; 'some strange malady'. A note of mock perplexity now crept into the Judge's voice:

> *'I could not discover quite whether it was diarrhoea or whether it was constipation. He would seem to infer that it was a mingling of both which seems to me to be a mixture of opposites.'*

Dickman, Coleridge went on, could not remember whether he had gotten into the field through a hedge or over a fence:

> *'It may be, as he says, his pain was so extreme as to take from him the power of observation.'*

Exactly. Nothing could have been more natural. But regrettably Coleridge chose to prefix Dickman's account with the words:

> *'It is strange obliviousness.'*

I doubt that anything could be less strange. On the other hand, nothing could be more strange than the performance of this Judge, sworn to uphold the law, and the principles of truth and justice enshrined in it, but who was now busily erecting the scaffold for Dickman's execution.

Coleridge dealt now with Dickman's sojourn in the field and his return to Morpeth station. Then he unleashed his next attack. Dickman had claimed that recumbency was the best remedy for piles, but instead of sitting in the waiting room he had chosen to stroll down to the town, intending to call in at the 'Newcastle Arms'. At that point he met Elliot and Saunderson.

Ah, so Coleridge was aware after all of the nature of the malady. He trips himself up here. Just for a moment the mask is torn away and we can peek behind it. What we see is not pleasant. A man who knew all along the nature of the prisoner's illness but chose to ignore it so that he could sneer and jibe at his defence. And, as we shall see, a man who only now admits to knowing what it was because he can use it to score further debating points in the Prosecution's favour. What he was implying was that Dickman would not have gone for an additional walk had he really had an attack of piles. Instead he would have sat down in the waiting room. But Dickman's explanation, not thought worthy of record by his eminence, was that he had begun to feel better. And after all he had sought Coleridge's 'obvious remedy' when he had lain down in the field. Furthermore Dickman had assigned a reason for his proposed visit to the "Newcastle Arms"; Hogg often lunched there. This also was ignored by the Judge.

The defence, Coleridge went on, had claimed, as a point in Dickman's favour, that he had seemed perfectly cool and collected to Elliot and Saunderson. But in his own inimitable style Coleridge turned this to a point in the Prosecution's favour.

> *'Apparently he did not acquaint them with his malady, or exhibit signs in his face of the suffering he had undergone.'*

With these words Coleridge subverted yet another element in the defence's case.

This portion of the summing-up came to its all too predictable end with Coleridge telling the jury that:

> *The story depends on his evidence, and his evidence alone, for he did not use the lavatory at Morpeth going or returning. He did not acquaint anybody with his malady; neither Elliot nor Saunderson whom he subsequently met. I know not how much this road may be frequented, it may be very little, but in fact he met no one on the road, and therefore has no corroborative evidence of his being on that road at all.'*

At this point Mitchell-Innes intervened:

> *'As you have been good enough to invite correction, may I remind your Lordship that it is the uncontradicted evidence on behalf of the prisoner that he has in fact been treated for this very malady at the prison.'*

Coleridge:

> *'I do not doubt that. I am glad to be reminded of it, and I do not think anybody has disputed he suffered from piles. Of that I have no doubt. He said he was so treated in the prison, and I do not gather there is any contradiction, or that any question was put about it, that he had suffered from piles.'*

'I do not think anybody has disputed he suffered from piles...' Yet a few minutes earlier he had sung a very different tune: '...he is attacked by some strange malady. I could not discover quite whether it was diarrhoea or whether it was constipation.' No further comment is required. Coleridge resumed, 'Now gentlemen, I pass that by.' And he did. He passed by every hole in the Prosecution's case.

Having omitted, or dismissed, every detail or argument which might have been of value to Dickman between the hours of 11:15 and 1:40 on March 18th, Coleridge then dealt with the defence's contention that the Prosecution's case depended very largely on Dickman's own statement, hardly the behaviour of a guilty man. 'What are we to say to that?' he asked the jury and it will come as no surprise to learn that the Judge had plenty to say about it on the Prosecution's behalf. The central theme of his argument was that on March 21st Dickman had no real idea of how much the police actually knew. He ended with these words:

> *'It may be consistent with his innocence, it may be consistent with his guilt.'*

A very neat way of perverting one of the main points in Dickman's favour. Semantics were substituted for logic; the feat of mental gymnastics involved was quite extraordinary. But it was successful. The defence argument was negated. We are asked to accept that because he had no real idea of how much the police knew, Dickman then proceeded to tell them exactly what they needed to know in order to hang him. Does this make sense, because it was precisely what Coleridge was arguing?

After pulling the rug out from under the defence on what was one of their strongest points, Coleridge might have been expected to redress the balance by commenting on one of the points claimed by the Prosecution in their favour: Dickman's wretched display in the witness box. In closing, Tindal Atkinson had told the jury:—

> 'They had an opportunity of watching him, seeing his demeanour, and of listening to the statements he had made. To a large extent, where the ring closed more closely than ever around him, the accused had contented himself with a flat denial of some of the principal facts sworn to by the witnesses for the Prosecution.'

Coleridge might have warned the jury that Dickman's performance was not evidence against him. But he did not. Was this fair? Was it impartial? Draw your own conclusion.

Coleridge next ventured to examine the evidence of the two pistols. Here the jury was faced with a straight choice between the Prosecution's contention that one murderer had used two pistols and the defence argument that there were two killers. Naturally enough, the Judge came down on the Crown's side; the two pistols could not be divorced from the rest of the evidence which suggested that Nisbet had only one travelling companion. Here, Mitchell-Innes had seen the issue in splendid isolation, telling the jury:—

> 'The reasonable inference from the presence of these shots, two kinds of bullets, was that two murderers did the deed.'

He never challenged the rest of the Crown's case which pointed to only one murderer.

Coleridge therefore was not obliged to put any alternative theory before the jury. However, we can be sure that he would have done had it been in the Prosecution's interest and not the defence's. He had given clear proof of this when turning Elliot and Saunderson's evidence against Dickman, and he would do so again shortly.

The penultimate item of evidence for judicial review was the forensic evidence. I will repeat my view which is that this minutiae should never have been brought against a man on trial for his life, and that to do so illustrated how thin the Crown's case actually was.

Needless to say, this was not a view shared by Lord Coleridge.

He began by very properly instructing the Jury to ignore the stain on the overcoat. Then he turned to the glove; the Prisoner had said that he was wearing different gloves on the day of the crime and the Jury might be inclined to give him the benefit of the doubt but for the fact that he had chosen to contradict Dr Boland's testimony that the stain was recent. Dickman did not deny wearing the trousers on the day of the crime and there could be no doubt that the stains in the pocket had come from the gloved hand being put into it.

Once again points very much in Dickman's favour were being used against him. Why, if he was lying should he have opposed Boland's evidence when he did not need to do so; when it was in his interests to go along with it? Mitchell-Innes had put forward an entirely feasible, everyday explanation of the stains which was now being distorted because of his clients own honesty!

Worse followed. Instead of examining, as he should have done, the issue of how, in that charnel house of a compartment, the alleged killer had escaped with only two faint smears of blood on the thumb and forefinger of a glove, the Judge turned the matter on its head and in effect implied that these minute stains supported the Crown's proposition that there would be very little blood on the murderer because the body would not bleed much until afterwards. There was said Coleridge, no evidence of any struggle before death. Here he was supplying his own analysis (entirely in the Prosecution's favour) because Tindal Atkinson had never mentioned a struggle either way. Was this not a throwback to the Miller case — a high order of intelligence being deviously used to get the desired result?

Let us see what the evidence actually was. John Nisbet's spectacles were crushed and broken; at one point either he, or his assailants, had pulled his coat collar over his head because the fatal bullet had been fired through it. The other serious wound had been inflicted from a range of only a few inches. There would have been a great quantity of blood at the time of death, before death (if the fatal wound was not the first) and after death. Blood in fact was still flowing from the wounds over thirty minutes later. The corpse, the seat and the floor of the compartment were extensively bloodstained. After killing Nisbet, with at least one point blank shot, the murderer(s) then pushed his bleeding body under the seat. Yet there were just two tiny specks of blood on a glove. You have heard what Coleridge and Tindal Atkinson tell you: what does logic say?

According to the Prosecution, the wet blood contaminated the trouser pocket? But not the ticket? Once again, apply logic.

But to return to Lord Coleridge, Mitchell-Innes had put forward a perfectly rational reason for the stains. Coleridge had to deal with it and deal with it he did in terms which might well stand as a classic definition of the word bias.

> '...he does not say, on such and such a day my nose did bleed, nor does he remember specifically blood falling on his gloves and putting his hand into his pocket.'

Well, where were you when you last had a nosebleed? Did you make, a note of it, "Dear Diary" and so on? By itself it is laughable, but this dialogue of death helped put a rope around John Dickman's neck, manipulated it into place, pulled the trapdoor from under him and snapped his neck like a rotting twig.

The dread summation was now, mercifully, reaching its end. The evidence had been dissected and discussed, not fairly and properly but according to

Coleridge's fancy; a fancy which leaned supinely towards the Prosecution. But he still had a few more sallies to make. For example:

> *'Now gentlemen, I believe that I have gone through, I do not say every fact [he could say that again!] but if I have omitted any fact material or immaterial, supply it for yourselves and supply the argument which you base upon that fact. I do not pretend to have exhausted every item in this case.'*

Presumably the defence case was one of the items which the jury was supposed to supply for itself.

The last piece of evidence was that elusive moneybag which had been so belatedly discovered in the mineshaft. Spooner's testimony, that the pit would have been inspected more than once between March and June, was ignored throughout. The jury, unless they all had exceedingly good memories, was left with the impression that the bag had been put down the shaft on March 18th. But then no omission was being spared to strengthen the Prosecution's case.

Part of the Judge's comments were as follows:—

> *'The Prosecution say he carried the bag with him when he got out at Morpeth Station. I think the learned Counsel for the Prosecution invited you to say, if that was not proved, he was not the murderer. I do not know that that quite follows. I can understand, whoever the murderer was, having many ways of disposing of the bag. The bag might have been thrown intact on a selected spot on the railway, and afterwards searched for, recovered and dealt with.'*

The fact that Tindal Atkinson had never put this suggestion before the jury implies that he thought it very unlikely; — and rightly so. But this did not deter Coleridge from putting it into his summing-up on the Crown's behalf. Clearly, he was quite willing to advance possibilities which were not in evidence when they favoured the Prosecution.

Now the finale and Coleridge's definition of circumstantial evidence, followed by reasonable doubt, a passage which Fenton Bresler aptly describes as 'deadly against the accused'[1]. The first part dealing with circumstantial evidence would not have been so damaging had it proceeded a suitable definition of reasonable doubt. Instead it provided a fitting climax for this second speech for the Prosecution. It was a brutally clever piece of work because having dwelt at length on circumstantial evidence Coleridge took no trouble at all with reasonable doubt.

If such a doubt assailed their minds, then the accused was entitled to go free; the Prosecution had a bounden duty to convince them of their case. He went on:

1   "Scales of Justice"

> *'Ask yourselves, then, what is the cumulative effect upon your minds of so many, so varied, so independent pieces of evidence all pointing, it is said, in one direction, all tending, it is said, to inculpate the prisoner, and the prisoner alone, in the commission of this crime. Summon to your aid your just and ordered reason. If it tells you that the guilt of the prisoner is reasonably proved, then the law and the oath which you have taken alike demand that you should act with firmness and with courage.'*

Which was an elegant way of repeating Lord Baxendale's infamous charge to a jury; — 'Come along gentleman and let me hang these scoundrels before breakfast.'

Before the jurors left their box there was still time for Mitchell-Innes to lurch headfirst into one more blunder. His Lordship, he complained, had not dealt with the possibility that the killer might have jumped from the train between stations. In fact he had and promptly said so. So the last thing which the jury heard before retiring was Dickman's Counsel being put firmly in his place.

But in fact Coleridge had omitted one item which he was legally bound to bring to the jury's attention: Tindal Atkinson's improper comment on Annie Dickman's absence from the witness box. Coleridge did not put this to the jury until they had actually returned to court with their verdict. He then asked whether it had influenced them. Predictably their answer was no. They were hardly likely to say otherwise!

The jury went out at 12:55. Coleridge's summing-up left little doubt as to what the verdict would be. At 3.32 the twelve men filed back into court and pronounced Dickman guilty.

We do not know what thoughts went through Dickman's mind during those two hours and thirty-seven minutes; whether the tension gnawed away at his stomach, whether his hopes rose and fell as he turned the case over and over again in his mind. Because basically John Dickman was a digit in the crime statistics. He was a name to be slandered on the streets of Newcastle, and read about as a macabre passing fancy by the rest of the country. We know nothing more about him really. A member of the middle classes fallen now from grace and consigned to the rogue's gallery, occasionally to be trotted out to fill up a few columns in some notorious crimes remembered series. Nothing more of him has come down to us beyond his last despairing cry from the dock on that summer's afternoon:

> *'I declare to all men that I am innocent.'*

And then he was gone from view, stumbling down the steps to the cells below.

I have dwelt at length on Coleridge's summation not to criticise the Judiciary as a whole. I have read summing ups which were models of fairness and accuracy; I have sat in Court and listened to a Judge sum up for acquittal. I do not say that Coleridge was in general a bad or unfair Judge. But in this particular instance he was. It will not do to say that the jury could have rejected his summation. Most juries are influenced, one way or another, by a Judge's summing up. And in this case Coleridge was inventing things which had never happened, distorting things that had happened, and making points for the Prosecution which they themselves had never made. The jury had sat for two days listening to the evidence. They cannot have been expected to remember each and every detail clearly so as to be able to say — 'no that never happened', 'that is not the way he says it is', or 'the Prosecution never said that — why?' They could only be guided by what they thought was established fact or even handed speculation from the bench.

Small wonder then that five of them later had a doubt when they found out they had been misled.

(9)

In 1910 the Court of Criminal Appeal had been in existence for a mere three years. New innovations sometimes take time to mature and the Appeal Court was no exception. Often, its role as an arbiter of justice proved stronger in theory than in practice.

The arch problem was the lack of safeguard against prejudice or incompetence by the Appeal Court Judges themselves. Many Judges believed that it was inconceivable that an accused person could be unfairly treated during his trial, or that a jury could reach the wrong verdict. In many instances, perhaps a majority, the Appeal Court was being asked to criticise either directly, or by implication, a trusted colleague who might also be a personal friend. In some instances the trial Judge might well be their senior on the bench. David A Yallop, in his definitive study of the Craig/Bentley case, argues these points very cogently indeed:—

> *'The situation is not unlike one in which three directors of a company are asked publicly to state that their managing director has made a mistake. It was perhaps situations such as this that had led one member of the legal profession bitterly to describe these hearings as presided over by a "court of criminal no appeal". In reply to any criticism of a particular Judge's behaviour, the reply all too often was "No fault is to be found with this impeccable summing-up".*[1]

And a Court of Criminal no Appeal it was to prove for John Dickman.
Of the 710 cases heard by the Court of Criminal Appeal in 1910, John

---

*   "To Encourage the Others" p219

Dickman's was certainly the most important. It created legal history as the first Appeal to be heard in fact as well as law.

During the first three years of the Court's existence appeals had been based purely on legal points, misdirections by the judge, or irregularities during the trial. But following Dickman's conviction, Mitchell-Innes had ferreted out the story of Hall and Spink's glimpse of Dickman prior to the identity parade, and also investigated his acquaintanceship with Cicely Nisbet. The upshot of all this activity was that Chief Constable Fullarton James wrote to the Home Secretary, Winston Churchill, and Mrs Nisbet was also persuaded to write to him as well. Churchill's response was to order the Appeal Court to hear factual as well as legal evidence at Dickman's appeal. In effect this meant a sort of mini retrial with both Hall and Mrs Nisbet summoned to give further evidence, if required, and a fresh analysis of the identification evidence as a whole. Additionally, Mitchell-Innes had drawn up the appeal on three other counts: misdirection of the jury by Coleridge, Tindal Atkinson's improper comment on Annie Dickman not having appeared in the witness box, and what he, Mitchell-Innes, termed as the withdrawal of evidence from the jury, although, as he explained, the last count was the same as the first by withholding evidence from the jury Coleridge had seriously misdirected them.

But the appeal was doomed from the start. In retrospect it seems clear that the three Appeal Judges resented Churchill's instructions to them. One of them in particular, Lord Alverstone, the Lord Chief Justice, may also have had a personal reason for disliking such a direction. Three years earlier Alverstone had presided at the trial of George Raynor for the murder of a wealthy store owner. In passing sentence on Raynor, Alverstone had told him that he could hold out no hope for mercy. But Churchill's predecessor had controversially reprieved Raynor. Although Alverstone himself was not the main focus of the controversy, it is possible that the Lord Chief Justice felt that he had been slighted. Certainly, at least one of Alverstone's remarks at the Appeal hearing implied that he thought that the Home Secretary was meddling in the case. Moreover, Dickman himself was not permitted to be present at the Appeal. There is no hard or fast rule about an appellant being present, but one would have thought that this was a case in which he ought to have in attendance.

In an age of legal greatness, historians have called it the golden age of advocacy, it is something of a mystery that a self-confessed mediocrity such as Alverstone succeeded in becoming Lord Chief Justice. Presumably, as a former Attorney General, political influence was the deciding factor. Two cases will suffice to show just how well suited he was to sit in judgement on his fellow beings.

Two months after John Dickman's execution, Dr Hawley Crippen was tried at the Old Bailey for the murder of his wife. Alverstone presided and came close to bringing the law into disrepute with some of his antics. At one point he invited a leading actress to share the bench with him. On another occasion he interrupted the hapless Crippen's cross-examination and snapped at him 'Do you really ask the jury to understand...?', a form of questioning which might well have brought him a sharp rebuke from at least one of his successors as Lord Chief Justice.* But the worst moment occurred after the jury had returned with their verdict. Not until the foreman was about to pronounce Crippen guilty did the Judge realise that the accused man had yet to be brought up to the dock.

A sorry display, but no worse than Alverstone's performance at the Appeal Court two years later in the case of John Williams.** Williams had been found guilty of murdering a Police Officer on evidence which was open to some doubt. He was represented by Sir Patrick Hastings, then at the outset of his glittering career of the Bar. It was the only occasion on which Hastings was to enjoy the dubious pleasure of appearing before Alverstone, and one was quite enough for him:—

> *'...I was not greatly impressed by his legal acumen. From the outset it was apparent that he was satisfied of the prisoner's guilt and no legal argument seemed to make the least impression upon him. Indeed in his judgement he never referred to it. The prisoner was guilty and that was enough. The appeal was dismissed.'*[1]

Old dogs, it is said, do not learn new tricks. 'Satisfied of the prisoner's guilt... no legal argument seemed to make the least impression... the prisoner was guilty and that was enough' are all phrases which fit Alverstone's performance at Dickman's Appeal to a tee.

The Appeal was heard on July 18th, and Mr Justice Lawrence and Mr Justice Phillimore flanked Alverstone on the bench.

Mitchell-Innes opened by dealing with Coleridge's directions on the value of motive. Evidence of motive could not be used as a substitute for lack of evidence to connect Dickman with the crime. Then, warming to his task, the defence Counsel set about trying to prove that the evidence against Dickman was: 'in the highest degree unsatisfactory'.

Firstly Raven's evidence: Mitchell-Innes submitted that Dickman had simply walked alongside Nisbet without realising it. Raven had said that the two men were not in conversation, but Coleridge had failed to put this to the jury. Next Hepple's testimony was reiterated. It had a certain force, admitted Mitchell-Innes, but only when it was taken in conjunction with Hall's evidence. Neatly developing his theme the defence Counsel went on:—

1   "Cases in Court" p303

---

*   Lord Hewart.
**   a.k.a. Lewis Mackay

> *'...if Hall's evidence is discredited that would materially effect the force of the evidence given by Hepple.'*

At this juncture Mitchell-Innes attempted to introduce into evidence the letter written by Fullarton James to Churchill dealing with the glimpse of Dickman afforded to Hall and Spink. But this move was blocked by Alverstone on the grounds that it was not the proper way to bring evidence before the Court. Tindal Atkinson then rose to say that Hall was present and without further ado the wages clerk was summoned to the witness box. What he had to say about his sneak preview of Dickman has already been recounted. It was a sorry story, and Hall's role in it quite despicable. Although he freely admitted knowing that such proceedings were, quote, 'most irregular' that had not deterred him from taking part in them. Quite the opposite. On finding that he could see nothing through the window, he had complained to the detective that it was, 'perfectly ridiculous' to expect him or Spink to get a view through it, whereupon they had been guided to the partially open door. Plainly, curiosity exercised a stronger pull on Hall than morality. It was, perhaps, characteristic of his performance throughout.

Hall's admissions made no impression whatsoever on their Lordships. Alverstone dismissed them on the following grounds:—

> *'...the question of identification by Hall is not so important as it would have been had the case for the defence been that Dickman was not on the train at all.'*

Endemic in this statement are the seeds of an unfortunate misunderstanding which was to bedevil the defence throughout the hearing. It was partly their own fault. By conceding Raven's identification, and agreeing that Hepple possessed a certain force, Mitchell-Innes had implanted in the minds of the Judges the misconception that the defence were not now disputing that Dickman and Nisbet had strolled side-by-side to platform five, and gone together to the head of the train. In fact the defence case had not changed. It was of course that Dickman had never consciously been in Nisbet's company; that he had not walked with him to the front of the train, and that he had travelled in a rearward compartment. Moreover, Mitchell-Innes had opened his submissions to the Appeal Court by stating that if Hall's identification was discredited then it also raised doubts about the accuracy of Hepple's. But the triumvirate on the bench did not understand this: they thought that the defence were no longer quarrelling with either Raven or Hepple's identifications, and that Mitchell-Innes was arguing that Dickman had left Nisbet at the front of the train and then walked back to a rear compartment.

Next Mitchell-Innes sought to gain the Court's acceptance of Cicely Nisbet's statement, pointing out that she had made it at the request of the Home Secretary. This almost went the way of Fullarton James letter. Declared Alverstone:—

> *'We have frequently declined to listen to statements of the kind you now suggest. No doubt the Home Secretary receives all manner of communications from interested friends or from the prisoner himself. The mere fact of their being addressed to the Home Secretary cannot make them evidence.'*

It is not clear whether the Lord Chief Justice was congenitally stupid or whether it was a defect he had acquired with age. Unless one sees them in the context of continued pique over the Raylor case then they are quite incomprehensible. Whatever the reason, they do Alverstone no credit and they contain one incredible *faux pas*. Cicely Nisbet had suddenly been transformed into an 'interested friend' of the prisoner.

Tindal Atkinson intervened again to say that Mrs Nisbet was also in Court, but in the most contradictory manner possible the bench decided that in this instance they preferred the statement after all!

Suffice to say, the contents were not of much interest to their eminences. On this occasion it was Phillimore who put the boot in!

> *'She does not say that it was Dickman she saw in the train; she says that the profile of the man she saw in the carriage was the profile of the man in the dock at the trial.'*

Ignore the legal hair-splitting and the fact that Phillimore was incapable of distinguishing between the trial and the magistrate's hearing. Put quite simply, if Cicely Nisbet really saw enough of the man's profile to identify him at the Magistrate's Court then she ought to have been able to recognise him as somebody she had known for a good many years.

Wearily, Mitchell-Innes announced that he was leaving the question of identification. His next submission concerned the empty money bag. Although the mine shaft had been examined between March and June, the bag had not been found until June 9th which meant that Dickman could not have put it there. Alverstone supplied his own answer to this particular riddle:—

> *'One would think that a man would have destroyed the bag instead of keeping it and then putting it down the pit. He had from March to June in which to dispose of it.'*

Was a glimmer of perception at last creeping into the proceedings? Alas, no. What Alverstone meant was that the bag must have been cast down the mine shaft on March 18th after all; otherwise the killer would have destroyed it — not retained it for three months. This was pure hypothesis: it completely ignored the actual evidence which suggested that the bag had been disposed of after Dickman's arrest.

Feeling no doubt that he was bashing his head against a brick wall, Mitchell-Innes soldiered on. The murder might have been committed after Morpeth; the Judge had been under the misapprehension that Stannington was the next stop after Heaton; there was no identification of Dickman after Heaton;

the murderer might have left the train whilst it was still in motion. At this point Phillimore decided to impose his own peculiar brand of logic on the case again:—

> *'There was doubtless plenty of opportunity for change. But appellant does not suggest that: he said "I never changed carriages".'*

It is not possible to decipher exactly what this ermined fool was getting at. Presumably he had misinterpreted Mitchell-Innes' remarks to such an extent that he thought that the defence was also arguing that Dickman could have boarded the train with Nisbet at Newcastle and changed compartments after Heaton. If so, then Mitchell-Innes might just as well have made his submissions in Swahilli to a bunch of backward schoolboys. They would have fared equally as well as Phillimore in following the case.

If Mitchell-Innes did still harbour any fond illusions about the reliability of the Appeal Court then he must have listened to Phillimore's remarks with a sinking heart. But on he trudged, reminding the hatchet faced trio in front of him that Dickman had volunteered the information about getting out at Morpeth, and that he had not been seen carrying a bag. His final points concerned the guns: the ballistics evidence pointed to two pistols but no gun had ever been traced to Dickman.

The defence Counsel concluded by drawing their Lordships attention to Tindal Atkinson's comment about Mrs Dickman's absence from the witness box. This, claimed Mitchell-Innes, must have unfairly influenced the jury. Citing precedents by the bushel he proceeded to ask for a new trial. There then followed one of those exchanges so beloved of legal purists, with a barrage of *rex versus so and so* flashing back and forth across the court room. Mitchell-Innes appeared to have scored more hits but obviously not in any vital organs because he lost this piece of legal fencing as well.

The Lord Chief Justice then conferred with his two colleagues and delivered their judgement. I do not intend to delve into it it detail. The following two statements accurately sum up its tone and tenor:—

> *'...we have come to the conclusion that, although Hall's identification of the actual individual might have been slightly influenced by what had previously taken place, it has so little bearing on the real merits of the case this it is quite impossible for us to interfere with the verdict on this ground.'*

Dealing with this particular remark by the Lord Chief Justice, Fenton Bresler first reminds us that the Judiciary were still coming to terms with the Infant Appeal Court before commenting tartly:

> *'Anyone can make their own assessment of how he (Alverstone) was faring.'* [1]

---

1   "Scales of Justice"

The second sentence requires no comments whatsoever:—

'The learned Judge... summing up... is one of the most able I have ever read.'

Running throughout the judgement is the very strong theme that the Appeal Court had entirely misconceived Mitchell-Innes' argument. They imagined that he was arguing that Dickman had either made his way from the front to the rear of the train before it had started, or that he had changed compartments after Heaton. In a situation where not even an iota of misunderstanding should have been present the judgement was rife with it. As a result the Judges were able to use Dickman's own evidence, contradicting his identifications by Raven, Hepple, Hall and Nisbet, to destroy the defence which they themselves were now wrongly attributing to him.

Every point of Coleridge's summing up, and the case for the Prosecution, was resolutely defended: every issue raised by the defence was brushed aside. The possibility of a miscarriage of Justice simply did not exist in the minds of these three old men who could quote verbatim from musty law books, but were quite incapable of even following a simple line of argument let alone reasoning along it. In a swinging sally against the Appeal Court which upheld Derek Bentley's conviction, David Yallop writes:—

'If God does indeed move in mysterious ways he could still learn a thing or two from these Appeal Judges!' [1]

If God was responsible for bringing John Dickman into a head on collision with the likes of Coleridge, Alverstone, Phillimore and Lawrence with his earthy fate entrusted to the care of Edward Mitchell-Innes, then God may well have learnt quite a bit about the way in which his earthly subjects conduct their affairs — none of it good!

✳✳✳✳✳

By the evening of July 18th only one man stood between Dickman and eternity: Home Secretary Winston Churchill.

One consequence of Capital Punishment was that it thrust upon the Home Secretary of the day a responsibility which no man could want or desire. As the ultimate arbitrator of Law enforcement policy only he could decide whether a convicted murderer should live or die. In effect, for a brief moment in time he assumed the role of God. Each successive Home Secretary was to describe this task as melancholy and disturbing.

---

1   "To Encourage the Others" p231

It was generally held that there were seven main reasons for commuting the death sentence. One of these is described by David Yallop in the following terms:—

> *'It has occasionally been thought right to commute the sentence of death in deference to a widespread or strong local expression of public opinion, on the ground that it would do more harm than good to carry out the sentence if the result was to arouse sympathy for the offender or hostility to the law.'* [1]

Another was summed up by Sir John Anderson, a Permanent Secretary at the Home Office and later a Conservative Home Secretary, in a debate on Capital Punishment in the House of Commons on April 14th, 1948.

> *'Where there is a scintilla... of doubt... the Home Secretary has invariably advised commutation.'*

When Churchill sat down to study the papers on the Dickman case he was confronted by both these considerations.

There was now a strong surge of feeling in Dickman's favour. Public opinion had changed dramatically since the jury had brought in their verdict. To quote Sydney Rowan-Hamilton:—

> *'After the trial of Dickman the papers were filled with this type of letter, denouncing the verdict... as "vicious and ill-considered" etc.'* [2]

Friends and supporters of Dickman were waging a campaign on his behalf and, as already mentioned, five members of the jury had added their names to the petition for his reprieve.

On the second point, there was very decidedly a scintilla of doubt: much more than a scintilla in fact. The "Concise English Dictionary" defines the words as an 'atom' or 'spark'. Dickman had been convicted on evidence which left room for considerable doubt. There had been Police misconduct, and the identifications of Dickman by Hall and Mrs Nisbet had been shown to be seriously flawed. 'Atom'? 'spark'?: a full current would be a more apt description.

But unfortunately it was customary for the Home Secretary to solicit the views of the trial Judge. If Churchill did consult Coleridge then we can be in no doubt that the latter told him that Dickman was as guilty as hell!

Never one to shirk or delay a decision, Churchill did not ponder long. His verdict was that the Law had to take its course.

We do not know exactly why Churchill decided against reprieving Dickman, and it would be fruitless to speculate. What we do know — and I return to

1   "To Encourage the Others" p262
2   "Trial of J A Dickman" p2

the introduction to this book — is that the Home Office ignored two of its own guidelines for reprieve. It also ignored Police misconduct, which should give those who believe in capital punishment additional food for thought.

*****

On August 9th, 1910 thousands of small cards were distributed in the streets, pubs and restaurants of London and Newcastle. They bore this terse little message:—

> *'Must Dickman be hanged tomorrow? No! No! No! Wire Home Secretary at once and wash your hands of complicity in the legal crime.'*

Innumerable circulars bearing a similar message flooded the streets of every major city in Britain. Sydney Rowan-Hamilton records that the men and women who fought for Dickman in those last desperate hours were from 'every rank and calling in Society'.[1] But even as the frantic campaigners scurried to and fro in the summer sunshine the executioner was already preparing to dispatch John Dickman into eternity. The public's protests were all ignored. There was to be no eleventh hour miracle.

On the morning of August 10th Dickman was taken to the execution shed at Newcastle prison. Just under five months earlier he had walked a free man to Newcastle Police Station. Now he made his final walk, this time to the gallows. From first to last he had never ceased to maintain his innocence. But the small group of men who escorted him on that last day were disinterested in such matters. They merely had an unpleasant task to perform. Even so they were impressed with Dickman on that long ago summer's morning. According to one of them:—

> *'Dickman appeared to be the calmest man of the little company assembled in the cell. He walked to his execution as a soldier on parade.'*

(10)

I dislike conspiracy theories. They go against my life experience which is that most people are decent people. The majority of such notions I have found to be holy grails of the frustrated, and the paranoid. But conspiracies have and do exist, and where they have been successful it is partly due to the unwillingness

---

1   "Trial of J A Dickman" p23

of people like myself to accept them.

I have always been very unwilling to believe that John Alexander Dickman was judicially murdered by conspiracy. But that theory does exist and it is my duty to put it before you.

In 1975 the B.B.C. included the Dickman case in their "Barlow & Watt Investigate" series. In it they told the strange story of Clarence Norman.

Norman was the Court shorthand reporter at the Dickman trial. According to him after the jury had retired, he was summoned to Lord Coleridge's Chambers to read back his notes on what Tindal Atkinson had said about Annie Dickman's absence from the witness box. He found Coleridge closeted with Weddell, Lowenthal and the Crown Solicitor. But they were not talking about the Nisbet case; instead they were discussing Dickman's possible involvement in a murder committed almost two years earlier.

Mrs Caroline Luard was the wife of Charles, a retired British Army General. In the early evening of August 24, 1908 General Luard discovered her dead body at their summer house near Sevenoaks, Kent. She had been shot twice through the head and her purse was missing; the rings on the fingers of her left hand had also been stolen.

An extensive murder hunt proved fruitless. A drunk confessed at Bow Street: when sober he retracted. A tramp was arrested: he was found to have been in prison on August 24th. Poison pen letters accused General Luard himself: he was exonerated at the inquest but in his grief took his own life. Finally, a discarded overcoat and a pair of boots were discovered on the banks of London's Regent Park Lane along with a note confessing to the crime. The writer, who signed himself 'John' or 'Jack' Storm, was never traced. Eventually the case faded from the newspapers and was consigned to the nether world of the unsolved murder, a curiosity to be occasionally wheeled out and put under the microscopes of perplexed criminologists.

Such then was the crime which, according to Clarence Norman, Coleridge, Lowenthal and Weddell were associating with John Dickman while the jury was out deciding whether he had killed John Nisbet.

Following Dickman's conviction, Norman claimed to have sought an interview with Lord Alverstone to whom he recounted the story of the meeting in Coleridge's Chambers. According to Norman the Lord Chief Justice told him that he, Norman should:—

> '...not refer to the matter in view of my [Norman's] official position.'

Later, said Norman, he discussed the affair with a Cabinet Minister named John Burns and the Editor of the "Daily News", a man named Gardiner. Gardiner, says Norman, refused to print the story while Burns, quote:

> 'conveyed my representations to Mr Churchill, but without avail.'

None of this takes us very far. For one thing, Norman, in his own words:—

'took a very different view to the jury; I thought the case was not conclusively made out against the accused.'

So, he was a supporter of Dickman's cause; not an impartial observer. He might therefore have been making the whole thing up. Might: — but apparently not. What follows is the text of a letter written to Norman by Sydney Rowan-Hamilton, the editor of "The Trial of J A Dickman":—

October 26, 1939

Sir,

Your interesting letter of the 24th August only reached me today. Of course, I was not present at the incident you referred to in the Judge's Chambers, but Lowenthal was a fierce Prosecutor. All the same Dickman was justly [convicted?] and it may interest you to know that he was with little doubt the murderer of Mrs Luard, for he had forged a cheque she had sent him in response to an advertisement in "The Times" (I believe) asking for help; she discovered it and wrote to him and met him outside the General's and her house and her body was found there. He was absent from Newcastle those exact days. Tindal Atkinson knew of this, but not being absolutely certain refused to cross-examine Dickman on it. I have seen replicas of the cheques. They were shown me by the Public Prosecutor: also see the note on the first page of the preface. He was, I believe, mixed up in that case, but I have forgotten the details.'

This is a rather strange missive. The "Trial of J A Dickman" was first published in 1914. A second edition was published in 1926 with a preface by W Teignmough Shore, as Rowan-Hamilton had by then been appointed Chief Justice of Bermuda. In the introduction, Rowan-Hamilton chooses his words very carefully, but it is clear that he believed that Dickman was not convicted beyond a reasonable doubt.

There is no mention in either edition of the Luard case.

Twenty-five years later, and now in retirement in Eire, Rowan-Hamilton's views appeared to have undergone a considerable change. Now he apparently believed that Dickman was guilty not only of Nisbet's murder but Caroline Luard's as well. He also refers to another murder in the 'preface' of his book. In fact it is Appendix 3 of the book and concerns the murder of a moneylender named Herman Cohen on March 8th, 1909. Cohen was battered to death in his office and his finger, on which he wore a diamond ring, had been hacked off. This, implies Rowan-Hamilton, was also Dickman's work.

The three murders, apart from all apparently having been committed for gain, have some very minor similarities, one to another. Like John Nisbet, Mrs Luard was shot behind the ear and under the eye. Her glove had been pulled off and her rings stolen whilst Cohen's finger had been cut off in order to secure his ring.

But these apart, there is nothing to link the crimes, certainly nothing tangible, and the Cohen murder is wholly dissimilar to Nisbet's.

There is not a shred of evidence to associate John Dickman with Herman Cohen's death[*]. Rowan-Hamilton claims to have seen evidence linking Dickman to Caroline Luard's, but nobody else seems to have done.

According to the notes which I scribbled down from the B.B.C. programme, the Newcastle Police wrote to the retired Chief Constable of Kent in 1929 (an inquiry possibly prompted by Norman) asking whether Dickman had ever been a suspect in the Luard murder. The answer was no.

The name of Percy Savage will be familiar to crime historians as the Scotland Yard Detective who arrested Patrick Mahon, the 'Crumbles' murderer. Savage was called in to investigate the Luard murder. Of it he later wrote:—

> '*It remains un unsolved murder. All our work was in vain.*'[**]

By 1939 Rowan-Hamilton seems no longer to have had a very close grip on things. He writes:—

> '*Tindal Atkinson knew of this, but not being absolutely certain refused to cross-examine Dickman on it.*'

Coming from a prominent Barrister and Colonial Chief Justice, this is an astonishing comment. Tindal Atkinson could not have cross-examined Dickman about the Luard murder because he was not on trial for it. A defendant cannot be cross-examined about other crimes unless he has raised his character, or the character of others, as issues, or the crimes connect to form evidence of 'system', and the case which established 'system', George Joseph Smith the 'brides in the bath' murderer, did not come about until 1915. Even then it would not have applied to Dickman; one similarity does not constitute a unique method of murder, which is what 'system' is.

Without wishing to be cruel, I do not think we can place much reliance on Rowan-Hamilton in his cottage. Certainly not as far as his *details* are concerned. But the general point is another matter because it seems plain that somebody, somewhere, did connect, or attempt to connect, Dickman with other crimes. Here we have the evidence of the Cohen appendix — hitherto a mystery — in "The Trial of J A Dickman" as early as 1914. And we have Norman's testimony of

---

[*]   Stories linking Dickman to this crime only appeared after his execution, i.e., at the same time as the 'paper bullet' theory when public concern that he had been wrongly hanged was at its highest.

[**] Bernard Taylor ("Perfect Murder") analyses the case against Dickman as Mrs Luard's murderer and concludes that it is without foundation. Judge Gerald Sparrow ("Vintage Edwardian Murder") and Roy Lewis ("Edwardian Murder") both reach similar conclusions.

Coleridge, Lowenthal and Weddell discussing the Luard case in the Judge's Chambers. That cannot be easily dismissed. Clarence Norman does not come across as a crank. A life-long member of the Labour Party, he was, apparently, on friendly terms with Ramsey McDonald and other senior party members. Norman was later to contend that Churchill, Coleridge, Alverstone, Lawrence, Phillimore and Tindal Atkinson were all friends of the Luards and formed a conspiracy to railroad Dickman to the gallows. Where does this take us?

First, there is no evidence whatsoever against Churchill and the Appeal Judges. The evidence here is an unreliable system not working properly.

Coleridge and Tindal Atkinson were vehemently against Dickman. Once again, this could be purely the fault of the adversarial system which produces such behaviour. But in this instance it could go further. It is all too easy when a person has been accused of one crime to associate them with others and Judges and Barristers are not more immune to the old game of Chinese Whispers than the rest of us, 'no smoke without fire' as the saying goes. Sometimes this may be right; other times spectacularly wrong. A case in point is that of Tom Mooney, an American Socialist and Trade Unionist, who spent twenty-two years in prison for murders which he did not commit.* Mooney was tried and wrongly convicted of a bomb blast which killed ten people because the authorities believed, entirely without foundation, that he had committed previous bomb outrages.

I opened this section by saying that I disliked conspiracy theories. In my book "The Killing of Leon Beron" I outlined a *possible* conspiracy by the British Establishment, ironically not to convict but to acquit, the murderers of three London Police Officers. Was there a plausible conspiracy in this case too; did Coleridge allow himself to be borne on the winds of unfounded suspicions elsewhere? He had done it before in the Miller case. At the end of the day, it is a matter for you to decide.

(11)

Over eighty years have passed since the bodies of John Nisbet and his supposed killer were consigned to the earth. If Dickman was not the murderer then who was? That question can never be answered because the trail has grown too cold. We can only examine the case in relation to Dickman.

In order for him to be guilty you have to be satisfied, first and foremost, that the identification evidence is reliable. We know that it is not; that Hall's identification was the result of Police misconduct, that he and Spink originally thought that Dickman was *not* the man they saw. That being the case then the

---

* He was finally pardoned in 1939. See "Frame Up" by Curt Gentry for a definitive account of the case.

connecting chain of Raven — Hepple — Cicely Nisbet — Hall is not merely broken but runs in reverse, *against* Dickman being Nisbet's travelling companion. That is reinforced by John Nisbet's behaviour that morning. He went to the head of the train even though he knew Cicely would be waiting at the rear. Why? The logical answer is that he hoped to shake off the man walking alongside him. If so then it was because that man was a stranger. Here, remember too the evidence of Raven, Hepple and Hall that no conversation was passing between them: also that Nisbet failed to draw his wife's attention to the man, which he would have done if he was an acquaintance of theirs.

After Heaton there is no identification, only a hodge-podge of illogicalities put forward by the Crown. They used Dickman's own, freely given, statement against him where they could, failing to explain the inconsistencies in their argument. Routine activities, such as we might all indulge in during the course of our everyday lives, were turned upside down and used against Dickman as a substitute for evidence. One gaping hole was how the killer left the train at Morpeth because Grant saw nobody get out of the compartment. Tindal Atkinson avoided this issue like the plague. He did not ask whether a man could leave the compartment by the far door, walk across the tracks and clamber upon the opposite platform. The train back to Newcastle was due in just eight minutes time (travelling on to Pegswood ran the risk of missing it). Here there was no attempt to examine the issues fairly, just twisting and turning with fingers crossed that nobody would spot the gaps.

All that we are left with is motive. By itself that does not mean anything. The Crown said Dickman borrowed because he was broke; he said it was a business investment. Frank Christie, who the Prosecution skilfully used against him, borrowed *ten times* Dickman's amount from the same money lender for the same reasons as Dickman. At no time was the point ever made on Dickman's behalf that the colliery's wages had been reduced by two-thirds because of the strike, yet the Crown alleged that he was familiar with the collieries. Here their own claims work against them.

That then was the Prosecution's case. Even if their theory of the murder was correct it does not bring it home to John Dickman. And if that theory was not correct then their case ceases to exist altogether.

Everybody assumed that John Nisbet was dead at Morpeth. Even Mitchell-Innes told the Jury:—

> *'Of course there was nobody on the seats at Morpeth.'*

But was this true? Maybe. But there were pieces of evidence which did not quite fit the jigsaw, clues which like little fragments of an incoherently constructed crossword puzzle cannot be reconciled with the complete picture.

Whoever killed John Nisbet made a thorough job of it. His head was reduced to a grisly mass of bone and tissue from which an obnoxious triplet of red streams wound their way across the carriage floor. His spectacles lay crushed and broken. But his other personal possessions were apparently intact. None of them seem to have fallen out of his pockets during whatever struggle he put up, or when his body was crammed under the seat.

Read now the testimony of the man who found the body, Foreman Porter Thomas Charlton, and the man who examined it, Dr Charles Burnham.

First Charlton:—

> *'I did not move the body myself, but called for the guard of the train and called one of the porters, and also sent for the Station Master. The Station Master found a ticket; it was a return ticket, third class, to Widdrington.'*

And now Burnham:

> *'It [blood] was all over the hand which was not covered with the glove, and it also covered the glove.'*

What do we glean from these two particles of evidence? First that the Station Master found a ticket. There is no suggestion that any of the four railwaymen touched the body in any way. The first person to make such a search was Constable Nisbet. But the Station Master found John Nisbet's ticket and under the circumstances it can only have been found on the floor of the compartment. Now Burnham: his evidence could not be clearer; only one hand was gloved, and the missing glove was next to the body. This item must also have been found on the floor.

If no other items, apart from Nisbet's spectacles, were divested during the course of the crime, then how did the ticket and glove come to be on the floor? Let us examine them individually.

Had Nisbet been holding the ticket all the way from Newcastle? Not a very likely proposition. On the other hand did he, like the overwhelming majority of passengers then and now have it ready in his hand because he was nearing journey's end and getting out at the next station.

Widdrington Station!

And the glove. Why was it not on his hand?

There are two likely possibilities; that he had both gloves off and was in the act of putting them on when he was attacked, and that he had his ticket inside the glove and took it off in order to get it out. If so then he was getting ready to leave the train.

And that takes us back to Widdrington Station!

Here now the double murderer theory comes firmly into play.

A man boards the train with Nisbet at Newcastle. An accomplice notes the compartment and when the train stops at Pegswood changes compartments. Or he boards the train at Pegswood having seen Nisbet's travelling companion, his accomplice, hanging out of the window, exactly as Nisbet did at Heaton, when he knew his wife would be on the platform. They then kill Nisbet between Longhurst and Widdrington.

This of course involves tossing aside Grant and Cosher's Testimony.

But Grant failed to notice someone else whom he should have seen, a young man who was travelling in the first compartment. He saw, in that compartment, a Mr Andrew Bruce, whom he knew, because Bruce was sitting on the platform side at Morpeth. Grant did not see Bruce's travelling companion, who was apparently on the far side of the carriage.*

Mitchell-Innes asked Grant:—

Q. It would be easier to see a man on the platform side rather than the furthest side?

A. Exactly.

Cicely Nisbet said that at Heaton, her husband's travelling companion was on *the far side of the compartment.*

John Spink at Stannington had *both Nisbet and the other man seated on the far side.*

Because of this Hall did not see the other man at all.

All of which leaves open the very clear possibility implicit in Grant's testimony, that he could have failed to see Nisbet and his travelling companion.

As for Cosher, his duty was a routine one, performed automatically. He, like Grant, could have failed to notice passengers on the far side of the carriage. To be objective, it has to be stated that he did see people in the first compartment, but he then walked down the train shouting out 'Longhurst Station', and the duty would have become more and more routine. He may also have been distracted by seeing Grant, whom he knew, alighting from the first compartment of the second carriage.

So there was an alternative theory of the crime, one that was never put before the jury. When you look at both theories, and consider the evidence as a whole, does it not point, at the very least, to reasonable doubt?

The last words I will leave to Fenton Bresler, a Queen's Counsel of distinction:—

'I personally am convinced that John Dickman should never have been hanged: the evidence simply was not there to justify the ultimate penalty.'[1]

---

1   "Scales of Justice"

---

*   He got out at Chevington, the stop after Widdrington.

John Alexander Dickman

Lord Coleridge

Edward Tindal Atkinson K.C.

Edward Mitchell-Innes K.C.

Walter Graham Rowland

David John Ware

The Corner of Deansgate and Cumberland Street

(Note the position of the street lamp.)

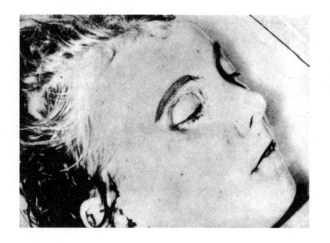

Olive Balchin

(Retouched mortuary photograph)

PART TWO

WALTER GRAHAM ROWLAND:
KILLER OR VICTIM

Before the Law there stands a guard. A man comes from the country begging admittance to the Law. But the guard cannot admit him.

Can he hope to enter at a later time?

'That is possible,' says the guard.

The man tries to peer through the entrance; he had been taught that the Law should be accessible to every man.

'Do not attempt to enter without my permission,' says the guard. 'I am very powerful. Yet I am the least of all the guards. From hall to hall, door to door, each guard is more powerful than the last.'

(Franz Kafka: *The Trial*)

WALTER GRAHAM ROWLAND:

KILLER OR VICTIM?

(1)

The Rowland case is not a complex one and can be told very simply in outline.

On the morning of October 20th, 1946 the dead body of a prostitute named Olive Balchin was found on a bomb site in Manchester. She had been bludgeoned to death with a hammer.

Six days later the Police arrested an itinerant labourer named Walter Rowland and charged him with her murder. On December 16th of the same year Rowland was found guilty of the crime at Manchester Assizes and sentenced to death.

Five weeks after this David John Ware, who was serving a prison sentence for theft, confessed that he was the murderer of Olive Balchin. Rowland appealed but the Appeal Court refused to hear Ware's evidence. Instead they recommended that the Home Secretary should set up an inquiry.

The Home Secretary, James Chuter Ede, subsequently appointed Mr James Catterall Jolly, K.C., to investigate Ware's claims. On February 22nd, 1947 Ware retracted his confession. On the 25th Jolly reported to Chuter Ede that there were no grounds for believing that Rowland had been wrongly convicted. On the 27th Rowland was executed at Strangeways Prison, Manchester.

Four years passed. Then a woman was attacked in similar fashion in Bristol. Her attacker gave himself up to the Police saying: "I have killed a woman. I don't know what is the matter with me. I keep on having an urge to hit women on the head."

The man was David Ware. He was found to be insane and sent to Broadmoor. What, if any, statements he made there about the Balchin murder are unknown. In 1954, whilst still detained at Broadmoor, Ware committed suicide.

So who killed Olive Balchin? Rowland, the man who was hanged, or Ware, the man who confessed? Was justice done?

(2)

The train of events which led Walter Rowland to the gallows was set in motion on Saturday, October 19th, 1946. At some time that afternoon, 5:40 according to the evidence at Rowland's trial, 4 o'clock if Ware's somewhat incoherent memory was accurate, a man entered a hardware shop in the Ardwick district of Manchester and purchased a hammer from Mr Edward Macdonald, the owner of the shop.

Later that evening, at 6:15 to be precise, Walter Rowland caught a bus from Lower Molseley, Manchester, to the town of New Mills in Derbyshire where his parents lived. Rowland was a criminal, a man with a distinctly unpleasant past. He was living a hand to mouth existence in Manchester, spending his nights in Hostels and seedy, run-down lodging houses, and his days in the company of petty crooks and prostitutes. His only real contact with a normal home life was provided by his mother who did his laundry for him. That day he had expected to receive a parcel of clean clothes from her at the Post Office branch in Spring Gardens. But his visit there, at 5:20 that evening, ended in disappointment; no parcel had arrived. Reluctant to wait until the following Monday, he decided to travel the thirteen miles to New Mills and collect the clean clothes himself. He arrived at his parents' home at 7:30., changed his shirt and collar and relaxed whilst his mother made up a brown paper parcel consisting of some shirts, socks, undergarments and a set of overalls. By 9:15 he was ready to return to Manchester.

Fate has a capricious nature. Events which influence or even decide the direction of our lives often take place without our knowledge or design. Thus it was with Walter Rowland on that Saturday evening. At the time he was setting foot outside the door of his parents' home, two women were having a fateful encounter in the streets of Manchester. Rita Leach was en-route to the City's Piccadilly area when she was stopped by a woman who asked her the way to Deansgate. Leach noticed that the inquirer was wearing a large beret and a coat with a double row of buttons down the front. She obliged the woman by pointing her in the right direction. Then they parted. A trivial, everyday incident; yet it helped to put a rope around Walter Rowland's neck.

Rowland could have stayed the night at his parents' home. Later he was to explain that he had decided against it because he was suffering from syphilis and felt that he would be insulting his mother by sleeping at home. But in all probability this was a lie dictated by the exigency of having to face a jury without giving away his criminal background. It is far more likely that he was planning to meet up with some of his underworld acquaintances in one of the Manchester pubs which they frequented. If so then he was unlucky. He caught the wrong bus and ended up in Stockport. This meant that he would have to catch another bus back to Manchester, and by the time he arrived the pubs would be shut.[*] Accordingly he decided to have a few drinks at a pub next to the bus station in Stockport before catching a late bus into Manchester.

Standing at the bar supping his pint, Rowland was blissfully unaware of the disaster which was steadily overtaking him, a disaster over which he had no control and which was shortly to escalate beyond the point of no return.

---

[*]   Saturday closing time was then 10:30.

The scene now shifts back to Manchester. Almost lost amidst the pubs and restaurants dotted around the City's Deansgate area was a small basement cafe known as the "Queens", a decidedly pretentious name to say the least. At 10:30 that evening two women and a man descended the narrow flight of stairs into the cafe. As soon as the trio were seated waitress Elizabeth Copley bustled over to their table and took their order. The two women both had something to eat but the man merely ordered a cup of tea. Business was slack that evening and Copley had plenty of time to observe them. One of the women was elderly and Copley recalled having seen her in the cafe before.

The second woman was much younger — about thirty-eight — and she was wearing a coat with a double row of buttons down the front. She was bareheaded, but Copley was later to claim that she had seen a hat on the chair next to her.

But it was the man whom Copley particularly noticed. He seemed to be annoyed about something and hardly spoke to the two women. A mix-up over the teas did not help matters. He was young and fresh complexioned with dark hair plastered down with grease. He had with him a long thin parcel wrapped in brown paper. At the time Copley did not recognise him as anyone she had seen before.

The threesome left the cafe at 11:00 p.m.

Three people enjoying a late supper in a cheap eatery would not have caused any shadow of apprehension to flicker across Walter Rowland's mind. But then he had not yet been charged with murdering one of them.

If Rowland's subsequent story was true then he left Stockport on the 10:45 bus. He decided not to travel into the centre of Manchester. Instead he got off at a stop in the suburb of Ardwick. He then bought some fish and chips and asked a soldier if he knew of a nearby lodging house where he could get a bed for the night. The soldier recommended a lodgings in the Chorlton District, no 81, Brunswick Street, owned by a man named Frank Beaumont. Rowland arrived there at about 11:15. When Beaumont opened the door to him Rowland realised that he had stayed at the lodging house on a previous occasion.

Beaumont was able to provide Rowland with a ground floor room for the night. This having been settled, Rowland asked whether he could go out and come back again, explaining that he was thirsting for a soft drink to wash the fatty taste of the chips out of his mouth. It was now 11:20 and Beaumont was getting ready to go to bed but he told Rowland that he could borrow the front door key and go out again if he wished. Rowland did, but soon returned when he discovered that all the shops and Cafes in the locale were now closed. Beaumont was still up and Rowland gave him back the key and retired for the night. He awoke shortly before 10 o'clock the following morning, had some breakfast, and departed, signing his name in the visitor's book before he went.

Such was Rowland's story. If it was true then he was in bed and asleep by 11:45 that night.

At the same time that Rowland said he was climbing into bed, David Ware was en-route to a common lodging house in Stockport. Ware was making the same bus journey as Rowland, only in reverse. On the run from the Police, Ware could not afford to be too fussy about his choice of accommodation. He would spend the night in a large dormitory style room in the midst of dossers and down and outs. The following day he would trudge wearily on to Chapel-en-le-frith.

Manchester had suffered heavily from bombing raids during the Second World War and the city was littered with bomb sites. One of them was situated on the corner of Deansgate and Cumberland Street. To publican Norman Mercer the bomb site had become part and parcel of the landscape. He walked past it every night when taking his dog for a walk. Normally the streets were deserted at midnight when Mercer and his canine companion enjoyed their nocturnal stroll. But tonight was different. Approaching the bomb site he could dimly make out the shapes of a man and a woman standing on the corner. As he drew nearer he heard the sound of their voices raised in anger. Mercer could see the man's features only in profile, but the woman was directly facing him. Later he was to say that as he passed them he was walking so slowly that he almost came to a halt. However once he had passed them his step quickened. A few strides later he was round the corner and out of earshot. When he passed the bomb site again on his way home thirty minutes later there was no sign of the couple.

Eleven hours later some children found the dead body of Olive Balchin on the bomb site. She was lying just a few inches away from a wall. Balchin had been battered to death by repeated blows to the right side of her head and face. The murder weapon, a hammer, was found nearby. Also found near the body were a piece of brown wrapping paper and a large beret. The latter had belonged to Balchin. She had sustained the most ghastly injuries, being struck with such force that her brain was protruding from her skull. At one point she had obviously tried to protect herself by putting her hands over her head because the nail of the index finger of her left hand had been torn from its bedding. She was fully clothed and had not been sexually assaulted. The coat she was wearing had a double row of buttons down the front.

Such were the brutal facts of the murder of Olive Balchin. She had been living in a hostel under the name "Olive Balshaw" and working as a prostitute. Balchin was forty years old and still reasonably attractive but her favours could be bought for as little as fifty pence. The prostitute's story is almost always a sad one. In Balchin's case we do not know what had pushed her into that life. Only one friend of hers was ever traced, a man named Angood who told the Police what her real name was.

A sad life had come to an end; another was soon to be ended.

The Police investigation into Balchin's murder was put into the hands of Detective Inspector Frank Stainton, operating out of Bootle Street Police Station. Within a short time of the body being found Norman Mercer telephoned the Police and told them about the couple he had seen quarrelling outside the bomb site the previous night. He made a statement and was then taken to the Mortuary where he identified Balchin as the woman he had seen. He also claimed to have recognised her coat. Exactly how valid these identifications were is a matter of dispute.

Newspaper reports of the crime on Monday, October 21st, were accompanied by two photographs. One was of a Policewoman wearing Balchin's hat and coat. The other was of the murder weapon, a leather dresser's hammer with a distinctive number '4' stamped on it.

The first photograph attracted the attention of Rita Leach. The woman she had spoken to on Saturday evening had been wearing a similar hat and coat, similar enough anyway to persuade her to go to the Police. She did so and was shown a photograph of the corpse. Like Mercer, she identified Balchin as the same woman.

The photograph of the hammer also produced a response. Edward Macdonald recognised it as the hammer he had sold the previous Saturday. For good measure he also identified the brown paper as that which he had used to wrap it in.

That Monday the Police also interviewed a man about the murder. After questioning he was released. Who he was we do not know, except that it was not Walter Rowland.

Whilst all this was going on in Manchester a seemingly trivial incident was taking place across the Pennines in Sheffield. On the Monday evening two men walked into a Sheffield Police Station and asked to see the Station Officer. One of them was a Salvation Army Captain. The other was David Ware. The Captain announced that he had come to hand Ware into custody, his having confessed to stealing some money from a Salvation Army Hostel in Stoke the previous Friday. Ware confirmed that this was true. For this crime he was sentenced to a term of imprisonment in Walton Gaol, Liverpool.

No one thought to connect Ware with Manchester or the murder of Olive Balchin. Nor could they be expected to. But by his later confession Ware was wearing a blood-stained raincoat from which he had removed and thrown away the belt.

Back in Manchester Stainton's next move was to send his men out into Deansgate with a photograph of Balchin's features, retouched to hide the dreadful injuries. For the next two days they scoured the pubs and cafes searching for witnesses who might have seen her on Saturday night. At the Queen's cafe they struck lucky. Elizabeth Copley identified her as the younger of the two women who had come in together that night. And she also told them about the man, — a man carrying a long, thin brown paper parcel which could have contained a hammer, a man who seemed to have been in a bad mood about something.

The Police now had four witnesses. Macdonald had spoken of a man buying the hammer, Leach of pointing the victim in the direction of Deansgate,

Copley of the victim coming into the cafe with an irritable man who carried a parcel which could have contained the murder weapon and Mercer of seeing the victim arguing with a man outside the murder site. It was, to say the least, very thin. One slightly contradictory detail was that Macdonald's customer had worn a dark fawn raincoat whereas the man seen by Copley and Mercer was not wearing a coat. Doubtless, the Police thought that he might have taken it off between the time of buying the hammer and meeting Balchin. But that raincoat was now to assume, albeit temporarily, great importance in the case.

Friday, October 25th. Five days had elapsed since the finding of the body and no viable suspect was in sight. But that day there was a visitor to Bootle Street, an American nicknamed "Slim". What his real name was we do not know. What we do know is that "Slim" dragged Walter Rowland's name into the case. 'Roland', said "Slim", had borrowed his raincoat on Friday the 18th and had not returned it.

What followed has never been adequately explained but as a result of the suspected theft of a raincoat, Walter Rowland became a suspect for the murder of Olive Balchin. In "The Trial of Walter Rowland" Henry Cecil writes:

> *'Sergeant Trippier who was... concerned in the murder enquiries decided to find out something more about... Roland. As a result he... learned that he frequented the Manchester area and had a criminal record which included at least two offences of violence...'* [1]

The Police themselves now take up the story claiming that Rowland: 'answered the description of the man seen in the company of the dead woman late on the Saturday night.'

The first of the above two statements is correct; the second is not.

Rowland had spent the week since the 19th stopping in lodging houses and hostels. On Sunday, the 20th, he spent the night at a lodging house in Hyde Road, Ardwick. The following morning he decamped to a Salvation Army hostel where he stayed for the next four days.

On the Friday, October 25th, he moved on to a Services Transit hostel. He was asleep there on Saturday night, October 26th, when Detective Constable Douglas Nimmo and Detective Sergeant Joseph Blakemore shook him awake and asked him to accompany them to Bootle Street. According to both Officers Rowland said:— 'You don't want me for murdering that fucking woman do you?' Rowland categorically denied making any such remark.

At Bootle Street Rowland was questioned by Stainton, Blakemore, and Nimmo. What he told them is a matter of considerable dispute, not so much in terms of what was actually said but in the context in which it was said. This is

1   "The Trial of Walter Rowland" p25

a controversy which we shall examine later. In the meantime there are certain things which Rowland did tell the Police and which are not in dispute. These were that he knew Olive Balchin, had had intercourse with her on two occasions, once on a bomb site and once in a shop doorway, and believed that he might have contracted syphilis from her. He had met her on the evening of Friday, October 18th in a cafe in Piccadilly, Manchester in order to try to find out if Balchin was suffering from the disease. He was not successful and in taking his leave of her had casually told her that he would see her the following night, an appointment he vehemently denied having kept. These admissions were serious enough but on top of them Rowland volunteered another tit-bit which really damned him: he stated that if he had been certain that he had caught syphilis from Olive Balchin then he would have strangled her!

In addition to the evidence which Rowland volunteered against himself he also made a serious mistake about where he had stayed on the night of the 19th. He thought that it was in Hyde Road where he had in fact lodged the following night, the 20th.

Had Rowland not made these statements then on the night of October 26/27th no case would have existed against him. The Police had no knowledge of his relationship with Balchin, the fact that he had syphilis was irrelevant because her autopsy had disclosed that she was not suffering from it and Frank Beaumont would have confirmed Rowland's stay at his lodging house with the visitor's book to support him. In fact though Rowland would have been wisest to have maintained his right to silence. The fact that he gave it up and made the error about Hyde Road enabled the prosecution to attack him quite ruthlessly at his trial. He was accused of lying about Hyde Road and of deliberately withholding the Brunswick Street alibi so that the Police could not check on it. Had he stayed silent then none of this could have been brought against him. Those who argue in favour of dispensing with the right to silence should ponder the Rowland case.

That however is hypothesis. Rowland did not stay silent and he played right into the hands of the Police. Before his statement they had not had even grounds on which to question him. The explanation that he 'answered the description' of the man seen with Balchin is one of the six impossible things which we are asked to believe before breakfast. When we come to examine Rowland's statement as a whole we shall see that we are also being asked to swallow the other five as well! For the moment however it is sufficient to say that Rowland did *not* fit the description given by Macdonald and Copley, whilst Mercer's could have fitted half the men in Manchester. Rowland was questioned purely because of his record: it was an attempt to fit him to the crime and unwittingly he went along with it.

According to Rowland the interrogation went on until four in the morning. He was then allowed to sleep and on Sunday afternoon put on an identity parade in front of Edward Macdonald and Elizabeth Copley.

Copley first. She walked slowly along the line, once, twice, three times. Finally she returned and touched Rowland on the shoulder with the words 'I'm not certain but I think this is him.'

Edward Macdonald had no such hesitation. He picked Rowland out immediately.

Rowland was charged with murder. Edward Macdonald went drinking with the Police.

Missing was Norman Mercer. But his time would come. According to his testimony at the trial he was interviewed again on either the 28th or 29th. On November 4th he attended a second identity parade at Strangeways prison where Rowland was on remand. Mercer walked the line without picking anybody out. He then asked to see the parade side faced. The line-up duly made a half turn to the right and Mercer picked out Rowland. Rowland had a prominent scar behind his left ear.

(3)

Rowland's trial was set for December 12th at Manchester Autumn Assizes. But before turning to it and examining in depth the evidence which sent him to the gallows it is advisable to look at his life history because although superficially it tends to strengthen the case against him, I believe that when viewed objectively it points more towards his innocence than his guilt.

Walter Graham Rowland was born on March 26th, 1908 at his parents' home in New Mills.

He left school at fifteen and served an engineering apprenticeship until he was eighteen at which point he joined the Army. From all accounts Rowland was an intelligent young man but inclined to be impetuous and hot tempered. Certainly joining the Army was an ill considered action which he speedily regretted. After only two months in the service he prevailed upon his parents to purchase his discharge. Back in Civvy Street his temper got the better of him in his next job and he was dismissed for insolence. He then decided to try the Army again but this time his sojourn in Her Majesty's Forces was of even shorter duration. He was discharged on medical grounds after only two weeks.

Shortly afterwards Rowland committed his first known criminal act when he attempted to strangle his fiancée, a girl named Annie Schofield. He then tried to commit suicide by hanging himself. Rowland claimed that he had attacked Schofield in a fit of rage and the Police apparently accepted this because he was charged not with attempted murder but grievous bodily harm. Even so Rowland still received a three year Borstal sentence.

He was released in 1929 and went to work as a labourer. In 1930 he married but unfortunately his wife died in childbirth ten months later. It was at this point that Rowland's life went into the downward spiral which culminated with his execution sixteen years later.

Rowland's immediate reaction to his wife's death was to steal a car. He was caught and in July, 1931 sentenced to two months in prison. On his release he married Annie Schofield, the girl he had almost strangled four years earlier. Schofield was then four months pregnant and it would appear to have been a classic case of marriage on the rebound with Schofield's pregnancy thrown in as an additional factor. Certainly, as events were to prove, it was not the recipe for a happy union.

In February, 1932 Annie Rowland gave birth to a daughter who was christened Mavis Agnes. In October Rowland committed a robbery and immediately afterwards tried to kill himself by taking Lysol. But he survived and again found himself in a prison cell, this time for a year. When he was released the depression was in full tide and he found it impossible to get a job. Obviously his lengthening criminal record was very much against him.

Things now went from bad to catastrophic. In March, 1934 Rowland bilked a taxi-driver and once again found himself hunted by the Police. He suggested to his wife that he should rob the gas meter but this she refused to countenance. The Rowland's domestic life was extremely unhappy and for Rowland this was the last straw. A terrible row ensued which ended with Rowland flying into a dreadful rage and strangling his small daughter. On the run he again bilked a taxi-driver and this time was arrested for it. Once in custody he was naturally charged with the infinitely more serious crime of murder. Once again he attempted suicide, this time with iodine.

At his trial Rowland tried unsuccessfully to blame his wife for their daughter's death. He was found guilty but the jury attached a recommendation of mercy to their verdict. The Home Secretary agreed with them and Rowland's death sentence was commuted to life imprisonment.

1942 found Britain at war and in need of able-bodied men and so Rowland was released on licence to join the Army and fight for King and Country. This time it was a case of third time lucky and Rowland succeeded in lasting out for the duration. He was demobbed in 1946 with an indifferent character reference, the result of striking a sergeant in a fit of anger. He had been demobbed for only a few weeks when he resumed his criminal activities by breaking into a warehouse. He was arrested by Detective Constable Nimmo. Rather surprisingly, in view of his past record, he was only put on probation.

This was to prove the opposite of a blessing in disguise.

At the age of 38 Rowland was a man with no marriage, no job, and precious little in the way of prospects. One thing that he did have, as he told the Police, was a pride in his body and finding that he had syphilis was a great blow to his ego.

But did it lead him to batter Olive Balchin to death?

I have gone into Rowland's life and criminal history at some length for two reasons. The first is objectivity. It would be quite wrong to harbour any illusions about Rowland's character. He was a dyed-in-the-wool villain.

It is obvious that his real reason for not living at home was that he wanted to indulge his taste for the Manchester underworld, and that his friends came from the same dubious milieu. When he was arrested Rowland had in his possession the overalls which his mother had given him and a card from the Employment Exchange sending him for employment as a joiner at a Manchester firm, but as the card was dated October 11th, and Rowland had not reported for work when he was arrested on the 26th, then it seems obvious that the purpose of both the card and the overalls were merely to convince respectable people that he intended getting a job when in fact his real aim was to carry on with his criminal career.

Objectivity may in this case have its price: the reader may already have formed a firm opinion that Rowland was quite capable of the murder of Olive Balchin. This then leads me on to the second reason for examining Rowland's past so thoroughly. I believe that his history strongly suggests that he was not the type to commit a premeditated murder.

By his own admission Rowland had a bestial temper and did things on impulse which he regretted later. His near strangulation of Annie Schofield was certainly not premeditated. Nor was the murder of his child. Child murder is rightly considered to be a particularly heinous type of murder and the jury would not have recommended mercy had they not been convinced that Rowland killed the child in a fit of blind rage. Indeed it is possible that had Rowland pleaded guilty to manslaughter the court would have accepted this.

The record above shows quite clearly that Rowland was a man who committed acts of violence in fits of sudden rage. There is nothing in his history to suggest that he was the type who could calmly plot a woman's death, buy a hammer, arrange to meet her that night and *then* batter her to death.

Moreover Rowland's three attempts at suicide are important in his defence. They show that after committing a serious crime he was affected by severe pangs of remorse. Rowland made no suicide bid following the death of Olive Balchin. He did not act like a guilty man and vehemently protested his innocence to the bitter end.

I ask the reader to bear these points in mind when he or she considers the evidence against Rowland.

(4)

Between John Dickman's execution in 1910 and Rowland's trial, it is arguable that the state had put to death no less than thirteen innocent men and women, a total which, if accurate, deserves to be called a state massacre.

The courts retained their archaic rituals, the Judge a seemingly omnipotent presence, the Barristers resplendent in their wigs and gowns, the adversarial system hurling them against each other like Pit Bull terriers. Even the quill pen remained in use until the Second World War. What it all had to do with justice and the search for truth is hard to see. Looking back on it the crime historian is at a distinct disadvantage. He or she cannot cut like a laser through the endless muddle of words and adversity, the innuendo and inference, to say what is and what is not truth. Objectivity has no place in the adversarial system. Truth is obscured by combat.

This system, which remains in force today – most of its shibboleths still intact, pitted Mr Basil Nield K.C.[*] and a second Basil, Mr Wingate-Saul, against the best which the poor prisoner's defence[**] had to offer Rowland, Mr Kenneth Burke and Mr H Openshaw – King's Counsel against Junior Barrister. The gap in stature between attack and defence is readily apparent from the trial transcript. Mr Justice Sellars presided. He would unfairly negate a crucial part of Rowland's defence.

Resources were also an important difference between the two sides. The state had them; the defence didn't. Nothing was available to track down people who could have been important to Rowland's defence; the old lady in the Queen's cafe and the soldier who had directed Rowland to Beaumont's lodging house, for instance. Of 32 witnesses called only 4 would be appearing for the defence (including Rowland himself) and one of these would turn out to be worse than useless.

Today almost fifty years later, we can assess Rowland's trial as objective observers. We can, hopefully, leave aside our personal feelings about a wretched miscreant who strangled a child, and our need to believe in the justice and integrity of authority figures, and weigh and sift the evidence as seekers after truth.

Many years ago Edward Marshall Hall, foremost of our defence advocates, made an historic speech about the scales of justice. Justice, he said, was evenly balanced but when the *presumption* of innocence was put into the scales then the weight of it caused the scales to drop in the accused's favour.

The presumption of innocence is what the Rowland trial is all about. Point and counterpoint appear to balance each other on an even keel. But when we add in the presumption of innocence the scales no longer balance each other

---

*   Later Mr Justice Nield.
**   Now called Legal Aid.

because they can only do so then through facts only explainable by guilt. No such facts exist in Walter Rowland's trial.

The first witness of importance was Dr Charles Jenkins, the pathologist who had carried out the autopsy on Olive Balchin. Death had been caused by a blunt instrument which the killer must have gripped very tightly. From the way in which the injuries had been inflicted blood would have spurted as well as flowed.

Cross-examining, Burke asked Jenkins whether he would have expected to find blood on the murderer's clothes. Jenkins stated quite categorically that he would and then went on to say that although it was not impossible for the killer to have escaped without blood on his clothes it was certainly improbable.

As we shall see, this was a crucial point in Rowland's favour.

Jenkins was followed into the witness box by Mr Edward Macdonald, the hardware shop proprietor. He told the Court that on the morning of Saturday October 19th he had purchased the murder weapon, a leather dresser's hammer, from a cobbler named Rawlinson. That afternoon he put the hammer on sale in his hardware shop and at about 5:40 a man came into the shop and bought it. Macdonald's court room description of the purchaser ran as follows:—

> *'Aged about 28–32, height — 5ft 7–8 ins. Build — medium. Face — thin. Features — very pallid, clean shaven. Hair — dark, well greased. Clothes — dark fawn raincoat, dark suit, white shirt with matching soft collar, dark tie, no hat. Quietly spoken.'*

Macdonald asked the man what he wanted the hammer for and he answered that it was for 'general purposes'. Macdonald told him: 'it's no use for that; it wouldn't knock a nail in.' The man replied, 'it will suit my purpose' and left. Macdonald identified Rowland as the purchaser.

Neat? Simple? Yes. That is if you don't examine it too closely. Then Mr Macdonald and his evidence do not add up.

The tendency with most witnesses is that details fade as time wears on. But not, it seems, Edward Macdonald whose Court Room description of the purchaser was amplified from the description he had given to the Police on October 21st. Then he had not been able to say what colour the man's hair was. Now it was 'dark'. But this did not fit Rowland at all; he had fair hair. So a caveat was inserted, 'well greased', which would give it a darker appearance.

Whether or not Rowland greased his hair was debated *ad nauseum* at the trial. We need only look at the salient points. Only one witness thought that Rowland's hair appeared well greased, Captain Thomas Reid, Superintendent of the Salvation Army Hostel where Rowland stayed from October 21st to the 25th. Rowland and his mother both testified that he never used grease, only water. But there was negative evidence in Rowland's favour. When he was arrested on the 26th his hair was dry and no grease was found amongst his possessions.

To return to Macdonald's description, his customer had a very pale, thin face; Rowland had a full, well rounded face with a florid complexion. Macdo-

nald's customer was 28 to 32; Rowland was 38. The man had worn a white shirt
and collar. Rowland, again supported by his mother, denied owning any white
shirts or collars:— the Prosecution did not challenge this. Finally, that elusive
raincoat again. Rowland disclaimed owning one; he said that he had borrowed
"Slim's" on October 18th and returned it within the hour. Here again, the
Prosecution did not dispute his story. Walter Harris, Manager of the Hyde Road
lodging house, had seen a raincoat draped over a dining room chair and had
assumed — no more — that it was Rowland's. Captain Reid was emphatic that
Rowland did not have a raincoat. And no raincoat was in his possession when
he was arrested.

The discrepancies in Macdonald's description were of course fully exposed by Burke during cross-examination. But they were by no means the most
serious flaws in his identification of Rowland. The main one concerned an
incident which had occurred in November at the committal hearings. On that
occasion Rowland had sat in the well of the Court alongside his solicitor.
Macdonald made his deposition and was then asked if he could see the man who
had bought the hammer in Court. There are two conflicting versions of what
happened next.

First Macdonald's:

> *He claimed that he looked carefully round the Court but was unable to
> spot the man to whom he had sold the hammer. Counsel for the Pros-
> ecution then asked him if he had picked a man out at an identity parade.
> Macdonald replied yes. He was then asked to have another look round
> the Court and this time he noticed a man sitting amongst some Barristers,
> Clerks, and Police Officers in the well of the Court. The man had his
> head bent. Macdonald asked him to stand up. It was Rowland and
> Macdonald identified him.*

Rowland's version was:

> *He had not had his head bent; Macdonald had looked him full in the face
> without recognising him, and had only picked him out when prosecuting
> Counsel ordered him, Rowland, to stand up and pointing to him had
> asked Macdonald if he was the man.*

Rowland's version was supported by his solicitor, Mr T H Hinchcliffe,
who was prepared to give evidence on his behalf. Burke decided that it was
unnecessary because yet again the prosecution accepted Rowland's evidence.
Nield did not ask Macdonald about it during re-examination and he pointedly
avoided cross-examining Rowland on it when he gave his evidence. As Prosecuting Counsel Nield was fully aware who was telling the truth and had no
quarrel with Rowland's version. Which means that a man who had picked the
defendant out of a line-up without hesitation on October 27th was unable to
recognise him again two weeks later. Why? The only logical answer is that he

was *helped* at the identity parade. And he needed help. His description of the customer bore little resemblance to Rowland. It did, interestingly enough, bear a resemblance to the man whom the Police interviewed on October 21st, the same day that Macdonald went to the Police. During his interview he was shown 'hundreds' of photographs by the Police and, again in Macdonald's own words, he put 'one or two' aside as having a 'similarity' to the man who had bought the hammer. Was one of these of the man the Police interviewed that day? If so, then not only did Macdonald's description not fit Rowland but he had already picked the wrong man out once.

And had Macdonald already failed to identify Rowland from *his* police photograph? Macdonald said no. Not unnaturally, so did the Police. But can we seriously believe that Rowland's was not one of the hundreds shown to Macdonald? There cannot have been too many convicted murderers walking the streets of Manchester.

Macdonald's failure to pick Rowland out at the Magistrate's Court effectively destroyed his identification. His inadequacy was demonstrated in other ways too. Burke asked him:

> *Q) Did his hair appear dark when you picked him out the identification parade?*
>
> *A) No. But I never forget a face.*

But a few moments earlier Macdonald had not been anywhere near as confident of his ability to recognise faces. Here Burke was questioning him about Rawlinson from whom he had originally bought the hammer on the morning of the 19th.

> *Q) Do you think you'd recognise him if you saw him again?*
>
> *A) I think so, I might do, I don't know.*

'I don't know' was the answer of this man who never forgot a face (except at committal hearings!!).

Burke continued to hammer away at this theme. When had Macdonald last sold a hammer prior to the one he claimed to have sold to the accused?

> *A) I sold one on the Friday [18th].*
>
> *Q) What sort of hammer was that?*
>
> *A) A Joiner's Hammer.*
>
> *Q) Is the man who bought the hammer personally known to you?*
>
> *A) No. A passing customer.*
>
> *Q) Could you describe him to the jury?*
>
> *A) He was an ordinary working man.*

Which was as far as Macdonald got. Pressed by Burke, he uneasily claimed that he could describe him to a certain extent but when invited to do so he hastily abandoned this position and decided that he had not taken any particular notice of the man.

So he could remember the type of hammer he had sold him but despite his boast that he 'never forgot a face' he could not describe him.

Perhaps just as ominous as the flaws in Edward Macdonald's testimony was its general tone and tenor. Even from the dry, hard prose of the trial transcript an impression emerges of a man who was completely bound up in his role as a prosecution witness. This is hardly to be wondered at. After Rowland's identity parade the Police had taken Macdonald out for a drink, made him feel like one of the boys, patted him on the back for getting it right. Consequently, Macdonald was unwilling to concede even the smallest point to the defence. For example:

> *Q) This man has not got a pale face has he?*
>
> *A) Well, he appears pale to me now.*

And a little later on:

> *Q) Did you say that he [the man who bought the hammer looked ill?*
>
> *A) No sir, I did not.*
>
> *Q) Do you remember giving evidence at the police court?*
>
> *A) Yes sir.*
>
> *Q) Do you remember saying to the learned stipendiary '...I said he had a pale face and may have said that he looked ill'?*
>
> *A) Not as I remember Sir.*

It is not surprising that as Macdonald stepped down from the witness box Rowland shouted at him: 'You're a liar!'

Next came Rita Leach. The defence did not challenge her identification of Olive Balchin. Precisely what was in Burke's mind we do not know. He seems to have wanted to leave the jury with a clear cut issue: was Rowland the man with Balchin that night or not? But he did rather half-heartedly contest Copley and Mercer's identifications of Balchin. Perhaps he was frightened of confusing the jury but if so then why raise the issue at all? The other side of the coin is that the jury was being asked to say that Copley and Mercer's identifications of Balchin were correct but that they were wrong about Rowland, a contradictory point which would certainly have been seized upon by the Prosecution. That a junior Barrister should be asked to make decisions like this with a man's life at stake is no advert for the Adversarial system.

Had David Ware confessed before the trial and not after it then Burke's strategy would have been clear; he would have attacked all three identifications of Balchin very vigorously. As it was he certainly should have at least cast some doubt on Leach's because by conceding that Olive Balchin was en-route to Deansgate at 9:15 he was adding credibility to Copley and Mercer's identifications.

Olive Balchin was murdered in Deansgate. But it is an important part of the case for Rowland's innocence that she did not travel to Deansgate by herself and that she was not the woman in the Queen's Cafe or the woman Mercer saw. So was Rita Leach's identification valid? Principally, she identified Balchin by her coat and her beret. The Prosecution set great store by these as if they were somehow unique to Olive Balchin. They were not. The coat was a cheap, mass produced line (my mother recalled owning one) and berets were the most common form of head wear for working class women in Britain in the forties (it was then usual for women to wear hats). Any number of women wearing similar hats and coats might have been out and about that night in working class Deansgate; — and probably were. Leach was unable to identify either item by its colour.

Apart from that Leach was shown a photograph of Balchin's features which she identified. She did not see the body. Even though Balchin's face had been washed the wounds were quite ghastly, whether too bad for convincing identification is a moot point, but Leach would certainly not have wanted to look at the photograph too long or too closely. And, crucially, the single photograph test is regarded as unreliable, just as a single person on an identity parade would be. Had an alibi witness for Rowland identified him from a single photograph then that would have been attacked by the Prosecution; — just as it was sixteen years later at the trial of James Hanratty.[*]

Leach was followed into the box by Elizabeth Copley. Her evidence about the trio who visited the cafe on October 19th has already been set out and we do not need to recapitulate it. Instead we can move on to what she said in cross-examination. Mrs Copley had by far the best view of the man the Crown said was Rowland. She was an honest witness who gave her evidence very fairly and with an open mind.

Burke opened by drawing attention to her uncertainty at the identity parade.

Q) Then when you'd picked him out... you said 'that looks like the man but I'm not sure' didn't you?

A) Yes, I think I did say that Sir.

In fact it would be more accurate to say that she was really picking Rowland out as a man whom she had seen in the Queen's Cafe before October 19th. He had been a customer in the cafe on two previous occasions as Mrs Copley confirmed.

Q) I understand you to say that you'd seen him twice before that?

A) Yes, Sir.

---

[*]   Hanged in 1962 for the A 6 murder.

But initially she had been unable to reconcile the man with Balchin as anyone she had seen before:

'I didn't know I'd seen him before until after [the identity parade] when I remembered when I first worked there.'

To summarise the position, although she had allegedly seen Rowland in favourable conditions for a period of some thirty minutes on the 19th she was not able to recall having seen him in the cafe before. Then, after very hesitantly picking him out at the identity parade, she only then realised that she had seen him in the cafe on two past occasions. This only makes sense if the man in the cafe was not Rowland but somebody she had never seen before.

Mrs Copley experienced no difficulty in recalling that she had seen the old lady once before and she did so without the benefit of an identity parade.

Q) You had seen that lady before?

A) Yes. At a time when I was on. When I was a waitress.

Mrs Copley had ceased regular employment at the cafe in mid-July and was only standing in for someone else in October. But it was during this earlier time, up to mid-July, that she remembered Rowland and the old lady coming in, not, it should be emphasised, together. Mrs Copley's memory serves to stress the point that if the man in the cafe had been Rowland then she would surely have recognised him there and then.

So this was a very definite point in Rowland's favour. Another one was the parcel which Balchin's companion carried.

Q) This was a thin parcel?

A) Yes Sir.

Q) And might have contained a hammer?

A) It might have done, yes.

Q) Not the sort of parcel which might have contained two shirts and some socks and an overall was it?

A) No, nothing like that.

'No nothing like that'. In other words it was not the parcel which Rowland was carrying when he left home that night, *on a journey which provides him with a complete alibi for the time he was supposed to have been at the Queen's Cafe.*

According to the Police theory of Rowland's movements he left home at 9:20, caught the bus to Stockport, and then boarded a bus to Manchester arriving in the Piccadilly area at 10:20. From there it was an approximate ten minute walk to Deansgate.

To support this thesis Detective Sergeant William Gallimore travelled by the same bus from New Mills to Stockport that Rowland had used. The bus reached Stockport at 9:59. Gallimore then boarded a bus to Manchester which departed at 10:03 and arrived in Piccadilly at 10:20.

Jack Baskeyfield, driver of the New Mills–Stockport bus on October 19th, stated that the bus was scheduled to arrive in Stockport at 10:09, but that he often arrived before the scheduled time, sometimes by as much as nine minutes. Laurence Hollingsworth, the driver of the Stockport–Manchester bus on the night in question, gave evidence that he had commenced his journey at 10:05 and reached Piccadilly at 10:25.

The time schedules were admittedly tight but they meant that Rowland could just about have been in the Queen's Cafe by around 10:30.

But Rowland had a very convincing alibi to prove that at 10:30 he was still in Stockport;— the Police themselves.

To recap on his story, he caught the wrong bus, wound up in Stockport instead of Manchester, and decided to have a few drinks before catching a late bus into Manchester.

The pub he went into was called the "Bottom Wellington". He had two or three glasses of beer and whilst he was standing at the bar the bar sink overflowed. Immediately after the last bell at 10:30 he went to the toilet. When he came out he was just in time to see two Policemen leaving the pub.

Called to give evidence for the defence, Police Sergeant Norman Jones stated that on Saturday, October 19th he and a Constable named Moores had paid a routine visit to the "Bottom Wellington" at 10:32. It was a duty which he carried out regularly, but not every Saturday night.

Here was impeccable support for Rowland's story. It was also supported by a man named Henry Somerville who unfortunately was not available to give evidence at the trial but later came forward to testify at Rowland's Appeal. Somerville had gone into the "Bottom Wellington" for a late drink at about 10:15. Whilst he was there he bought a packet of cigarettes from a man whom he identified as Rowland, and he also recalled the incident of the bar sink overflowing.

This meant that it was quite impossible for Rowland to have been in Deansgate between 10:30 and 11:00. The earliest he could have reached there was 11:15.

But was it possible that Mrs Copley had made a mistake about the time? It is of course a very easy thing for a person to misjudge.

The answer is a very decisive 'no'. Mrs Copley had a method of fixing the time accurately as she revealed during cross-examination.

> *Q) You looked at the clock didn't you when they left the premises at eleven o'clock?*
>
> *A) Yes, I always do.*
>
> *Q) That is why you've got eleven o'clock fixed in your mind?*
>
> *A) I generally look at the clock because sometimes we have customers*

coming in and sometimes they want to know if a person comes in what time they go out and I generally tell them.

Q) Did you look at the clock when they came in?

A) Not just when they came in. Previous to that I looked at it.

Q) These people you are speaking about who were in the cafe that night came in at 10:30?

A) Yes, sir.

Q) And left as near as anything on the stroke of eleven.

A) Yes.

And twice earlier in her testimony Copley had categorically stated the time as being between 10:30 and 11:00.

Rowland could not have been in two places at the same time. The evidence proves beyond doubt that he was in the "Bottom Wellington", Stockport, until after 10:30 which means that he cannot have been in the Queen's Cafe at that time. This factor must also be taken in conjunction with the other two major flaws in Copley's identification of Rowland; if he was the man then surely she would have remembered at the time that she had seen him before, and he ought to have been carrying a second parcel which contained some clean clothes. Here the Prosecution's own timetable works in Rowland's favour for even if he had had a place to deposit the parcel of clothes then he would not have had the time to do so in order to reach the cafe by 10:30.

Walter Rowland cannot have been the man whom Elizabeth Copley saw. And if she was wrong about Rowland then she could equally have been wrong about Balchin. She identified Balchin by her coat and her photograph. Exactly the same criticisms apply here as with Rita Leach's identification.

Clearly, much light could have been shed on the matter if the third member of the trio, the elderly woman, had come forward. She did not. Why, we shall never know. Perhaps she did not read the Newspapers (Copley testified that she herself rarely took notice of them); perhaps she did not want to get involved, a common enough trait; perhaps she failed to make the connection between herself and the person being spoken about. Whatever the reason, she stayed mute. But her very presence that night is a dagger thrust into the heart of the Crown's case. We are asked to believe (and apparently the jury did) that Rowland not only allowed her to accompany him with a woman he intended to kill, but that he still went ahead with it afterwards; and that Balchin allowed an old woman to tag along with herself and a client. Does this make sense because it is exactly what the Prosecution was arguing? What it really points to is not Rowland, nor Balchin, but three people having a bite of supper before going home.

The final identification witness was Norman Mercer, licensee of the "Dog and Partridge", Deansgate. Mercer's sighting has already been outlined but we need to add that the woman had her back to a wall and he glimpsed her full faced, whilst the man was facing her and he saw him in left profile. He described the man as 30-35 years old, about 5' 7", 'proportionate build', full, round face, clean shaven, wearing a blue suit, with dark hair which 'could have been well greased to give a darker appearance'. Asked whether he had any doubt that Rowland was the man Mercer replied, 'no doubt whatsoever'. We shall see whether such certainty was justified.

To begin with we need to look at the conditions under which Mercer saw the couple. A photograph was taken of Deansgate approaching Cumberland Street (the jury do not seem to have been shown it) and is reproduced here as plate 7. I invite the reader to study it and take particular notice of the one and only street lamp in the vicinity. It is situated a good way down Deansgate from the corner and the lamp post itself is sited on the edge of the pavement with the actual lamp jutting out over the kerb. This means that the sole street lamp was located some distance from the couple arguing on the corner. It was midnight and without the aid of a lamp the corner would have been pitch dark.

This meant that the couple were shrouded in darkness. Yet Mercer described them as though it was broad daylight. The man had a full, round, clean shaven face, dark, well greased hair and was wearing a blue suit. The woman had lightish brown hair. Can we believe this?

Significantly, there were two things which even in the darkness Mercer should have seen if the couple were Rowland and Balchin. The man ought to have been clutching two parcels. Mercer did not notice them. The woman should have been wearing the beret which was later found next to Balchin's body. It was a very large beret and when the Police photographed the Policewoman wearing it, the beret virtually covered her hair. Mercer could not have failed to see it, particularly as he claimed to have noted the colour of her hair. Yet he saw no hat.

In addition to this Mercer ought, if we can take him seriously, have noticed the colour of the woman's coat. It was not included in his evidence. Rowland's suit he said, was blue. This is partially right because Rowland was wearing a blue suit that night, a fact which he never sought to deny. But it was a blue *pin-striped* suit and if it was Rowland and Mercer can be relied on then he should have observed the stripes. He also claimed to have seen the couple clearly enough to discern that Balchin's hair was *lightish* and that Rowland was clean shaven. If so then the scar on the back of Rowland's neck should have been visible. But no, he did not see that either. Perhaps we should not expect people to notice such details in the darkness which brings us back to where we started: how was it possible for Mercer to have had such a clear vision of two people standing on a dark corner at midnight?

Like Edward Macdonald, Mercer's recollection seems to have improved with time. When he came to give his evidence at the trial he averred that the man's hair was 'well greased'. Burke reminded him that he had never said that before. Oh, but he had, according to Mercer and this led to a remarkable statement:

'I said it appeared dark to me, but it could have been well greased to give a darker appearance.'

This is what Mercer claims to have said to the Police on Sunday, October 20th. But why should somebody who had seen a man with dark hair then add quite gratuitously that it could have been well greased to make it look dark. If this is what Mercer actually meant — and a careful reading of the trial transcript supports this interpretation — then it was a quite extraordinary suggestion to volunteer. And if he did make it then why did the Police not write it down?

Norman Mercer's was a memory which gained in certainty as time passed. Olive Balchin for instance.

*Q) Did you say in the Police Court 'Her features were **similar** to those of the woman whom I saw the previous night'?*

A) That is right.

Q) Would you like to be sure it was the same woman?

A) I was as positive then as when I saw the woman.

That does not really sound like the case and it brings us back to Mercer's identification of Balchin. He identified her coat and was taken to see the body. The same argument about the coat applies equally to Mercer as it does to Leach and Copley. The woman he saw did not have a hat. As for the body, he was only able to say that Olive's terribly battered features were 'similar' and as with the single photograph test so the single person test is also fallible.

There is a very decided hint that the Police were not overly impressed with Norman Mercer as a witness. He made his statement on October 20th and after viewing the body went through the "rogues gallery" of Police photographs picking nobody out. We are assured that Rowland's photograph was not amongst them. As he was a convicted murderer this is very strange. But if Mercer did fail to pick out a photograph of Rowland it might explain why he was not taken to the identity parade on October 27th. There is no suggestion that he was unavailable. In addition his story was an odd one, a couple encountered in darkness yet described as in the light, and interestingly, although he had almost stopped as he passed them, he was quite unable to provide the gist of what the quarrel was about or even pick up some of the words spoken.

Mercer was re-interviewed on either the 28th or 29th according to his evidence. Why, we are not told, but only after that was a decision made to have him attend an identity parade. Here Burke attached much weight to the scar on Rowland's neck implying that Mercer had not looked at his profile full on but at a right angle thus suggesting that he had been told about the scar and was looking for it, a suggestion which he also put directly. Mercer of course denied it. Can we be sure? After sifting his evidence can we share his jaunty confidence that Rowland and Balchin were the couple the couple he saw? Or do we have our doubts *even before* examining the strongest point in Rowland's favour?

In order for Norman Mercer's identification to become even remotely credible Rowland's alibi needs to be completely overturned. He said he did not go into the centre of Manchester that night; that he never went anywhere near Deansgate. He got off the bus in Ardwick and stayed the night at Frank Beaumont's lodging house in Chorlton arriving at 11:20 and departing at about 10:00 the following morning. Frank Beaumont completely supported this. Rowland signed his visitor's book. The signature was of course tested by the Police and proved to be Rowland's. Contesting the alibi the Prosecution had to fall back on two feeble alternatives. One was that Rowland had left the house again after Beaumont had gone to bed, which Beaumont described as 'far fetched'. The other was that Rowland had stayed there on the previous night. But if he was offering this, a phoney alibi, then Beaumont could easily have disproved it. Instead the lodging house keeper was adamant that Rowland had stayed there on the night of October 19th/20th. At the end of the day the jury preferred Norman Mercer's identification to Frank Beaumont's alibi. Why, only they knew. We are making our own independent assessment of the same evidence, and at our leisure — a luxury not enjoyed by a jury — which means that we can weigh this and sift that with all the points and counterpoints at our disposal, another advantage not enjoyed by a jury. What do we prefer, Mercer's glimpse in the dark or Rowland's supported alibi?

Three witnesses had identified Rowland, not three out of thirty-three, but three out of three, a fact which no doubt impressed the jury. But eyewitness identification is notoriously unreliable even when it is unanimous. Adolph Beck has already been discussed in part one of this book. I will mention here just two other cases which are relevant. The first is the Broughty Ferry Case in 1912 in which an elderly woman was murdered. Five people saw a man loitering near her home on the day of the murder. His description fitted an itinerant Canadian named Charles Warner and all five witnesses identified him as the man they had seen. But Warner was able to prove that he had been in Belgium on the day of the crime. In 1932 a prominent local Councillor named Braddock was convicted of causing a riot. He was identified by no less than fourteen Police Officers. Braddock was subsequently able to prove that he had been attending a council meeting at the time and had been mistaken for a man named Boggin. The Appeal Court quashed his conviction.

Macdonald's customer had a pale, thin face; Copley's was fresh complexioned. Rowland had a full, round, florid face. Mercer's description more fitted Rowland but even if he had seen him in broad daylight then it was still a very general description and it conflicted with Macdonald and Copley's. Now of course witnesses descriptions of the same man often vary enormously but that does not make discrepancies valid; it only serves to prove how unreliable —

eyewitness identification is. All three witnesses described a man with dark hair; Rowland's was fair. Only Mrs Copley said right from the start that it was well greased; Macdonald and Mercer added this in later when the Police had to find an explanation for the radical difference in colour. Only Macdonald's identification was not contested by sound alibi evidence. The prosecution said, very unconvincingly, that these were phoney alibis based on things that had happened on other days. If that was true then why did Rowland not try to concoct an alibi for Saturday afternoon? He simply said that he had 'knocked about town and had a wash' before going to the Post Office. Even here he made no attempt to coincide his visit with the time Macdonald said he had sold the hammer. When Rowland's evidence does not challenge the Prosecution's then they accept he is telling the truth; when it does, and he produces witnesses to support him, then he is lying.

I will not reiterate my criticisms of Leach, Copley and Mercer's identifications of Olive Balchin; — repetition will add nothing. It does have to be fairly said that the Police were at a disadvantage; they could hardly arrange an identity parade of dead bodies or produce myriad photographs of women with their heads battered in. But that does not make suspect tests reliable.

Before leaving this part of the case we need to make one more analysis, one that has hitherto been overlooked in the Rowland case. The testimony of Macdonald, Leach, Copley and Mercer was not only important for identification purposes but also enabled the prosecution to fix their timetable of events leading up to Olive Balchin's murder. This ran as follows:—

> October 18th: Rowland arranges to meet Balchin in Deansgate the following evening.
>
> October 19th: 5:40 p.m. buys hammer
>
> 6:15 catches bus to New Mills
>
> 9:15 Rita Leach directs Balchin to Deansgate.
>
> 9:30 Rowland catches bus to Stockport
>
> 10:05 catches bus to Manchester arriving 10:25 and walks to Deansgate
>
> CIRCA 10:30 meets Balchin. Together with old lady they go to the Queen's Cafe for a meal.
>
> 12:00 Rowland and Balchin seen arguing by Norman Mercer.
>
> 12:00–12:30 Rowland murders Balchin.

But if we look in depth at this seemingly neat little package, flaws emerge which are equally as disturbing as the weaknesses in the identification evidence.

Why should Rowland require a hammer to murder Balchin? He said, in words which he came to regret, that if he had been certain that he had contracted syphilis through Balchin then he would have strangled her. His record shows that he was perfectly capable of killing in this manner.

Rita Leach claimed to have encountered Balchin at 9:15. If the Crown's theory was correct then she was on her way to Deansgate to meet Rowland.

But at 9:15 Rowland was still at his parents home in New Mills.

Either Balchin was very early or Rowland was very late.

If Rowland had an appointment to meet Balchin in Deansgate at 9:30 then why did he not leave New Mills earlier? He caught the bus at 9:30. Even if he had travelled directly to Manchester he could not have arrived there until well after 10:00. On the other hand if he had arranged to meet Balchin at 10:30 then why did she turn up an hour too early?

The evidence that Rowland was not the man in the Queen's Cafe is overwhelming; so powerful that it has convinced even some who ascribe to Rowland's guilt. After weighing it carefully Judge Henry Cecil Leon, Editor of "The Trial of Walter Rowland" decided that the Crown was mistaken on this point. But Judge Leon goes on:

> *'If Copley saw somebody else at her Cafe and not Rowland then this does not mean that Mercer and Macdonald were also wrong.'*[1]

Does it not? Well, what we are being asked to accept is that Rowland and Balchin finally made their meet at between 11:15 and 12:00, 11:15 being the earliest that Rowland could have been in Deansgate. This meant that Balchin, a working prostitute, was hanging about in an area which the prosecution said she was unfamiliar with for at least two hours waiting for him. And that Rowland, having missed their appointment by a minimum of an hour, still travelled all the way into Deansgate on the vague off chance that at approaching midnight she might still be waiting for him. Surely the only sense that this makes is nonsense.

That is the identification evidence and that is the Crown's timetable. Have the Scales of Justice tipped in favour of guilt or in favour of innocence?

(5)

Day two of the trial opened with Rowland's mother in the witness box. She was succeeded by Walter Harris and Captain Reid. We do not need to examine their evidence individually; it will be given in the context in which it is relevant.

The bulk of the evidence on this day was provided by four Police witnesses. Sergeant Trippier identified the Crown's exhibits, Sergeant Blakemore gave

---

1   "The Trial of Walter Rowland" p48

evidence of Rowland's arrest and Inspector Stainton occupied the witness box at some length. In the main his testimony was about Frank Beaumont's visitor's book and Rowland's interrogation. What he had to say about the latter was a duplication of the evidence given by Detective Constable Nimmo, the most junior member of the team, who put Rowland's statement into the record and carried the ball over his questioning. After the identification witnesses Nimmo was the most important witness against Rowland and it is to his testimony that we must now turn. The Police either stand or fall by it.

Douglas Nimmo was a young officer of great ability and promise, a promise which was realised because in the next twenty years he rose to become head of Manchester C.I.D. A photograph taken of him then shows a smiling, avuncular pipesmoker, the sort of comfortable man whose wife and children look forward to his coming through the door at night. Not the sort of man to be embroiled in controversy you might think. Think again.

In 1967 Nimmo became involved in the case of James Hanratty, a young burglar convicted and hanged for the murder of a research chemist in a lay-by off the A6. The case has many similarities with Rowland's. After Hanratty's conviction a number of respectable witnesses came forward to support his alibi of being in Rhyl, North Wales, at the time of the murder. Five years after Hanratty's execution misgivings about the verdict had reached alarming proportions. The Home Office instructed Nimmo to go to Rhyl and interview the witnesses. He did and presented a report of some 250,000 words (about three average novels) which concluded that the new evidence was not of great substance. But this did not coincide with statements made at the same time by the witnesses to Hanratty's family, so Nimmo was then ordered to repeat the exercise. His conclusions in the second report were no different from the first. Neither report has ever been released for us, the public, to judge and a solicitor present at the second batch of interviews concluded that the witness statements did effectively support Hanratty's alibi. Let us now look at Nimmo's testimony against Walter Rowland. It is for you to decide whether this too was controversial.

Nimmo told the court that on Saturday, October 26th he and Sergeant Blakemore had woken Rowland at the Services Transit Hostel at about 11:00 p.m. Rowland allegedly said:— 'You don't want me for murdering that fucking woman do you?', clearly an incriminating remark if he did make it. Then, whilst he was getting dressed, Rowland asked:— 'Is it about that raincoat?' Rowland did not dispute making this second remark.

Rowland was then taken to Bootle Street Police Station where, according to Nimmo, he was interrogated for the next two hours by himself, Detective Sergeant Gallimore, Detective Sergeant Blakemore, and Detective Inspector Stainton.

Stainton began the interview by telling Rowland that he was making inquiries into the murder of Olive Balchin. He explained the circumstances of her death and told Rowland that he fitted the description of a man seen with her on the night of the murder. He asked Rowland to account for his movements on the evening of the 19th.

Rowland then proceeded to launch himself into a series of wildly incriminating statements. First he said:

> *'I am admitting nothing because it is only a fool's game to do that. I can account for where I was. I was at home at New Mills when she was murdered. I did not come back to Manchester that night.'*

This did not satisfy Stainton who repeated his question:— where had Rowland stayed on the night of October 19th?

Rowland answered with a question of his own:— had Stainton seen his mother? When Stainton replied that he had not, Rowland told him:

> *'Well I did come back to Manchester. I got a lift in a car and then went into a pub for a drink. I didn't go into Deansgate. I stayed in the Ardwick district and had a bit of supper and stayed at Grafton House [the name of the lodging house at number 36, Hyde Road]. I didn't get in until after one o'clock.'*

Later in his statement Rowland first told the Police that Grafton House was number 36, Hyde Road and then altered the number to 67.

Stainton told Rowland that he would have to visit Grafton House and check this out whereupon Rowland immediately changed his story again saying:

> *'Well I didn't stay there [Grafton House] I stayed at 36, Hyde Road and I only stayed there one night.'*

The interrogation then switched abruptly to Rowland's relationship with the dead woman. Rowland admitted knowing Balchin — whom he knew as "Lil" — and asked Stainton whether he had a photograph of her. Stainton replied:

> *'I've only got a photo of her after she was dead. It isn't pleasant to look upon. I don't propose to show it to you. She's been badly knocked about and it would be difficult to identify her.'*

It was then that Rowland made the most damning of all the remarks attributed to him by the Police. He said:

> *'Things like that don't happen to decent women and whoever did it didn't do it without a cause. You can't see what you've done in the dark. Let me see it and I will tell you if it is the same woman.'*

It would be hard to imagine a more incriminating statement;— or a more callous one. The clear impression is of a man burning with hatred and longing to gloat over the evidence of his handiwork.

Stainton showed Rowland two photographs of Balchin taken at the Mortuary. This led to Rowland making another highly damaging statement:

> *'Yes, that her but I've got a fighting chance and I'm going to hang on to it.*

I've got an uncontrollable temper but that's not evidence is it? I'm sure I didn't do that. It's possible the hammer was got to do a job with. I was not going to do a job that night. I'm not admitting anything. I came back on the 9:30 bus and got off at Ardwick.'

Rowland went on to tell the Police that he had borrowed a raincoat from "Slim" on the 18th and returned it within the hour. The final part of the interrogation dealt with his very frank admissions about having syphilis, and his belief that he had caught it from Balchin. He said:

'I wanted to know where I got it. If I had been sure it was her I would have strangled her. I did think it was her. It's hard to say it was her now. Has she got V.D.? If she gave it to me, she deserves all she got.'

If Rowland was guilty and the Police's version of the interrogation was correct then he had made statements sufficiently incriminating to put his head half-way into the hangman's noose.

Following the interrogation Rowland made a formal written statement in which he volunteered two additional pieces of information:— that he had met Balchin at a cafe in Piccadilly on the 18th to try to ascertain whether she had syphilis, and that he had had a drink in the "Bottom Wellington" Stockport on the night of the 19th.

The overall impression that one gleans from the Police testimony is of an almost gentle interrogation during which Rowland, in a sort of murder's charge of the light brigade, consistently pointed the finger of guilt at himself.

However Rowland's version of the interrogation was markedly different. He agreed that he had made most, although not all, of the seemingly incriminating remarks attributed to him, but he disputed the Police's version of the context in which they had been made.

This is what he said.

Nimmo and Blakemore had woken him at the Services Transit Hostel. His reaction was to ask Nimmo:— 'What do you fucking want me again for?' Nimmo's response had been to tell him to get dressed. Whilst he was thus engaged Rowland asked:— 'Is it about that coat?'

If the Police's version was correct then Rowland's mind had jumped from the murder of a woman, for which he could be hung, to the pure mundanity of the petty larceny of a raincoat.

Does this make sense?

On the other hand Rowland's version was entirely consistent. First he asked what the Police wanted him for. He received no answer but the reason which sprang most readily to mind was the raincoat which he had borrowed from "Slim".

Whose version was the more logical?

Next Rowland accompanied Nimmo and Blakemore to Bootle Street Police Station and at 11:30 p.m. the interrogation commenced. The Police account gave the impression that Rowland had been treated decently. Not so according to Rowland. He had been subjected to a sustained barrage of questions lasting not two but four and a half hours and the atmosphere had been anything but friendly. He had twice asked if he could get some sleep — not surprising as he had been rooted out of bed at 11:00 p.m. — but Stainton had told him; 'You'll get no sleep until this is cleared up.'

According to the Police account Stainton first asked Rowland to account for his movements on the 19th to which Rowland answered:— 'I am admitting nothing because it is only a fool's game to do that', followed by the remarks that he had been in New Mills when Balchin was murdered and had not returned to Manchester that night.

Rowland however stated that he had no recollection of telling the Police that he had been in New Mills at the time of the murder. He agreed that he had said — 'I am admitting nothing... it is only a fool's game...' but claimed that this was not in answer to any question about his movements on the night of the murder. According to Rowland:

> *He [Stainton] had been questioning me in regard to why I had been living in Manchester under the conditions that I was — no settled address. I tried to explain that it was purely a private and domestic matter. The suggestion was made that I had been living on my wits. That was when I said I am admitting nothing. That is only a fool's game.'*

It is important to note that at this point Rowland had not been charged with murder. If he was innocent then he would also have been anxious to avoid being arrested for some lesser crime that he was guilty of. The Police knew that Rowland was a criminal. They had arrested him before, and as Henry Leon states:

> *The Police have little doubt that he kept himself mainly on the proceeds of crime.'*[1]

It was of course Rowland's past record which made him a suspect in the first place.

If Rowland did volunteer the information that he was in New Mills at the time of the murder then it was certainly an astonishing remark for him to have made. He must have been aware of how easily this could be disproved.

Rowland did admit saying that he had not returned to Manchester that night, but claimed that the Police had taken the remark out of context. He explained it in the following way:

> *I was implying [in] my term there as Manchester meant the centre of town. I was no nearer Manchester that night than Ardwick.'*

---

1   "The Trial of Walter Rowland" p16

Ardwick is an outer suburb of Manchester and Rowland's story was that he got off the bus from Stockport in Ardwick and wound up staying at Beaumont's Lodging House in neighbouring Chorlton. Beaumont was later to give evidence to this effect and there was no dispute as to the fact that Rowland had spent the following evening in an Ardwick Lodging House.

According to Nimmo, Stainton's next question was:— 'Do you care to tell me where you stayed on the 19th?' Rowland was alleged to have responded by asking Stainton whether he had seen his mother and when the Detective said no, he launched into the story of returning to Manchester that night after all via a lift in a car, and of staying at Grafton House arriving shortly after 1 a.m.

Let us study this carefully. Although Rowland has allegedly just told the Police that he was in New Mills, Stainton nevertheless repeats the question. Rowland's reaction is to ask whether they have interviewed his mother, but although the answer is no he very conveniently (for the Police) changes his story. Now his tale is of hitching a ride back to Manchester in a car and having a drink in a pub followed by a bit of supper. Although the Police have not been to see his mother he entirely discards his story of staying at home and ends up in an Ardwick lodging house where he arrives after 1 a.m., which very conveniently gives him plenty of time to have battered Olive Balchin to death in Deansgate.

Rowland seriously disputed this. Some of the answers he denied having made at all, and those which he had given were, he claimed, taken out of sequence by the Police.

This was his story.

Yes said Rowland, he had asked Stainton if the Police had seen his mother, but not in response to any question put to him. He had initiated the inquiry himself because he was concerned that the Police might have interviewed his mother and upset her.

He had 'no recollection' of telling the Police that he had returned to Manchester; he had 'definitely not' told them that he had gotten a lift in a car; and 'to the best of his knowledge' he had not said anything about having a drink in a pub. he had 'emphatically' told Stainton that he had not gone into Deansgate that night. It was 'quite true' that he had claimed to have stayed at Grafton House that night and at the time he 'believed it to be true'. That had been 'an honest mistake'. 'Very possibly', he had told the Police that he had gotten in after 1 a.m. but as he now knew he had stayed at Grafton House on the Sunday night and he had arrived there 'late at night'.

After he had told Stainton that he had stayed at Grafton House the Inspector had detailed two Detectives to go there and make inquiries. Upon their return a whispered conversation had ensued between Stainton and the two Detectives after which the Inspector said to him:

'Just as I thought. You never did stay there that night.'

To this Rowland replied that he was convinced that he had stayed at Grafton House.

Does Rowland's version make sense?

He was clearly very close to his mother. It would be natural for him to envisage her being upset if she learnt that he was suspected of murder. The Police said that Rowland had initially claimed that he was at home in New Mills on the night of the killing. Surely he would have asked the Police whether they had seen his mother before making this statement, not after it. If he really did make such a remark followed by the question about his mother then does it really make sense that on finding out that the Police had not been to see her he abruptly changed his story?

Rowland told the Police that he caught a bus to Stockport and had a few drinks at the "Bottom Wellington". But if we are to believe the Police version he also told them a completely contradictory story of getting a ride in a car from Stockport to Manchester, and then having a drink in a Manchester pub. If he did then it seems strange that the police did not invite him to enlarge upon it. Did they not want to know anything about the car or its driver? Were they not interested in finding out the name of the pub or the district in which it was located? Apparently not. Nor do they appear to have been curious as to why Rowland should give them two conflicting accounts of his movements.

A week later Detective Sergeant Gallimore travelled the bus route which Rowland indisputably said that he took. Gallimore discovered that by catching an earlier bus from Stockport to Manchester than the one which Rowland claimed to have travelled on he could reach the Queen's Cafe in Deansgate by 10:30. This formed the basis of the Prosecution's theory of Rowland's movements on the night of the murder. The car and the Manchester pub were quietly shelved except for the fact that they were useful in implying that Rowland had given conflicting accounts of his movements. Had there not been a bus available to deposit Rowland in Manchester in time to be at the Queen's Cafe by 10:30 then perhaps the car would have been substituted for the bus. After all, a weak link is better than none.

Rowland of course denied saying anything about a car or a drink in Manchester. He was able to give a lucid account of his movements that night: he did not need to invent a cock and bull story about them.

Which leaves us with a clear cut choice between Rowland's denial and the strange case of the story which the Police failed to investigate.

When Rowland went into the witness box and gave his evidence he claimed that he had made an honest mistake in telling the Police that he had stayed at Grafton House on the 19th. The question here is whether he would have told the Police an outright lie which could be disproved within the hour, and indeed was if his account of the nocturnal visit to the lodging house was correct, or whether he was indeed genuinely mistaken.

He first told the Police that Grafton House was number 36, Hyde Road. Later, in his statement, he altered the number to 67 which was incorrect because he had been right the first time.

The Police account makes no mention of any visit to Grafton House in the early hours of Sunday, October 27th. Think about this. Was it in the Police's interest to have Rowland still maintaining that he had stayed at Grafton House on the 19th even after they had established that he had not stayed there that night? The answer is obviously no. That would have made Rowland's story of having made a genuine error very convincing indeed. This in turn would have had the effect of adding weight to his subsequent recollection of spending the 19th at Frank Beaumont's lodging house.

When did the Police visit Grafton House? We do not know but Rowland's second mistake may give us a clue to the answer. Remember, he initially told the Police that Grafton House was at 36, Hyde Road; later he altered this to number 67. No reason was offered for this alteration but a logical explanation is that Rowland came to the conclusion that he had made a mistake about the number of the house after being told by the Police that he had not stayed at number 36 that night. If so then this pinpoints the Police's visit to Grafton House as taking place during the early hours of Sunday, October 27th exactly as Rowland contended.

In this context we should also examine Captain Reid's testimony. His evidence was that Rowland had told him that on Sunday, October 20th he had spent the night at a place called Sinclairs Hotel in Brunswick Street. This was the same street in which Frank Beaumont's lodging house was situated.

Captain Reid's testimony on this point clearly confused Rowland. Cross-examined about it he said: 'I don't see why the name Sinclairs could be in my mind at all.' On the face of it this is a rather tangled web. We know that Rowland stayed at Grafton House on the 20th and not at any address in Brunswick Street. Yet the following day he told Reid that he had stayed not at Grafton but at Sinclairs. Reid was unlikely to be mistaken about this; on the other hand Rowland had no reason to lie about where he had stayed on the Sunday night. The obvious conclusion is that Rowland was making a mistake; that he said Sinclairs because it was fixed in his mind at the time that it was on the night of Saturday, the 19th that he had stayed at Grafton. This was five days *before* he was questioned by the Police.

Captain Reid's evidence is therefore indirect corroboration of Rowland's claim to have been making an honest mistake.

But the matter does not end there; it goes further.

Rowland told Reid that he had spent Sunday night at Sinclairs. He was wrong. But if we accept that it was a genuine mistake then it logically follows that he was getting the two nights in the wrong order; that the correct sequence was first Sinclairs and then Graftons, where he indisputably stayed on Sunday.

Sinclairs was in Brunswick Street and Rowland had not stayed there on either night. But Beaumont's *was also* in Brunswick Street. Rowland was never able to remember the number of Beaumont's; the lodging house was identified by the description he gave of it. Nor did he recall Beaumont's name. Was he therefore confusing Beaumont's for Sinclairs in the same street? It is surely reasonable and logical, to think so. If that is the case then it means that he was indirectly telling Reid that he had spent Saturday night at Beaumont's. It is a complex little knot but when it unravels it does so in Rowland's favour.

We now come to the most sinister of the remarks which he made to the Police, his declaration that 'things like that don't happen to decent women and whoever did it didn't do it without cause. You can't see what you have done in the dark.' This, according to the Police, was volunteered by Rowland after Stainton had refused to show him a photograph of Balchin.

But Rowland claimed that Stainton showed him two photographs of Balchin taken at the mortuary and then told him; 'That is your handiwork, you know.'

Rowland naturally denied it and, referring to the photographs, said: 'Things like that do not happen to decent women. Whoever did it didn't do it without a cause.'

Stainton then remarked; 'It must prick his conscience,' to which Rowland replied: 'You can't see what you've done in the dark.'

If Rowland's version was correct then we are left with a perfectly innocuous conversation about a couple of photographs and here the evidence is decisively in Rowland's favour, as Burke revealed in a classic piece of cross-examination.

It was common ground that later on in the interview the Police had shown Rowland two photographs of Balchin's face and head, but Rowland claimed that the earlier photographs he was referring to were different altogether in that they showed her whole body. Two such photographs had indeed been taken but they were not introduced into evidence until after the trial had commenced. Burke took the matter up with Nimmo during cross examination.

> *Q. Did the Inspector put down on the desk photographs of this dead woman and say that is your handiwork, you know?*
>
> *A. No.*

At this point Burke produced the two photographs in question and went on:

> *Q. As they were not exhibited at the Police court the accused could not have seen them there, could he?*
>
> *A. No.*
>
> *Q. Did the Inspector...?*
>
> *A. They were not.*
>
> *Q. They were not?*

A. No.

Q. Can you think how it is that Rowland is able to instruct his Solicitor with a complete description of these photographs if he has never seen them?

A. No.

It was a most uncomfortable moment for Nimmo and he was not allowed to wriggle off the hook for Justice Sellars now intervened and under his stern questioning Nimmo's 'no' became a grudging 'He may very well have seen them.'

Burke now resumed his cross-examination and asked:

'Were photographs of this kind left lying about so that people could casually glance at them?'

'Well they were,' replied the hapless Police officer, a rather contradictory remark considering that he had earlier stated quite categorically that Stainton had told Rowland:

'I've only got a photo of her after she was dead. It isn't pleasant to look upon and I don't propose to show it to you.'

An unhappy minute or so in the witness box for Nimmo ended with him admitting that the photographs had been present on Stainton's desk.

This exchange supports Rowland's evidence and kicks the props out from under the Police's account. It also vanishes in a puff of smoke the impression of a gentle, leisurely interview which the Police sought to create at the trial.

The final conflict between Rowland and the Police concerned the two photographs of Balchin's head and face which Stainton showed Rowland. Upon seeing them Rowland allegedly said: 'Yes, that her but I've got a fighting chance and I'm going to hang on to it. I've got an uncontrollable temper but that's not evidence is it? I'm sure I didn't do that. It's possible the hammer was got to do a job with. I was not going to do a job that night. I am not admitting anything.'

Rowland denied making the remark about having a fighting chance. From the witness box he told the jury:

'I've no recollection of using those terms. Nothing about the fighting chance.'

Had he told the Police that he had an uncontrollable temper? No. According to Rowland the phrase was used but not by him. It was Stainton who had suggested that he had an uncontrollable temper and he, Rowland, had replied: 'That is not evidence.' Pointing to the photographs he had gone on to say: 'I am sure I wouldn't do that.'

Rowland agreed that he had made both the comment about the hammer and the remark that he had not intended to do a job that night. But concerning his alleged statement about admitting nothing he told the court that he had no recollection of saying this and added: 'I had nothing to admit. My conscience was perfectly clear.'

Whose version was right? Simple logic suggests Rowland's.

According to the Police Rowland, when confronted by the photographs, said: 'Yes that her but I've got a fighting chance and I'm going to hang on to it.' This would make sense if he were seeing the photographs for the first time but as we now know he had already seen two other photographs of Balchin's dead body. This fact makes nonsense of that statement. Nor would it have made any sense whatsoever for Rowland to have claimed 'I've got a fighting chance' only to have undermined it in his very next breath by stating that he had an uncontrollable temper. On the other hand the Police knew all about Rowland's past and were well aware that he was capable of savage rages. Who was the more likely to raise this particular issue, Rowland or the Police?

I have examined the controversy between Rowland and the Police step by step, point by point, because of its importance to the case. In addition to making a number of highly damaging admissions about knowing Balchin and believing that he might have contracted syphilis from her, Rowland was alleged to have made a series of highly incriminating remarks which tended to further point the finger of guilt at himself. These remarks he either denied or said that they did not come about in the way in which the Police claimed.

If we accept the Police version then there can be no doubt that the case against Rowland is strengthened. But there is a stark sense of unreality about it. It is rather like watching a three act play performed out of sequence. Act three follows act one and act two is performed last.

On the other hand we have Rowland's version. Unlike that of the Police it does not require a miracle of alchemy to turn the base alloy of improbability into the pure gold of likelihood. The account which Rowland gave was consistent and cogent. When he went into the witness box and gave his evidence he was subjected to a severe cross-examination about his version of the answers which he gave to the Police. He did not stumble or falter or contradict himself. If he was making his answers up then he had certainly learnt them off by heart. But if he was telling the truth then it must be conceded that his answers bore the stamp of an innocent man. His behaviour at the Police station does not suggest that he had anything to fear. At no point did he request the aid of a solicitor and he unhesitatingly volunteered information that was damaging to him. Does a guilty man admit knowing the victim; admit having probable cause for harbouring a grudge against her; admit that he would have satisfied that grudge if suspicion could be turned into certainty? Rowland was not a stupid man; nor was he naive. There is no suggestion of his being troubled by a bad conscience. All these factors are hallmarks of innocence, not guilt. A guilty man twists this way and turns that way in his bid to avoid retribution. He does not stand in the shadow of the gallows and assist in knotting the rope around his neck. Yet

Rowland did precisely this and the only logical explanation is that he genuinely believed that he had nothing to worry about.

But the Police clearly had a different perspective on the matter. It seems that Rowland's frankness coupled with his mistake about the lodging house hardened suspicion into certainty. At that point their minds closed like a steel trap.

This, and not the deliberate frame up, is the fault to be looked for in the British Police. It is a criticism made from all sides of the spectrum. From the heart of the British establishment Lord Hunter, an eminent Scottish Jurist, writes:

> *'There is sometimes a tendency, particularly with hindsight, to ascribe to dishonesty events which were in fact the results of inefficiency, lack of determination and a failure to keep an open mind.'*[1]

Very decidedly not from the establishment is Channel Four's "Trial and Error" team on whose behalf David Jessel states:

> *'Once the Police have formed a suspicion, they find it hard to let go of it—a healthy enough attitude, generally speaking, in the Police, but also a path along which many dangers lie. Time after time, our experience tells us and bears us out, a miscarriage of justice has its roots in the tenacity with which the Police seize upon on initial suspicion—and will not let it go. It happens, usually, when they have a suspect who they are certain, in their own minds, is guilty; from that point on, the investigation ceases to be a neutral inquiry, but is dedicated to collecting proof of the individual's guilt. Evidence which points to innocence is, often in all good faith, discarded as irrelevant. A tunnel vision, a blinkered focus on the fixed idea of a particular conviction, sets in.'*[2]

If we look at the Police performance in the Rowland case from these standpoints, and we remember that the interview took place in the small hours of the morning, a time when people are not at their best, then what it betokens is not dishonesty but narrow-mindedness.

The final part of the Prosecution's case was unfurled by Dr James Firth, Director of the Home Office Laboratory at Preston. In his opening speech to the jury Nield had confidently predicted that he would produce scientific evidence linking Rowland 'with that place at that time'. We shall now see just how far this expectation was realised.

Dr Firth told the court that he had made a minute examination of both Rowland's and Balchin's clothes and personal effects. He had also examined the murder weapon and the paper in which it had been wrapped. The results were as follows.

---

1   "The Hunter Report into the Patrick Meehan Case. Volume One" p305
2   "Trial and Error" p33

In the turn ups of Rowland's trousers were found a quantity of debris common to the bomb site on which Balchin had been murdered.

Strands of human hair which might have come from Balchin's head had been discovered on one of the lapels of Rowland's jacket.

On the inside heel of Rowland's left shoe there was a tiny human blood stain.

The wrapping paper around the parcel in which Rowland had been carrying his clean clothes was faintly smeared with blood.

Balchin's coat and hat were both drenched in blood.

The hammer was extensively blood stained but its wrapping paper had not been stained at all and had obviously been divested before the attack commenced.

This analysis is remarkable not for what it reveals but for what it doesn't.

Olive Balchin had been struck repeatedly with a hammer, and with such horrifying force that her brain was left protruding from her head. Earlier Dr Jenkins, the Pathologist, had stated that blood would have both spurted and flowed from the murdered woman's wounds. Indeed, blood had spurted onto a concrete block near to the body. Yet with the exception of some almost imperceptible smears of blood on one of Rowland's shoes and the parcel he was carrying there was not a single speck of blood to be found on his person: in particular, not even the most microscopic quantity of blood was present on his clothes.

Let us examine the very minor forensic items which were found.

The strands of hair: Dr Firth described these as being 'consistent' with Balchin's hair, but he could not quote: 'put it any higher than that [there was] no definite identity.'

The hairs might have been Balchin's; Rowland admitted intercourse with her on two previous occasions. Alternatively they might have come from some other woman. They have no relevance to the issue.

The debris in the turn ups: Dr Firth stated that it would be reasonable to find such debris on any bomb site. Once again, the point has no relevance. Any man picking his way across a bomb site could have picked up rubble in his turn ups; moreover Rowland had previously had intercourse with Balchin on another bomb site.

The blood stain on the shoe: described by Firth as being 'insufficient to group it'. Rowland offered two possible explanations for it. A Police Officer had cut him whilst shaving him (the Police confirmed this) and a dab of blood could easily have fallen onto his shoe. On the other hand he might have trod in some bloody spittle. Whatever the reason, such a tiny particle of blood was too insignificant to have a bearing on the case.

The blood smears on the paper: according to Dr Firth these were 'too faint' to be identified. The prosecution made no issue of them. They were wise not to. It would have been difficult for them to explain how Rowland could have gotten blood on his parcel but not his clothes. The likeliest explanation of these blood smears is that blood was transferred to the paper after Rowland had nicked himself whilst shaving. Once again, the matter is irrelevant.

Balchin's hat and coat have no bearing on the matter, but the hammer and its wrapping paper do. What fingerprints were found on them?

The answer is we do not know. Astonishingly, no evidence was elicited on this point.

There should have been three sets of fingerprints on the hammer, the killer's, Edward Macdonald's and the man Rawlinson from whom Macdonald purchased the hammer. On the wrapping paper there ought to have been the fingerprints of the killer and Macdonald.

Sydney Silverman M.P.[1] suggests that the fingerprints may have been too blurred to afford identification. Very possibly. The hammer was extensively blood stained and the stains may well have extinguished the prints. The paper could well have been of the type which does not yield clear prints. But had there been identifiable fingerprints which were not Rowland's, Macdonald's or Rawlinson's then they would have destroyed the Prosecution's case. That however is mere speculation. The fingerprint evidence was entirely non-existent.

The main bulk of the defence's cross-examination of Dr Firth was directed at the complete absence of blood on Rowland's clothes. It was common ground between the defence and the Crown that Rowland owned only one suit and that it had not been cleaned up to the day of his arrest. Dr Jenkins had told the court that it was improbable that blood would not have spurted onto the killer's clothing; he would certainly have expected it to.

All of this was neatly in the bag for the defence. The forensic evidence most emphatically did not link Rowland with that place at that time and when taken in conjunction with Dr Jenkins' evidence it pointed directly to his innocence. All of this Burke had established. He did not need to go further. Unhappily, he did, and the effect was to pull the wool over evidence which was decisively in his client's favour. The cross-examination deteriorated into a very long wrangle with Firth over the lack of blood on Rowland's clothes. Firth stated that Balchin might have lingered on for some appreciable time after the attack, this accounting for the extensive bleeding. This was fine as far as it went, but it

1   "Hanged and Innocent"

did not go far enough because Firth tried to ignore the fact that blood had spurted as well as flowed. That was Dr Jenkins' evidence and also the mute testimony of the concrete block. This being the case it was extremely unlikely that blood had not spurted onto the killer and, as we have seen, there was no blood on Rowland's clothes. But, said Firth:

'That does not mean anything. The absence of it is not elimination.'

It is difficult to avoid the conclusion that Firth, allegedly an impartial forensic expert, was trying to shore up the Prosecution's case, an impression borne out by his subsequent answers.

Q. And would cause spurting blood. Did you hear him [Jenkins] say that?

A. In my opinion it does not follow that the assailant ever felt spurting blood.

Which was not the answer to the question he had been asked.

Q. I am putting it to you that if you would regard the presence of blood on this man's clothes as of importance then surely the absence of blood is equally as important?

A. I agree it is of some importance but what I say is that the absence of blood is not necessarily elimination.

It will be noted that once again Firth chose to supplement his answer in aid of the prosecution.

Doggedly, Burke carried on.

Q. You say it is of some importance now. Did you not say earlier that it means nothing?

A. I may casually have used the word to stress that it did not provide elimination.

Q. However, we have got this far, that it is of some importance?

Even now Firth was reluctant to give a straight answer to a simple question. Although he had just admitted that it was of some importance he avoided answering Burke's question directly, replying:

'There is no blood on his clothing.'

Dr Firth, it seems, took his role as a Prosecution witness rather literally. Answers to the defence were augmented in favour of the Crown; points in the defence's favour were grudgingly conceded. I raise the issue because this was not to be Firth's only involvement in the case of Walter Rowland.

During his testimony he referred to a similar murder in Blackpool in which the culprit's clothes had escaped blood staining. This being the case we are entitled to mention another similar murder, that of Leon Beron who was bludgeoned to death in London in 1911. The Pathologist, Dr Frederick Freyberger, concluded that the murder weapon would have dripped blood: 'it might in that way drop upon the hand or the arm of the person who was using the instrument and it might also drop upon his collar.'[1] The hammer used to kill Olive Balchin was covered in blood. Blood would have run down it and could be expected to drop onto the killer's sleeve. There was no blood on Walter Rowland's sleeves, nor on any of his clothing even though it had spurted out of the wounds. Absence of it might not provide complete elimination but it did add up to very reasonable doubt. It most definitely did *not* support the case against Rowland.

This ended the Prosecution's evidence. The Police's account was riddled with improbability; Rowland's irresistibly coherent: the lack of forensic evidence pointed overall to innocence. Once again we have to ask whether the scales are tipped in favour of guilt or innocence?

(6)

On the afternoon of the second day of the trial Rowland went into the witness box and commenced his evidence. That, and the rest of the defence case, would last until the end of day three.

We have already examined in detail Rowland's answer to the Charge and it is therefore unnecessary to repeat his evidence. We have no appraisal of what effect his testimony had in Court beyond the bare fact that the jury found him guilty. From the transcript he appears to be giving his evidence well but of course that can be misleading. Nield's cross-examination was at times harsh but never unfair; the unfairness is in the system, not the man. Right at the end Justice Sellars, who up to then had refereed the proceedings impeccably, saw fit to intervene. Had Rowland made any attempt to contact the man "Slim" from whom he had borrowed the raincoat? The answer of course was no. The question really ought to have been addressed to the Prosecution. Where indeed was "Slim"? His raincoat had dragged Rowland into the case. After that he disappeared from it. At no time did the Prosecution challenge Rowland's account of returning it on the 18th. The point has no great significance except that it perhaps shows the way in which Sellars' mind was moving. Certainly, his performance with the next witness indicates that the defence was not making much of an impression on him.

We have already noted that the Police corroborated the Stockport part of Rowland's alibi. Just after closing time he had gone to the toilet. When he emerged he saw two Police Officers leave the bar. The "Wellington" was built

1   "The Trial of Steinie Morrison" p15

on two levels and had an upper bar and a lower bar. The two Policemen had exited from the lower bar.

Called to give evidence Sergeant Norman Jones said that at 10:32 on the night of October 19th he and a Police Constable named Moores had visited the "Wellington". They first went into the "Top Wellington" and then descended the short flight of stairs into the "Bottom Wellington". They walked through the bar and exited by the door which led out into Mersey Square. Jones told the Court:

'Incidental to my duty I visited Licensed houses in the Town. It is not a systematic part of my duty; it is a duty I carry out at my own discretion.' Cross-examined, he said: 'They can be visited any night, but one can rely that at weekends they are visited.' His visiting the "Wellington" was subject to his tour of duty but: 'Other Officers would probably have done so.'

So although the Police did not carry out a definite routine of visiting the pubs it was nevertheless a regular duty and Rowland might have taken a desperate gamble on the Police having called in at the "Wellington" that night. But this is extremely unlikely, and other factors really put the matter beyond doubt. Rowland could not have been certain that two Officers would have visited the pub; he could not have known that they would enter the "Bottom Wellington" from the "Top Wellington"; or that they would exit from the "Bottom Wellington"; he could not have been able to gauge the time so accurately.

This was a very convincing piece of evidence. Unfortunately, its effect was marred by the inexplicable failure of Justice Sellars to comprehend even its meaning, much less its importance. As Sergeant Jones' evidence unfolded the Judge interrupted, asking:

'Mr Nield, do you take any point as to the admissibility of this evidence?'

Nield answered:

'It seemed to me doubtful, but I did not feel that I ought to object to it.'

He was showing considerable prescience. Had Jones' evidence been vetoed then the Appeal Court may well have been forced to quash Rowland's conviction. Nield was certainly aware of this danger and avoided it very skilfully. His answer was a masterpiece of clever phraseology. On one hand he negated a crucial defence point whilst on the other he scored points for fair play.

Sellars continued to pepper Jones' evidence with interruptions, chiming in next with a query as to the relevance of the layout of the "Wellington". Eventually he allowed the witness to continue, but only after he had made it crystal clear that he regarded the issue as being of no importance whatsoever. Worse followed. Burke inadvertently forgot to ask Jones about the time of his visit and needed Sellars permission to belatedly put the question. Like the layout, the time was of crucial importance, but clearly his Lordship did not think so as his reply makes abundantly clear:

'I observed you did not ask him. If I had thought it was relevant I would have assisted him; since I did not, I did not. You can ask him.'

All of this took place in front of the jury and can only have persuaded them that the matter was of no consequence. As Judge Leon admits, 'I do not think that the Judge fully appreciated the effect of the evidence.'[1] The plain fact is that there can be no reasonable doubt that Rowland was in Stockport until 10:45 and that the very earliest he could have reached Deansgate was 11:15.

We now come to the second and most crucial part of Rowland's alibi — Beaumont's lodging house. Rowland said that he had no idea of the number of the house but that it had a small, white enamelled plate screwed to the door which said 'No Canvassers'. He recognised the proprietor having stayed there in August (with a friend), but he did not know his name.

All this was confirmed by Frank Beaumont. So too were the other material parts of Rowland's story: the time he had arrived and his going out again (although Beaumont thought that it was for fish and chips), and Rowlands leaving the following morning and signing his visitor's book which was produced in court. Beaumont had filled in the arrival and departure dates. The latter read '19/10/46' but as Beaumont explained, the departure date was an error: 'I didn't know it was disputed.' Rowland had not had a mackintosh with him.

Here then was clear cut testimony, supported by documentary evidence, that Rowland had spent the night in Chorlton. So what went wrong?

The adversarial system is not a quest for truth. When the protagonists sit down to plan their strategy they do so with winning in mind. It can be likened in part to a bullfight; in other parts to a tennis match with the net as the truth and the object to get the ball over the net. When Barristers discuss tactics they say, 'Well on our side of the net he is guilty, so how do we combat this, how do we knock this down?' And so on. That is not to imply dishonesty; it is the view seen from the particular side of the case on which Counsel is appearing. Rowland's alibi provides a classic example of this. Nield had laid the foundations during his cross-examination of Rowland, inferring that he had not told the Police about Beaumont's lodging house because it would not stand up to scrutiny.

Q. During the Police investigation inquiry before the Magistrate, right up to the time you see your solicitor, have you ever before said that you were at 81, Brunswick Street?

And, following Rowland's answer:

Q. Isn't that better than lying about it?

---

1   "The Trial of Walter Rowland" p47

Note the word "lying". It was not justified by the answer which Rowland gave but it was used anyway, implanted into the minds of the jury. And again:

Q. Did you stay there on the 14th August?

A. I did.

Q. They why did you say you couldn't identify the place sufficiently to satisfy the Police?

Nield was not in any way being deliberately unfair here. He was simply carrying out his role in the adversarial system. A subjective believer in Rowland's guilt, he was preparing the ground for the next subjective step; dismantling, if possible, the Beaumont alibi. His attack was two pronged.

The first contention was that Rowland had slipped out of the house again after Beaumont had gone to bed, returning later without awakening anybody. Beaumont described this idea as 'far fetched' and went on to explain:

'He could have done that but he wouldn't be aware of the fact... he would not have been aware that it was possible... he would not know the arrangements in my house, he had only been there one night. You could walk through the back door or... you could go out through the window but it would not be a very nice job.'

And it was also a blatant absurdity.

Rowland retired at 11:40. We are asked to believe that he then left the house, on the very unlikely possibility that Balchin was still hanging around waiting for him and managed to get to Deansgate by midnight. Afterwards having successfully constructed an alibi for the night, he did not mention it to the Police when they interviewed him! That is perfectly ridiculous. Moreover, the Prosecution was contradicting its own argument. Rowland, they said, had not mentioned the alibi because it would not stand up; instead he had told the Police a provable lie about Grafton House. They cannot have it both ways. Either Rowland was a cunning murderer who had established a highly credible alibi or he was an innocent man making a genuine mistake. Instead, the win at all costs and bugger the truth system argued, with total illogicality, both contradictory points against him.

But, if you still do not wish to believe in Rowland's innocence then there does remain a get-out Clause, the Prosecution's second hypothesis which was that Rowland had not stayed at the lodging house on the night of October 19th/20th, but on a previous October night.

There was no dispute that the signature in the visitor's book was Rowland's but the dates were problematic. Here is what the prosecution told the jury about them:

'It appears to record that Rowland arrived on the 9th October and departed on the 19th. The prosecution do not, however suggest that he

stayed there for ten days and that he arrived on the 9th... you will probably think, when you look at this book closely, that it is a singularly inaccurate record, and one from which you could not draw any satisfactory conclusions as to dates. The next two dates after the entry showing the arrival on the 9th or 19th, whatever it is supposed to be, are two entries, the dates of which are smudged. They are smudges so as not to be properly legible and, if you look back through the book, they are probably the only two seriously smudged entries in the whole book, and are a singular and remarkable coincidence, if it is one, and they appear to record the date of arrival of the next two visitors... as being either the 15th and 16th, or the 25th and 26th. If, in fact, they record arrivals on the 15th and 16th, it would mean that the entry relating to Rowland's arrival would be unlikely to be the 19th because it would then be out of date... look at the date of the entry showing the arrival of somebody, whose name is illegible, on the 16th or 26th. If you turn over the page and look at the back of it, you will see that the "2" of the "26th" has come through onto the back, whereas the "6" has not, suggesting that the "2" was possibly written in after or inked in more heavily later... If, as the defence suggest these figures here are "19" and not "9", if the book does in fact show that Rowland arrived on the 19th and left again on the 19th, because there is no doubt as to the leaving date — the '19' is written quite clearly — it means that, if that is accurate, he arrived sometime after midnight on the 18th... the Friday... and left again the same day, perhaps after his breakfast on the Saturday morning. That would fit in with 19th arrival and 19th departure. If that is not so, then the book is inaccurate somewhere, and you may think that the inaccuracy is this... he stayed there on the Friday night, the 18th, and, when the book showed he was leaving on the 19th, that is quite accurate, and the date of his arrival has been wrongly entered and should read the 18th.'

Thus was the trial reduced to a melancholy exercise in book-keeping whilst a man's life hung in the balance, its slender thread of continuity depending on which clerical error the jury accepted as valid.

But here at least, the Prosecution's suggestion did not involve contradicting themselves. What they were saying is that Rowland had stayed at the lodging house just prior to the night of the murder, had lied about Graftons and had subsequently taken refuge in another lie about staying at Beaumont's. Well then, let us examine the issue and see where the evidence takes us.

According to the visitor's book Rowland had arrived on October 9th and left on the 19th. Had this stood alone then it would have been a major point *against* his innocence. But it did not stand alone. Rowland had definitely not arrived on the 9th and stayed ten days as Mr Wingate-Saul was forced to concede:

'The prosecution do not, however, suggest that he stayed there, for ten days, and that he arrived on the 9th.'

Wingate-Saul then went on to refer to the two entries after Rowland's. The arrival dates appeared to have been altered. I find no quarrel with this but, inferred the Prosecution, they had been smudged to make them illegible. Perhaps Mr Wingate-Saul was doing some smudging of his own here. We do not know precisely what his comments meant, but he appears to be suggesting that the visitor's book had been deliberately tampered with. If that is the case then the implication is that it was either Rowland or Beaumont in Rowland's favour, presumably to make it appear more likely that Rowland had arrived on the 19th. But if either of them was concocting, or helping to concoct, a phoney alibi then a '1' would have been put before the '9' for the arrival date and the departure date would have been altered to '20', which is in fact quite easy to do, especially with the help of a bit of smudging. All that it really amounts to is that Beaumont realised that his records were inaccurate and changed the '15' and '16' to the correct '25' and '26'. Record keeping does not seem to have been his forte; a guest who had left on the 17th was wrongly shown to have departed on the 19th. Nor was he the only culprit; Captain Reid's Salvation Army Hostel had issued Rowland with a bed ticket for the 19th instead of the 21st: they had omitted to change the date stamp.

We are therefore left with the Prosecution's twin alternatives of Rowland arriving either on the 18th or 19th and leaving on the 19th. I think we can dispense with the 18th. Even by the standards of Frank Beaumont's patchwork book-keeping he was unlikely to have put down the 9th for the 18th. The arguments are the same against both anyway. It really boils down to a clear cut choice — no smudging required — between Rowland arriving after midnight on the 19th and departing later that morning after breakfast, or his arriving late at night on the 19th and leaving on the morning of the 20th, in which case he is innocent.

The Crown's hypothesis is of course a credible one. For instance, Rowland appears to have arrived at Grafton House after midnight of the following day. But where then did Rowland himself say that he stayed on the night of the 18th/19th? Here is what he told the Police:

'On Friday night, 18th October, I went to Littlewoods Cafe in Piccadilly and I saw Olive Balchin there... I left there at about quarter or half past nine... and I left her... and went down towards London Road Station for a drink in "The Feathers". Later I went to the NAAFI and stayed there.'

The Police produced no evidence to gainsay this. Nor was it directly challenged by Nield during cross-examination. But we do know that Rowland was staying at the NAAFI during the week ending the 19th because it was there that he borrowed the raincoat from "Slim".

Rowland said that he arrived at Beaumont's at about 11:20 p.m. on the 19th and went to bed at 11:40. In this he was entirely supported by Beaumont. If we accept that he was in Stockport until 10:45 then that is wholly consistent with his arrival in Brunswick Street at 11:20. Rowland's timetable that night is cogent and reliable; the Crown's, as we have seen, is shot through with illogicalities.

The Crown claimed that the Beaumont alibi was manufactured but if we return to Captain Reid's evidence then indirectly Rowland appears to have told him on the 21st that he had stayed in lodgings in Brunswick Street that weekend. Rowland himself had no recollection of mentioning Sinclairs Hotel to Reid. This is intriguing. If Rowland was lying then surely it would have been in his interest to have said, 'yes, I did say that and I now know that I was confusing the nights and mistaking the name of the lodgings.' Think about it. Is it or is it not oblique support of Rowland's alibi?

Last, but not least, we have Frank Beaumont's testimony about which night Rowland stayed. Asked whether he had any interest in Rowland, he replied: 'on the contrary'. Initially, he had some difficulty in recognising him in court and at one point he referred to him not as 'Rowland' but 'Brotherton'. But he gave unswerving support to Rowland's alibi. He said: 'Walter Rowland definitely did arrive on the Saturday [night]', and he was puzzled when Rowland showed him the card from the labour exchange *because the following day was a Sunday* and then it occurred to him that Rowland was going into work that day *because Sunday meant double time.*

To summarise the position, in order to accept the Crown's thesis that Rowland stayed at Beaumont's the previous night you have to be convinced on each of the following points:

That Rowland did not stay at the NAAFI on the 18th/19th although no evidence was produced to contradict it.

That the Crown's timetable is preferable to Rowland's alibi timetable.

That the point about Sinclairs has no substance.

That an ineptly maintained record book, in which the arrival date is certainly wrong, can only be explained in the Crown's favour and not equally in Rowland's.

That Rowland was definitely not at Beaumont's that night, even though the Crown did not suggest where else he might have stayed after killing Balchin.

That Beaumont's unshaken testimony is wholly wrong.

Finally, that Rowland's alibi was a series of desperate gambles which amazingly came right for him when he was supported first by the Police and then by Frank Beaumont.

In order to accept Rowland's guilt you have to accept that the Prosecution's theory, supported only by a date in an erroneous visitor's book, overrides the defence on each and every one of the above seven points. If you have a doubt on a single one of them then that is reasonable doubt.

Overall, are the scales tipped in favour of the Prosecution, are they neutral, which again means reasonable doubt, or do they lean towards outright innocence?

(7)

The final witness was a man named Charles Bolton. All published sources on the case omit his evidence entirely as nothing he said could be relied upon.[*] But he was called by the Defence and so the last thing the jury heard on day three of the trial was an unsatisfactory witness for Rowland.

Sunday, December 15th, was a day of rest. When the court re-convened on Monday Burke and Wingate-Saul made the closing arguments, Justice Sellars summed up and, at 4:40 p.m., the jury retired. They were back at 6:35. Guilty!

Rowland gasped: 'May God forgive you; you have convicted an innocent man.'

Asked whether he had anything to say 'why sentence of death should not be passed according to law?' Rowland seized the opportunity with an eloquence rarely surpassed in the annals of British justice:

> *'My Lord, I have never been a religious man, but as I have sat in this court these last few hours the teachings of my boyhood have come back to me, and I say in all sincerity and before you and this court that when I stand in the Court of Courts before the Judge of Judges I shall be acquitted of this crime. Somewhere there is a person who knows that I stand here an innocent man. The killing of this woman was a terrible crime, but there is a worse crime been [sic] committed now, my Lord, because someone with the knowledge of this crime is seeing me sentenced today for a crime which I did not commit. I have a firm belief that one day it will be proved in God's own time that I am totally innocent of this charge, and the day will come when this case will be quoted in the courts of this country to show what can happen to a man in a case of mistaken identity. I am going to face what lies before me with the fortitude and calm that only a clear conscience can give.'*

Judge Leon asks:

'It would be interesting to know if any member of the jury changed his view about Rowland's guilt when he heard this.'[1]

Interesting indeed!

---

1   "The Trial of Walter Rowland" p13

*   See Appendix 1.

(8)

Christmas, 1946 was the first real peacetime Christmas since 1938. It was the first Yuletide out of uniform for most of Britain's five million servicemen and women, Rowland included. None of them could have spent such a miserable Christmas as he did, back in the same death cell he had occupied twelve years earlier. 'Why?', he was later to write in a letter full of whinging self pity, 'did I not meet my end in Italy? Why should I come through that to have to die for some other's crime?' In fact, according to one acquaintance who soldiered with him in Italy, he had spent the greater part of his service there organising black market rackets. But that, neither morally or legally, can ever be a justification for executing the wrong man. Nor can his earlier murder, sickening though it was.

1946 slipped into 1947. Rowland's ex-comrades raised their glasses to the New Year and looked forward to their first full year in civilian collar. But the condemned man in Strangeways Prison raised no glass and rejoiced not at all. His entire world now revolved around one thing;— his appeal, his one slender lifeline to a future.

Slender it was too. Rowland's appeal should have been an ideal mechanism for Section 4 of the Criminal Appeal Act which provides for a direct challenge to the verdict of a jury when it is against the weight of evidence. But that clause exists mainly in theory. Only once in a murder case has it proved successful; that of William Wallace which I mentioned in part one of this Book. And there was a particular circumstance connected with the Wallace case: a special meeting of union delegates summoned to decide whether his union should pay his legal costs had, after hearing both the prosecution and defence cases, voted unanimously in favour of his innocence.[*] In the Rowland case the jury had overridden doubt upon doubt upon doubt in order to pronounce him guilty. There can be little dispute that in America that would have led to a retrial. But in Britain no retrial facility then existed in criminal cases. (It does now but once again the theory has proved stronger than the practice.) What it means is that a jury can totally ignore reasonable doubt and the Appeal Court will rubber stamp its findings. On the other hand a jury can get it completely right and have its verdict set aside on a technicality. Cock-eyed is the term which comes most readily to mind.

What therefore should have been Burke's strongest ground of appeal was, because of the limitations of the Appeal Court, a non-starter. *There was no question of an appeal based on a point of law.* He might have raised, as a point of appeal, Justice Sellars negation of the Stockport alibi but the appeal Judges response would undoubtedly have been that as the jury had heard the evidence

---

*   See "The Killing of Julia Wallace" by Jonathan Goodman.

then it was a matter for them. So he was forced to rely on what is termed as 'new evidence', i.e., evidence not available at the trial, and here he sought to call three further witnesses in support of the Stockport alibi, Henry Somerville, a Mrs Coppock, the Landlady of the "Wellington" Hotel and a cinema manager named Walter Ellwood. But the sum total of their evidence amounted to no more than a very forlorn hope.

Then came a sensational development. During his speech from the dock Rowland had said: 'Somewhere there is a person who knows that I stand here today an innocent man.' On January 22nd, 1947 David John Ware, claiming to be that person, made a sixty-four word statement to the Governor of Walton Gaol, Liverpool, in which he said that he had killed Olive 'Balshaw' (*sic*) with a hammer.

David Ware was thirty-eight. He originated from Skewen in Glamorganshire. Fifteen years earlier he had made a particularly clumsy attempt at blackmail and earned himself twelve months hard labour. Upon his release he married but five years later he deserted his wife leaving her with two small children to bring up. The ensuing five years are largely a blank save for a short spell which he spent in a Buckinghamshire mental home. Mental illness was to be a constantly recurring problem for Ware, culminating in his incarceration at Broadmoor in 1951.

In 1942 Ware enlisted in the Army. A year later he was discharged on the grounds that he was mentally unbalanced. His complaint was diagnosed as manic depressive psychosis. During the next two years he was twice imprisoned for theft. A curious feature of these crimes was that on both occasions he gave himself up to the Police. When not in prison he flitted from one hostel to another, living the life of a down and out. Finally, on October 18th, 1946, he stole some money from a Salvation Army Hostel in Stoke and fled to Manchester. The rest has already been described.

On January 24th Ware was interviewed by Inspector Stainton and Constable Nimmo, to whom he made a brief but detailed statement. A week later he made a longer one to Burke and Hinchcliffe who were acting on behalf of Rowland.

The gist of Ware's two statements was as follows:

He arrived in Manchester on the evening of October 18th with the money from the Salvation Army Hostel robbery in his pocket. He picked up a girl and spent the night with her at a lodging house. The following morning, the 19th, he left the lodging house and the girl. The money he had stolen, a paltry £1.75, did not figure to go very far and so he decided to buy a hammer for the purpose of robbery (if Ware's story was true then Rowland was being uncannily prescient when he told the Police:— 'It's possible the hammer was got to do a job with.'). He purchased a hammer at a shop which, in his own words:— 'was situated on the main road from the railway station to the Hippodrome theatre... on the left hand side of the road some little distance after passing under the bridge which passes over the road below the railway station and a little further down from the shop it inclines to the Manchester Hippodrome.' He made the purchase from a man whom he described as :— 'Middle-aged...of stocky build'. He also recalled that whilst he was in the shop another customer came in and bought a screwdriver.

After buying the hammer Ware decided to treat himself to the cinema in order to 'kill time till it got dark', to quote his own eerie phraseology. Outside the Hippodrome he encountered Olive Balchin and took her along with him. They re-emerged at 9 p.m., had a cup of coffee, and then caught a bus to Deansgate. At this point Ware decided to 'spend a while with her'. They went onto a bombsite where, in Ware's words, 'We were quite close to each other.' A certain odd prudishness creeps into Ware's statement when he describes his relations with Balchin. 'Spend a while with her' clearly means that he had made up his mind to have intercourse with her, and 'quite close to each other' is obviously a euphemistic way of saying that they were kissing and cuddling. Whilst they were so engaged he felt Balchin's hand in his pocket. Sexual desire turned abruptly to hatred. He suggested that they move further into the bombed building, and as they were picking their way across the rubble he launched his attack. What followed makes chilling reading.

> '...I struck her a violent blow on the head [I should say the right side]. She screamed, and before her scream lasted any length of time I struck her again. This time she only mumbled. Her hands were on her head protecting it. The second time, she fell to the floor up against the wall, and I repeated the blows. Blood shot up in a thin spray. I felt it on my face, and then I panicked, threw [down] the hammer, and left everything as it was.'

Ware goes on to tell how he ran zig-zagging his way up and down the dark streets until he reached Salford station. There he caught first a bus back to the Hippodrome, and then another to Stockport, where he spent the night at Richards' lodging house. On the Sunday he tramped first to Buxton, and then on to Chapel-en-le-frith where he stayed the night at yet another of the interminable lodging houses which seemed to mark his miserable existence. On the Monday he hitch-hiked to Sheffield. Whilst in Manchester he had worn a cap and a belted mackintosh. During the murder blood had spurted onto the mackintosh. He decided not to discard it altogether, but on arriving in Sheffield he threw away the belt, along with his cap, because he feared that they could lead to his being identified as the man who had bought the hammer. He then turned himself in for the Salvation Army theft.

The Appeal had been scheduled for January 27th. In view of Ware's confession a two week adjournment was granted. Rowland, quite naturally, was cock-a-hoop at this development. According to one source, he was so certain of winning the Appeal that his mother booked him a holiday and turned up at the Appeal Court on February 10th with his rail ticket in her pocket. Alas, they knew not the ways of British Justice.

The three Judges who heard the Appeal were Lord Goddard, the Lord Chief Justice, and Justices Humphreys and Lewis. They opened the proceedings by announcing that Mrs Coppock would not be heard because her evidence had been available at the trial. This was perfectly fair: it is difficult to understand why she was not called then and her evidence, about the bar sink overflowing, emerged anyway during Somerville's testimony.

But the Judges next ruling effectively killed Walter Rowland. David Ware would also *not* be allowed to give evidence; they would give their reasons later in writing.

Rowland sat in stunned disbelief whilst his defence team soldiered on as best they could. Somerville was called. We have already seen what he had to say. Walter Ellwood's testimony need not detain us long. He confirmed that a film which Somerville had watched before going to the "Wellington" had been playing at his cinema on the night of October 19th and gave some evidence about the time it would take to reach Manchester from Stockport, a matter which was hardly in dispute anyway.

Both Burke and Nield then addressed the court. They were simply going through the motions. The Judges had already decided that Somerville and Ellwood's evidence would not have affected the minds of the Jury. The Appeal was dismissed.

When this was announced Rowland exploded with anger:

> *'I am an innocent man. This is the greatest injustice which has ever happened in an English Court. Why did you have the man who confessed here and not hear him? I am not allowed justice because of my past!'*

Goddard curtly ordered that Rowland should be taken down, but the convicted man clung desperately to the dock and shouted:

> *'It would have knocked the bottom out of English law to have acquitted me and proved my innocence, I say now I am an innocent man before God!'*

And with that final roar of defiance Walter Rowland was wrestled out of the dock and into the cells below. He now had just seventeen days left to live.

A week later Goddard, Humphreys and Lewis delivered their written judgement on why they had not permitted Ware to give evidence. The judgement is reproduced here compressed into its key passages:

> *'...the court of appeal is not the proper tribunal to hold such an inquiry. It is no light matter to reverse the finding of a Jury... the mere statement of a person... that the convicted man is innocent because he himself is guilty... would not justify quashing the conviction of the other person but would only be the beginning of an enquiry which would involve... the recalling of many witnesses and probably the calling of several fresh ones. If we had allowed Ware to give evidence... the court would have been impelled to form some conclusion as to his guilt or innocence and to express that opinion in open*

court... therefore the court would have been... usurping the function of a Jury. In the event the findings of this court could not fail to be prejudicial to his chance of an impartial trial.'

Their Lordships concluded by suggesting, with all the aplomb of a trio of robed and bewigged Pontius Pilates, that the Home Secretary should order an inquiry into the matter.

Earlier we looked at the Appeal Court's performance in the case of John Dickman. At that point the Court had only been operating for three years and the excuse was made — although it seems to me to be a woefully inadequate one — that the Judges were having difficulty in getting to grips with it. No such excuse is possible with Walter Rowland; the Appeal Court was now 40 years old.

There can be no doubt that the guiding influence in refusing to hear Ware's evidence was that of Rayner Goddard, the Lord Chief Justice.* Goddard was one of the most controversial characters in English Legal history. His enemies, of whom there are many, have branded him as a blinkered and prejudiced reactionary. I am not altogether sure that this is fair. Certainly he was a hanger and flogger, but today the pendulum sometimes seems to have swung too far the other way. Goddard would certainly not have issued derisory sentences for rape or had any sympathy with abysmal excuses for it such as "contributory negligence". And we can be absolutely certain that he would not have kicked common sense in the teeth by sending violent criminals on "anger courses". He was also a pioneer of the retrial facility.

That having been said, Goddard — and Humphreys and Lewis — went horribly wrong in the Rowland case. Correctly putting aside his belief in Rowland's guilt, Judge Leon writes:—

'I should have thought that these facts (Ware's confessions) plainly constituted a very exceptional circumstance which made it incumbent upon the Court to hear his evidence.'[1]

Leon makes the point that the Appeal court would not have been trying Ware; it would only have been deciding whether the jury would have reached a different verdict had they heard his evidence, a subtle but important distinction.

Sydney Silverman M.P. in his book "Hanged and Innocent?" advances the same argument and also reminds us of the aforementioned case of *Rex v Braddock* which satisfactorily met the definition of new evidence, although whether the political element of that case was a factor can only be guessed at.

Let us look in detail at the Judgement.

---

1   "The Trial of Walter Rowland" p21

*   Although Humphreys wrote the Judgement.

The Judges were correct in stating that the Appeal Court was not the proper place to conduct such an inquiry. A new trial before another jury would have been altogether more suitable. Unfortunately, no such facility then existed in British criminal law. Quashing a conviction also had the effect of dismissing the indictment as well. There was no such thing as a retrial. Inadequate though it was, the fact remained that in 1947 only the Appeal Court was capable of holding such an inquiry within the setting of a court of law.

The Judgement states that reversing the findings of a jury is a momentous decision. So too is hanging a man by the neck until he is dead;— especially if he happens to be innocent!

We are told that Ware's confession would not by itself have been sufficient to set aside the original verdict; that the Appeal Court would have needed to call witnesses old and new to give evidence.

Certainly, we can agree that Ware's claim to be the guilty party would not by itself have determined anything. Other witnesses would indeed have been necessary in order to test the value of his evidence. But was this sufficient reason not to call Ware? I think not. The case had moved abruptly in a whole new direction, and all the roads and avenues of this new direction led from David Ware's confession. A completely new inquiry, with Ware's evidence as its centrepiece, undertaken in public and bound by the rules of evidence, was called for.

The Appeal Court was simply not in a position to know whether or not the original verdict should stand without hearing Ware's confession, and the evidence of any other witness whose testimony had a bearing on it. Had it become obvious that Ware's story was unreliable then the question of quashing Rowland's conviction would not have arisen. But on the other hand, had Ware's story stood up and implanted a seed of doubt in the mind of the Court, the Judges would have been perfectly entitled to take the view that if the jury had also heard Ware's evidence they too would have experienced similar doubts about Rowland's guilt. The Appeal Court was not being asked to reverse the findings of the jurors on the evidence they had heard; it was being asked to determine whether new evidence would have led to their reaching a different conclusion. This duty, to justice and to Walter Rowland, it shirked. Nor was it the only instance. In 1936 Charlotte Bryant was convicted of murdering her husband. The main prosecution evidence was provided by a pathologist named Lynch. Following the trial an eminent scientist approached the defence and told them that Lynch's evidence was blatantly wrong. But when the defence attempted to call him at the Appeal the Judges, *who included Justice Humphreys* refused to hear him. The rest of the story is best told by Sean O'Brien in his book "Bloody Ambassadors":—

> *'It was not the business of the Court of Criminal Appeal to pronounce on the guilt or innocence of Charlotte Bryant. What the Judges... had to determine was, if Professor Bone's additional evidence had been available and they had been aware of the gross inaccuracies in the testimony of the*

Crown's scientific expert, would the Jury... have arrived at a different conclusion? His Lordship thought they would not. Charlotte's prosecutor, Sir Terence O'Connor who told Casswell (defence counsel) privately that "Lynch has certainly made a dreadful mistake", thought they would and was in Court to repeat his belief. But he like Bone, was told by Lord Hewart that his presence was not required.'[1]

The Appeal Court not only refused to hear expert testimony that the scientific evidence which convicted Bryant was wrong; it also refused to listen to the Prosecution which accepted that it was wrong! Charlotte Bryant was executed on July 15th, 1936. She left behind five children and a dying declaration of her innocence.

There is not much more to say. Rowland's Appeal Court Judges baulked at the prospect of substituting themselves for a jury. In fact that is exactly what they had done when deciding that Somerville and Ellwood's testimony would not have influenced the jury. They were right to be concerned about Ware's interests but they also had a bounden duty to protect Rowland's. It was hardly right that he should die if the real murderer was prepared to confess to it. Whatsoever resulted from that confession was not the business of the Appeal Court; that was a separate issue to be decided in another place. In 1976 Patrick Meehan was pardoned after two other men made well publicised confessions to a murder in Ayr. One of them, Ian Waddell, was later tried for that murder, withdrew his confession and was acquitted.

At the end of the day the Appeal Court failed utterly to do its job. It was guilty not merely of incompetence but moral cowardice as well; just as it had been with Charlotte Bryant a decade earlier.

(9)

With the execution set for the 27th, Rowland's defence was running out of time.

They applied for leave to appeal to the House of Lords but the fiat was rejected by Sir Hartley Shawcross, the Attorney General. Appeals to the House of Lords are granted upon points of exceptional importance. One would have thought that this was just such a case. One man had been convicted on highly tenuous evidence; another had made a credible confession. But the fiat was refused. Step by step the system was failing Walter Rowland.

Now only one possibility remained. The Appeal Court had recommended

---

1   "Bloody Ambassadors" p122

that the Home Secretary should set up an inquiry. Such inquiries into cases of murder had been held before but only to test sanity, not culpability. As far as I am aware no inquiry had ever before been set up in a murder case to determine whether a condemned man was guilty. In effect the Appeal Court had dumped the whole kit and caboodle into the lap of an official, the Home Secretary, with far less facility to deal with it than the Court had. Whether there was a political dimension in this, (the Judiciary was overwhelmingly Tory and the comparatively new Home Secretary James Chuter Ede a Labour Minister representing a party with strong anti-capital punishment elements), is for the reader to judge. Whatever the case, Chuter Ede was honour bound to take up the baton. In doing so he could only rely upon the same people, lawyers, Judges and policemen, who had already condemned Rowland. On February 21st Chuter Ede appointed John Catterall Jolly, a King's Counsel with judicial experience, to conduct the inquiry. Assisting him would be two Metropolitan Police Officers, Detective Superintendent Thomas Barratt as assessor and Detective Inspector Herbert Hannam to do the leg work. An unhealthy precedent was being created.

Chuter Ede decided not to postpone the execution. Jolly commenced his inquiries on February 22nd which meant that he had just five days to present his report. It was the classic recipe for a bodge-up.

The Rowland case was a tragedy in three acts: part one, the arrest and trial; part two, the Appeal Court hearing; and now the third and final stanza which was just about to unfold.

Jolly commenced his investigation by interviewing Ware. Also present were Barratt and Hannam. Ware was not legally represented; nor were Burke or Hinchcliffe allowed to be present to oversee Rowland's interests.

Jolly described the interview as follows:—

> *'...I, together with Mr Barratt and Mr Hannam, interviewed Ware and investigated the three statements which he had made. After persisting at first in maintaining that his former statements as to the murder were correct, Ware admitted that they were false, saying, "I'd better turn it in."* [*]

Ware then proceeded to completely retract his confession. Now he claimed that he had not arrived in Manchester until 7:30 p.m. on Saturday the 19th and went on to tell a very different story from the one he had told earlier. He said that it was the 19th, and not the 18th, on which he had spent the night at the hotel with the prostitute, and that he had stayed at the Stockport lodging house on the night of the 20th, and not the 19th. But in fact Ware was hopelessly confusing his dates. Events which he claimed had taken place on the 20th could not possibly have occurred on that day, an error which went unnoticed at the time. It is now common ground that Ware did in fact arrive in Manchester on Friday the 18th, as he originally claimed, and that he confused the Saturday with the Sunday.

*

Asked why he had made his confession in the first place, Ware offered this explanation:—

> '...[it was] out of swank... I also thought I was putting myself in the position of a hero. I wanted to see myself in the headlines. In the past I wanted to be hung... life was not really worth living... I read all about the murder from the newspapers... and from conversation with other prisoners... one being Frank something and another a Scotsman.'

Jolly had been appointed, as he himself put it:—

> 'to inquire into the confession made by David Ware... to consider any further information which may have become available since the conviction of Walter Rowland... and to report whether there are any grounds for thinking that there has been any miscarriage of justice...'

But following his interview with Ware Jolly tossed Rowland's interests overboard. It is not unfair, or uncharitable, to say that he spent the remainder of the inquiry looking for evidence to support Ware's retraction. He closed his mind to the possibility that Ware might have been telling the truth in his previous statements. In fact the question needs to be asked as to whether Jolly did not actually set out on his task with the preconceived idea of disproving Ware's confession. Lawyers and politicians possess an almost pathological fear of admitting that an innocent person can be convicted. This attitude was reflected in two statements made in the House of Commons in 1948. The first emanates from Sir David Maxwell-Fyfe K.C., M.P., who was later to become Home Secretary in the Conservative Government of 1951.

> 'As a realist I do not believe that the chances of error in a murder case... constitute a factor which we must consider... there is no practical possibility... a jury might go wrong, the Court of Appeal might go wrong, as might the Home Secretary; they might all be stricken mad and go wrong. But that is not a possibility which anyone can consider likely. The Honourable and Learned Member is moving in a realm of fantasy when he makes that suggestion.' (Hansard 14/4/48)

The second comes from the lips of Sir John Anderson, formerly a Permanent Under Secretary at the Home Office. Anderson left that post to go into politics. Like Maxwell-Fyfe, he was destined to become a Conservative Home Secretary.

> 'The risk... of the capital penalty being executed on anyone who was not guilty... is so small, indeed so infinitesimal, that that consideration can be dismissed.' (Hansard 14/4/48)

Apparently, a belief in the infallibility of the judicial system is a prime qualification for the job of Home Secretary.

Despite the veritable flood of proven miscarriages, and the serious doubts which attach to many convictions still standing (Rowland's included), the Establishment continues to quail at the prospect of admitting error. Henry Leon regales us with this classic piece of myopia in his book "The Trial of Walter Rowland":—

> *'I do not believe that anyone who has never committed a crime... stands in real danger of being convicted of a serious crime of which he is innocent.'*

Thus stands Judge Leon, a legal Horatio protecting the gates of judicial infallibility without appearing to notice that the surrounding walls have already crumbled. Herbert Bennett, John Dickman, Norman Thorne, Timothy Evans, Edith Thompson, Charlotte Bryant, Robert Hoolhouse — the list is by no means exhaustive — were all standing in the dock for the first time when they listened to the Clerk of the Court intoning the charge of murder against them. It is Leon's prerogative to ignore them if he wishes, but every day they silently remind his hallowed legal system of its shortcomings. There is a piece of doggerel which describes the situation very aptly. I have amended it slightly to fit the context.

> *'As I was going into court I met some people who weren't there. They weren't there again today. I wish, I wish, they'd go away.'*

Following Ware's retraction Jolly arranged for him to be put on an identity parade before Edward Macdonald, Elizabeth Copley and Norman Mercer. None of them recognised him. Then each of the three witnesses confronted Ware individually, and all three said that they had never seen him before.

A number of points arise from this episode.

Having already identified Rowland, Macdonald and Co. were hardly unbiased witnesses. They knew that their identification had played a dominant role in convicting a man who was just a few short days away from being launched into eternity. Psychologically, they could not have permitted any vestiges of doubt to have lingered in their minds.

Jolly asked Copley to walk along the line and see whether she could see anyone resembling the man who had been in the cafe on October 19th.

The same question was put to Mercer, except of course that he was asked whether he could spot anyone resembling the man he had seen quarrelling with the woman at midnight. Later, the same question was again put to them when they were brought face to face with Ware by himself. Their replies: Copley, 'no definitely'; and Mercer, "definitely no"; could hardly have been otherwise. In fact their non-identifications were quite worthless.

Ware had never claimed to have visited the Queen's Cafe, or to have stood quarrelling with Balchin at midnight. In his statements he spoke of killing Balchin before midnight after they had travelled directly from Piccadilly to the Deansgate bombsite. Ware's confession did not actually contradict Copley and Mercer's identifications of Rowland... although this logically arose out of it... it opposed instead their identifications of Balchin.

Only Edward Macdonald was relevant to Ware's confession. Here there was a subtle but crucial difference between the question put to Copley and

Mercer, and the question which was put to the shopkeeper before he was sent out to view the identity parade. Copley and Mercer had been asked whether they could see anyone who resembled the man they had seen. But Macdonald was asked, quote: 'whether he could see anyone who resembles the man Rowland!' Needless to say, Ware bore no resemblance to Rowland, although interestingly enough he did resemble Macdonald's description of the man who had bought the hammer, a point made by Ware during his retraction:—

> *'Having... noticed the description of the suspect it struck me how much I was like him.'*

Having summarily disposed of the question of identification, Jolly next tackled the time of Olive Balchin's death, and quoted an interview with a man named Wilfred Gosling. Like Norman Mercer, Gosling was the Landlord of a Deansgate pub. He stated that on Saturday, October 19th, he had taken his dog for a walk at about half-past ten that evening. He and the dog had spent about five minutes on the bombsite. It was, 'rather a vicious dog', and he was certain that if Balchin's dead body had been present on the bombsite then it would have smelt the blood. Gosling had made a statement on October 20th. His evidence had not been sought at the trial because the Pathologist had decided that Balchin had been murdered after 11 p.m.

Ware originally claimed that he had slain Balchin sometime around 10 o'clock. The evidence of both Gosling and the Pathologist ruled this out. But in fact Ware only mentioned the time in his first, very brief statement to the Prison Governor. In his succeeding statements he made no attempt whatsoever to fix a time for the murder.

Jolly then goes on to deal with Ware's motive for the murder. He claimed that Balchin had picked his pocket and stolen a ten shilling note from him. A ten shilling note was found in Balchin's coat pocket, but it was carefully folded and lay beneath some coins inside a paper cash packet. The packet itself was underneath a welter of papers, letters, and bed tickets. Jolly states:—

> *'Had Balchin stolen the ten shilling note in the circumstances described by Ware, it could not possibly have been found where it was in fact found.'*

Moreover, Ware had told the Prison Doctor that after killing Balchin he initially retrieved the note from her. Then he altered his mind and threw it down at the body.

But no ten shilling note was found on the ground nearby.

Maybe there was no ten shilling note; maybe Ware simply needed a reason for an insane act. But what he allegedly told the Doctor (Jolly was not interested in the possibility that he and not Ware was mistaken) contradicted his formal statements anyway. In those he spoke of making no attempt to recover the money and of panicking and running away, exactly as one might expect after committing a murder.

The ten shilling note is a mystery, although in my view only a minor one. Ware could have concocted it to justify his actions; he could have thrown it down (as the Doctor claimed) and it might have blown away or been pocketed by an onlooker after the body was discovered. And it *could* have been the ten shilling note found on Balchin. There are two possibilities here. One is that she did not steal it; Ware gave it to her for sex but did not like to admit it. In his statements he spoke of spending the previous night with a girl, certainly a prostitute, but made no admission about paying her. Balchin was a working prostitute and prostitutes traditionally ask for their money before, not after, sex. The other is that Balchin did pick his pocket. Some prostitutes do that. Jolly was wrong in saying that she could not have surreptitiously folded it and put it into her cash pocket. It can be done. But in fact Balchin did not need to do so anyway. Here is what Ware actually said (ignored by Jolly) in his confessions:—

> *'She took the opportunity of going through my pockets... I... suggested that I'd like to make water and went further into the building. In there... I took the brown paper off the hammer... I went back to her.'*

Which meant that Olive had ample opportunity to fold the note and put it into her cash packet whilst he was away.

Others may take a different view — you are the assessors here — but I do not attach much weight to the issue.

In his retraction Ware told Jolly that he had obtained the details of the crime from reading about it in the newspapers and discussing it with other prisoners. Ware was remanded in custody from October 22nd to January 15th. During that time he had had access to newspapers, but in his confession he states:

> *'I read all about the finding of the woman's body but did **not** read any report of either the police court proceedings or the trial of Rowland. The last I read was a paragraph which said that an arrest in connection with the Manchester "blitz site murder" was expected at any moment. I then purposely avoided reading the newspapers, as I did not want to read anything more about the murder.'*

But in his retraction Ware sang a very different tune:—

> *'During my remand and whilst awaiting trial at Quarter Sessions I read all about the murder from the newspapers and continuously built up a story so that I knew all the details of it. It was during this time that I made up my mind to confess to the murder at a convenient time... I set myself to get all the details of the murder in my mind and continuously repeated the story to myself until I knew it right off. Whilst I was awaiting my trial Rowland was sentenced to death and I read about it in the paper and I also read that he was going to appeal... the matters which I stated I had learned from reading the newspapers and from conversations with other prisoners, some of whom came to the prison after the murder. I cannot name the prisoners with whom I discussed the murder apart from one being Frank... something... and*

*another a Scotsman. I tried to get all the facts I could from other prisoners...
I also played on the fact that the real prisoner made such a strong claim to
innocence.'*

In these passages Ware was quite clearly saying that he had continued to
study the case and accumulate details about it throughout the period of his
remand. No doubt this was precisely what Jolly wanted to hear at that time, but
once Ware had made the statement learned Counsel suddenly found himself on
the horns of a dilemma because what Ware was now saying made absolutely no
sense whatsoever.

If he had made the whole story up from a continuous study of press reports
and discussions with other prisoners then why was it so at odds with the evidence
given both at the Police Court and the trial? How was it that he had no idea of
Balchin's proper name? Why did he not time his meeting with her after her
supposed encounter with Rita Leach? Why did he not claim to be the man who
allegedly accompanied Balchin to the Queen's Cafe? Why was he so strangely
ignorant of Norman Mercer's testimony... so ignorant in fact that he claimed in
his confession to have killed Balchin before midnight? And why was the time
he gave for the murder so at variance with that of the pathologist?

The only way in which Jolly could resolve these difficulties was by altering
his stance and treating this aspect of Ware's confession as being truthful, a classic
example of expediency overriding integrity. But even here Jolly accepted
Ware's statement only in part. He conveniently ignored his claim not to have
read any newspaper reports *after* Rowland's arrest and instead examined items
which had appeared in the press as late as November 6th. Such machinations
would have made a wonderful addition to the trial scene in "Alice in Wonderland"; in an allegedly impartial inquiry with a man's life at stake they can only
be described as utterly disgraceful.

By dint of such tactics Jolly was able to "prove" that Ware could have
gleaned some... but not all... of the details from the newspapers.

First, the items which Ware might have culled from the Press, assuming
of course that he read the same newspapers from which Jolly compiled his list
of clippings.

There is no confirmation of this in the report.

In his confession Ware said that Balchin had worn... 'a dark blue or dark
brown... double breasted' coat. Now of course a picture of the coat had appeared
in the press on October 21st and Jolly states that a 'comment is made of the
distinctive nature of the buttons'. But whether these reports made any mention
of the colour of the coat is another matter. Jolly makes no mention of it and the
published photograph was of course in black and white.

Ware said that he paid 17½ pence for the hammer and this price was quoted
in the newspapers. The newspapers also reported the finding of the wrapping
paper a short distance from the body.

Two of the press reports mentioned the name "Balshaw". Jolly thought it 'noteworthy' that Ware referred to her by this name, conveniently overlooking the fact that if Ware had been telling the truth in his retraction then he would have known her real name when he came to make his confession. There is in fact nothing in Jolly's 'noteworthy' point except that it actually supports Ware's claim not to have read the newspaper reports after Rowland's arrest. Prostitutes do not give their real names to clients (Rowland knew her as "Lil") and "Balshaw" was the name she was living under at the time.

A few days after the crime one newspaper had reported:—

'there were severe injuries to the head and the nail of the index finger of the left hand was missing.'

In his confession Ware said:

'Her hands were on her head protecting it.'

The implication here is that Ware deduced that Balchin's hands were protecting her head from the fact that one of her fingernails was missing. But Ware's criminal career portrays him as a near idiot, quite incapable of drawing an intelligent conclusion about anything. A perfect illustration of his low mentality is to be found in his ludicrous attempt at blackmail in 1931. On that occasion he attempted to extort money from a man he accused of adultery without having the slightest proof of it. Not surprisingly Ware quickly came to grief. The consequences of making a threat which he could not sustain appears to have been beyond his powers of reasoning. This incident depicts Ware as a person to whom consecutive thought was an alien concept.

Finally Jolly quotes from the November 6th report which was mentioned earlier, giving further details about Balchin's injuries. Her right cheekbones had been broken in two places from the effects of 'many blows'. In his confession Ware had spoken of hitting Balchin on the right side of her head (he thought) and of repeating the blows. But the point here is the fact that Jolly had to go all the way up to November 6th to find what he was looking for. This perfectly illustrates the highly selective nature of his report. He temporarily discarded Ware's retraction in favour of his confession because it suited his purpose in "proving" his point. Then, with immaculate sleight of hand he ignored the part of the confession which did not fit in with his argument. The word cheating springs most readily to mind. Based on this performance Jolly would have made an outstanding pavement bunco artist: Now you see it; now you don't.

Such were the details which Ware might have gleaned from the newspapers, provided of course that he read the same journals as Mr Jolly, succeeded in finding one which mentioned the colour of Balchin's coat, suddenly acquired a depth of thought which had thus far in life eluded him and carried on reading about the crime up to November 6th.

Much more interesting are the details given in Ware's confessions which did *not* appear in the press.

Macdonald's shop:

> '*[The] shop which was situated on the main road from the railway station to the Hippodrome Theatre. The shop was on the left hand side of the road some little distance after passing under the bridge which passes over the road below the railway station. The road declines from the railway station and a little further down from the shop it inclines to the Manchester Hippodrome.*'

If Ware did not get these details from the newspapers then how did he obtain them unless he did visit the shop?

Edward Macdonald:

Ware gave a brief description of him which I quoted earlier. Jolly does not disagree with it. It is also a very singular fact that Ware says in his confessions:

> '*After buying it I said to the man who supplied it, this will be suitable.*'

Now this very closely resembles the conversation which Macdonald had with the purchaser. Moreover it was a conversation which was never made public until the trial. It received its first airing during Macdonald's evidence. Asked why he had never mentioned it before, the shopkeeper replied:

> '*I was told that this must not be spoken until later.*'

Ware could not have gotten the details of the conversation until after the trial had commenced.

Purchasing the hammer; Ware said:—

> '*In the window of the shop there were a number of what appeared to be second hand tools displayed for sale. Whilst I was buying the hammer a man came in and bought a screwdriver. He was served whilst the shopkeeper was attending to me.*'

Ware was saying that he first saw the hammer in Macdonald's shop window. The hammer was second hand and Macdonald placed it in the window at three o'clock that afternoon. He also put some other items up for sale at the same time and they were alongside the hammer. They had been purchased from Rawlinson only that morning.

The cinema:

Ware's statement:—

> '*After meeting the woman at the Hippodrome Theatre, we got on a tram car the indicator of which read "Belle Vue". We left the tram car at the stadium and then walked up the road for quite a long way until we came to a third rate picture house on the right hand side of the road. We went into the picture house together.*'

The above is extracted from Ware's third confession (to Rowland's defence). In his second confession (to the Police) he also mentions that Balchin and he had a cup of coffee opposite the cinema after leaving it.

Tram cars with Belle Vue indicators; a run down cinema with a place opposite where a cup of coffee could be bought; was this all invention? Had Ware been a regular visitor to Manchester then it would have been irrelevant. But he was not. He said that he was a virtual stranger to the city and this was never disputed.

The bombsite:

Ware takes up the story again:

> *'On returning to Manchester we left the bus at Piccadilly. We walked forward until we came to the shops down the road to the left and then turned to the right eventually coming to the bombed ruin.'*

It is admittedly a very general description of a journey from Piccadilly to Deansgate but it may well ring true for a man who was a stranger to the place and was taking no particular note of the surroundings. Certainly Mr Jolly found no holes to pick in it.

The murder:

Describing the murder, Ware says:—

> *'She... had only a few paces to go before reaching the wall.'*

Balchin's body was found just a few paces from a wall. The police photograph of her corpse taken on the bombsite confirms this. That photograph was not of course released to the newspapers.

Ware carried on:

> *'Blood shot up in a thin spray.'*

But no newspaper mentioned that blood had spurted prior to the trial when Doctor Jenkins gave his evidence.

If Ware did not get these details from the press then how did he come by them? An intriguing question: unfortunately it held not one iota of interest for Mr Jolly. But had it done so then he might have been forced to face the unpalatable truth that Ware's confession was highly convincing.

The final part of Ware's statement worth quoting deals with his movements after the murder:—

> *'I found myself at a railway station... an elderly man... told me it was Salford station. ...I got on a tram car close by. I asked the guard if I was going to the Hippodrome. He said "no" and pointed out to me the buses at the bus station.'*

Salford station, a tram car nearby, a bus to the Hippodrome. Once again the point is that Ware was almost a newcomer to Manchester, and yet once again Jolly finds no fault with this part of his confession. The morality seems to be:—

if you can argue against it, however tenuously, then do so. If not, ignore it.

Edward Macdonald's shop; Edward Macdonald himself; the hardware items; the cinema; the route to Deansgate; the wall; and finally the flight. All are rich in detail that only the murderer could know. There is no other practical source. Jolly did not see it: he was not a stupid man; he did not see it because he did not want to see it.

The sad saga of the press cuttings is now at an end. We can now move onto the next part of the report. It is just as sorry.

Jolly pounces on the time given by Ware for the purchase of the hammer... around 4 p.m.... which of course was seriously at variance with the time put forward by Edward Macdonald... 5:40. Assuming that Macdonald's time was accurate... naturally Jolly treats it as holy writ... then Ware appears to have tripped up badly. However, Sydney Silverman answers this point very adroitly:—

> *'But what does Mr Jolly want? If Ware gets his details right, that is because he got them from the newspapers. If he gets them wrong, that proves he is lying. The fact is that in all his written statements Ware gives no time at all for the purchase of the hammer, except that it was in the afternoon and before six o'clock.'* [1]

The only occasion on which Ware mentioned the time of 4 p.m. was during his interview with Jolly of February 22nd. At this point Ware was still holding fast to his confession. Later, he gave way and retracted it. Arrayed against him during this session were the trained minds of an eminent King's Counsel and two senior Police Officers, all richly skilled in the art of interrogation. Naturally they would have concentrated on any minor deficiencies in Ware' story, such as the fact that he had never pinpointed a time for buying the hammer. We have already seen how John Dickman was harried into playing guessing games. Perhaps, like Dickman, Ware merely took a stab at the question. This does not prove that he was lying... only that his memory was vague on this particular question. If his confession was true then he visited many shops that Saturday afternoon and it would hardly be surprising if his mind failed to keep track of the time properly. The only time he was positive about during this period of the day was encountering Balchin at 6 p.m.

Some interesting points arise out of this episode.

First, Ware's subsequent retraction. In it he claimed to have studied the case whilst on remand and to have continuously built up his knowledge of the case. If so then he might have been expected to know the time at which the hammer was purchased. That he did not undermined the value of his retraction,

---

1   "Hanged and Innocent" p70

a point which Jolly does not seem to have noticed. At this point the bunco game has gone slightly awry. The left hand does not seem to know what the right hand is doing.

Secondly, Ware's confession. Jolly treated it throughout as a tissue of lies. But for the moment let us assume that Ware was telling the truth and see where it takes us.

He said that he picked Balchin up outside the Hippodrome at 6 p.m., and implied that he walked directly to the theatre after buying the hammer. Although Ware was clearly oblivious to the fact, this would place the time of his visit to Macdonald's shop at around 5:40, thus matching the time given by Macdonald himself.

If we accept this as a possibility then, by reverse logic, if Ware did indeed buy the hammer at 5:40 then the time of his meeting Balchin can be verified as 6 p.m.

Here an interesting point arises. The police quickly established that Balchin was a prostitute but were not, apparently, able to find anybody who could testify to her movements on the evening of October 19th prior to Rita Leach at 9:15. Clients were unlikely to come forward, but the police seem to have interviewed the staff of various cafes which Balchin frequented. There was no suggestion that she was seen in her usual haunts that Saturday evening. But if Rita Leach was mistaken, and Balchin spent the evening with Ware, then that would explain why nobody recalled seeing her.

Jolly of course did not study the issue from any of these angles. Quite simply, he aimed to prove that Ware's confession was phoney, and the whole thrust of his analysis was bent towards this end.

To move on to the next issue, in his retraction Ware stated that on the afternoon of Sunday, October 20th he went to a cinema and saw:—

'A wartime picture with aeroplanes and parachutes jumping out.'

The price of admission was 14 pence.

He left the cinema at around 5:30, had a meal and then spent the evening in a pub called the "Oxford".

After leaving the "Oxford" he travelled to Stockport and stayed the night in Richards lodging house.

Jolly brings these events forward to October 19th. Here I have no quarrel with him because it is plain that Ware got his dates out of synch. It is clear that the events of the Sunday took place on the Saturday.

Jolly goes on to say:—

'My belief is that Ware, realising that the time of his arrival at Stockport could be checked, was obliged to fix the time of the murder which he was saying he had committed at an hour (10 p.m.) which would be consistent with his journey to Stockport and arrival there.'

Once again Ware has acquired a mental agility which would normally be associated with somebody of much higher intelligence.

Examining this part of Jolly's report, Sydney Silverman correctly attacks him for failing to notice that Ware was confusing the events of the 19th and the 20th. But he then goes on to say:—

> *'Whether a mistake was made or not, there the statement stands.'*

Silverman duly treats the retraction as being accurate as it stands which of course has the effect of rendering it meaningless.

This simply will not do. Black cannot become white because Mr Silverman wishes it so. It is absolutely obvious that Ware was mixing up the two days and that for the most part Jolly did not notice the error. We must therefore assess the retraction as referring to the Saturday and not the Sunday which means that if it holds water then Ware's confession flounders and sinks.

To investigate these issues Jolly detailed Inspector Hannam to locate the cinema (with Ware's help) and carry out inquiries at the lodging house.

Herbert Hannam. Much has been written about him, most of it uncomplimentary. Bob Woffinden in his book "Miscarriages of Justice" has this to say about the good Inspector:—

> *'Hannam's subsequent career was a chequered one... "Daily Express" chief crime reporter Percy Hoskins recalled that Hannam's method of conducting the investigation into the 1953 Towpath murder case was "At best unsavoury" ... the paper was prepared to back Hoskins in 1957 in his unpopular defence of Bodkin Adams the Doctor hounded to the Old Bailey (and almost to the scaffold) by Hannam.'*

Remember these words as we follow Hannam around Manchester and Stockport.

Hannam and Ware located the cinema and ascertained that a film about the battle of Arnhem entitled "Theirs is the Glory" was playing on October 19th. The film depicted parachutists jumping out of aeroplanes.

At first sight this seems to bear out Ware's retraction. Predictably, Jolly makes the most of it: it was, he thought, 'extremely significant'.

In fact it was a *non sequeter*. Ware gives no details beyond what he could have gleaned from walking past the cinema. The general content of the programme and the admission charges would both be clearly visible to the passer-by. He recalled nothing about the performance saying:—

> *'...there was nothing outstanding in the programme which I can remember. I was tired and had a sleep. There was a clock on the right hand side of the screen which I noticed was half past five when I woke up.'*

"Theirs is the Glory" is in fact a fine little war film. The 'aeroplanes and parachutists' which Ware did claim to have seen feature only in the first quarter of an hour of the picture. If he was telling the truth then he must therefore have been awake for at least the opening fifteen minutes. That being the case then he really ought to have been aware of an almost unique feature about the film: it contained no professional actors whatsoever, a point strongly emphasised in the opening credits. It is frankly inconceivable that Ware could have failed to notice such a detail.

And what of the clock? By itself its existence would prove nothing. Almost every cinema had one. But interestingly enough there is no confirmation from Hannam that this particular cinema had such a clock. And if it was not there then Ware was clearly lying.

What of the next part of Ware's story? According to him he had a meal and then visited a pub called the "Oxford" where he stayed until closing time. He encountered a man and two women and remained in conversation with the man throughout the evening.

Jolly makes no comment about this Saturday evening drinking session. Although Hannam drove Ware around Manchester until they found the cinema and although he followed this up by visiting the Stockport lodging house, a curtain of silence descends on the evening spent in the pub. There is not even a confirmation of the description which Ware gave of the place. Obviously it was not possible to substantiate this part of the retraction.

In fairness it must be pointed out that no barman would be likely to recall a casual customer four months later. But what of the people whom Ware claimed to have spent the evening with? He provided descriptions of them; in particular a very full description of the man. Given the time at Jolly's disposal any attempt at tracing them would probably have been futile but at least he could have tried. A story in the newspapers might have brought results. But then they might also have brought forth stories which Jolly did not want to hear because it is conceivable that Ware encountered the trio at some other time, maybe even at another pub that weekend. Perhaps the oddest thing about them is that they do not appear to have been blessed with names! Ware claimed to have stayed with the man until closing time and the two women for an hour. And no names were exchanged? Of course, if he was making them up then it is difficult to give an identity to a figment of the imagination.

After returning Ware to prison, Hannam next made tracks for Stockport. It is not disputed that Ware stayed at Richards lodging house in Stockport on the night of the 19/20th. Here the questions are why he went there and what time he arrived.

This is what Ware said in his confession:—

> *'I was frightened of going on the station [after the murder] so decided to go to Stockport.'*

Compare this with what he said in his retraction:—

> *'I knew I should not get a bed in Manchester but knew I should get one in Stockport...'*

This simply does not make sense. Ware was a virtual stranger to Manchester. How on earth did he know that he would not get a bed there? He was anyway quite wrong: as Rowland's nocturnal meanderings show there were plenty of lodging houses which stayed open late. But what makes the statement particularly incomprehensible, absurd even, is that Ware had stayed in a Manchester lodging house the previous night. The explanation does not hold water.

On the other hand what Ware says in his confession is entirely credible. After killing Balchin he ran zig-zagging through the streets, found himself at Salford station, was too frightened to go on the station and instead caught a bus. Murder is a far more rational explanation for leaving town.

The other question is what time did he arrive at Richards lodging house? Says Hannam:—

> *'I... interviewed... an old Gentleman named Ernest Plant. Following the inspection of the register by the Police... the book was destroyed but Mr Plant pointed out to the Police Officers the entry made in the book on the 19th October, showing that Ware slept on the premises that night. He remembers Ware's arrival because... there was a joke over the spelling of his surname... he says the man occupied bed 31 which I also inspected and found to be at right angles to all the other beds in the room. To the best of Plant's recollection Ware arrived... between 11:15 and 11:30 and produced his identity card.'*

How does this dovetail with Ware's retraction? The answer is, perfectly.

> *'I would have been at the lodging house at between 11:15 and 11:30. I saw an old man in charge... and [he] asked me if I had my identity card. I produced my card. The... bed... was the first bed on the right in the first room on the first floor, this bed being turned at right angles to other beds... a number of residents were in the general room talking around a stove.'*

Earlier I commented that bar staff at a pub would hardly have recalled an insignificant customer four months earlier. Yet this is precisely what Mr Plant, an elderly man, managed to do. We can accept the number of the bed, it was doubtless in Plant's register which Stainton and Nimmo had inspected only a month earlier. Because of the Police interest it would have then stayed in Plant's mind. But it is scarcely credible that he could recall the conversation and surely beyond any credence whatsoever that he remembered so well the time of Ware's arrival. But it coincided exactly with what Ware said about the time. Is this believable? Or was Ernest Plant spoon fed the answers?

And what of the missing register? According to Hannam it had been destroyed by the proprietor following Stainton and Nimmo's visit.

Why? Nobody knows.

What does Hannam say about it? Nothing.

Did he ask the proprietor about it? Seemingly not.

Was Jolly not curious about it? No.

And Stainton and Nimmo. Can they confirm what Plant said? Answer comes there not.

It is all very unsatisfactory.

According to Ware's retraction he left the "Oxford" at closing time. States Jolly:—

> *'Which was in fact 10 p.m.'*

A little later Jolly makes the statement which I quoted earlier; that Ware was obliged to fix the time of the murder at an hour consistent with his arrival in Stockport.

Unfortunately for Jolly there is a glaring error in his reasoning. Closing time on the 19th was 10:30 not 10:00, a point made by Ware himself. Jolly is not entitled to juggle around with Ware's retraction to suit himself. Doubtless learned counsel thought this a clever little point. When examined it dissolves into a tissue of irrelevance.

The plain fact is that it is not possible to pinpoint the time of Ware's arrival at Richard's lodging house. Nor is it possible to confirm Ware's story of spending the evening at the "Oxford". Jolly realised this. He therefore attempted to buttress Ware's retractions by intertwining the time which Ware gave for the murder with pub closing time. Unfortunately for him he came unstuck. The spectre of Ware as the killer could not so easily be banished.

Looking at the overall picture which this part of the report paints, it fails to prove anything beyond the fact that Jolly was, to put it kindly, riding a merry-go-round of rash and ill conceived notions. Like its accessory parts it is quite worthless.

The next portion of Jolly's document dealt with forensic evidence...or rather it didn't!

Ware's clothing was examined by Dr Firth at the end of January. Firth revealed his findings to Jolly. For once Burke and Hinchcliffe were permitted to attend. Why they were not present during any other part of the inquiry is not explained. Draw your own conclusions.

We learn from Doctor Firth that he could find no bloodstains on Ware's trousers and that the contents of his turn-ups was in 'marked contrast' to what he had found in Rowland's.

Yes, and what else?

We do not know. Jolly does not tell us. But what we do know is that there were bloodstains on Ware's raincoat. Here is what he said in his confession:—

> *'On the bus I noticed spots of blood on the left sleeve of my raincoat.'*

Jolly could not remove these blood spots by sleight of hand. They had existed, not only on the left sleeve, but also on the right sleeve and the front of the raincoat. How then did Ware seek to explain this away in his retraction?:—

> *'Whilst I was on remand... I stitched mailbags to earn some money; in doing so I often pricked my fingers. I used to wear my raincoat whilst*

doing the mailbags and I accordingly got some spots of blood on the front of it. When I was preparing my mind to confess to the murder I deliberately put spots of blood on the lower forearm of the two raincoat sleeves. I later washed these spots off with a piece of wet rag and burnt some of them off with the tip of a cigarette.'

Ware makes not attempt to explain why he was wearing his raincoat in a prison workshop. Nor is there any confirmation of this strange sartorial habit from the prison officers who supervised him. In fact there is not even any confirmation that he was ever engaged in sewing mailbags. He tells us that he also smeared blood on the sleeves of the coat to make his confession more convincing. But then he offers the strange explanation that he tried to obliterate the stains.

Does this make sense?

Surely the answer is no. A much more rational explanation is that he attempted to remove the bloodstains in the immediate aftermath of the murder because he feared that they would draw attention to him. This tallies with his original statement that he threw away his belt and cap before surrendering at Sheffield in order to alter his appearance following the publication of the description of the man who had bought the hammer.

Jolly's failure to examine the issue of the bloodstained raincoat, is quite incredible. There were bloodstains on the raincoat, an attempt had been made to expunge them and yet in this allegedly impartial investigation with a man's life in the balance nobody was prepared to take on such a vital question. Instead what we have from Jolly is the rather puerile statement that Dr Firth could not find the same debris in Ware's trousers as he found in Rowland's, and that it was not the type of debris to be found on bombsites. Manchester was littered with bombsites and Rowland freely admitted having had intercourse with Balchin on one of them. Ware on the other hand came from outside Manchester and if he did kill Balchin then he was on the bombsite for only two very short periods of time, once when unwrapping the hammer, then when committing the murder. He would not necessarily have gotten any debris in his turn-ups.

Having dealt only with the trousers Jolly goes on to summarise Firth's actual conclusions which were as follows:—

'From my observations in this case I am of the opinion that the description given by Ware of his attack on the deceased is not consistent with the facts in this case. There is no evidence from his clothing that he was ever on the site under the conditions described by him.'

After copying out Firth's conclusions I went back over that part of the report. Was it possible that Jolly had provided him only with Ware's trousers? The answer is no. Jolly specifically refers to Ware's 'clothing'; moreover it had been handed to Firth at the end of January, over three weeks before Jolly was appointed. Yet the only reference to bloodstains is that there were none on Ware's trousers.

To return to the raincoat, it was bloodstained. But Jolly — and seemingly Firth too — found this of no interest. If Ware was telling the truth in his retraction then the stains should have matched his blood group. If, on the other hand, his confession was true then the bloodstains should have matched Balchin's. Possibly they had a common group, but that should not have precluded mention of the issue.

Yet mention there was not. If the blood matched Ware but not Balchin, end of story. The rest of the report would have been superfluous. But there is not any reference to whose group the blood matched.

Why?

Jolly ignored or covered up — decide for yourselves which is the more appropriate term — the entire matter.

As for Firth, we have met the good Doctor before, at Rowland's trial. There he decided the complete absence of blood on Rowland's clothes did not eliminate him. But after analysing Ware's clothing, which included a raincoat from which he had attempted to obliterate bloodstains, he concluded that Ware could safely be eliminated from the case.

I make no comment. I leave it to the reader to decide whether any double standard was employed here.

After this the report peters out amidst details of Ware's history and a flurry of personal opinions from Jolly and the prison medical staff. One is tempted to ask what the prison visitors thought! There is an opinion that Ware was a hoaxer, an inference that he made a habit of confessing to murders and from Jolly himself the conclusion that Ware was morbidly obsessed by murder. The opinion is irrelevant, there is no evidence to support the notion that Ware habitually made confessions to murders and a morbid interest in crime would hardly absolve him of murdering anybody himself; quite the contrary.

There are however two glaring omissions from Mr Jolly's cast list. Conspicuous by the complete absence are 'Frank Something' and 'The Scotsman'. Remember them? They were the two convicts who allegedly helped Ware build up his knowledge of the case. Although Ware said that he did not know their surnames, in itself a dubious proposition if he was telling the truth, there should not have been any great difficulty in identifying them. Instead they disappear without trace. Why? We do not know, but perhaps we can guess.

The last item of any importance in the report related solely to Rowland. It was a statement made to Jolly by Mrs Ida Hollenschade who was the part owner of Grafton's hotel where Rowland stayed on the night of October 20th. It will be remembered that one of the points at issue during Rowland's trial was whether or not he greased his hair. According to Hollenschade, Rowland's hair had been greased during his stay at the hotel. She had insisted on him resting his head on a piece of calico whilst he slept so that he did not smear the pillowcase with grease.

Mrs Hollenschade did not give evidence at the trial. There is no indication that she ever told anybody about this prior to speaking to Jolly in late February, 1947. One would have thought that it was particularly important for Burke and Hinchcliffe to be present during her evidence, just as they would have been had she appeared in Court. But as usual Rowland's interests were ignored.

For the record, after an important trial all sorts of people lurking on the periphery of its events make claims which they have never made before. Jolly was well aware of this. He was also aware that Hollenschade's evidence would not have been permitted at the Appeal Court. It would have been excluded on the same grounds as Mrs Coppock's. Walter Harris, the co-owner of the hotel, did give evidence at the trial and made no mention of this incident. The kindest comment which can be made about Mrs Hollenschade is that her memory improved somewhat late in the day. Yet Jolly does not question the validity of her statement. He does not warn the Home Secretary that this so called evidence would have been inadmissible at the Appeal and perhaps even at the trial itself if Hollenschade had only come forward after the issue had been raised. He does not even ask her why she had failed to come forward before! Instead he includes her testimony without question and without comment. This was grossly unfair to Rowland. The inclusion of such a dubious piece of evidence in an allegedly impartial report borders on anarchy. But then it perhaps accurately conveys the whole tenor of the inquiry in-so-far as Rowland's interests were concerned.

For the record, Jolly's conclusions were as follows:—

> *'Having inquired into the confession made by David John Ware of the murder of Olive Balchin, and having considered further information which has become available since the conviction of Walter Graham Rowland for the murder of Olive Balchin. I report that I am satisfied that there are no grounds for thinking that there has been any miscarriage of justice in the conviction of Rowland for that murder.'*

What exactly did Jolly's investigation accomplish? In reality, nothing. The report was one false start from beginning to end. Its conclusions were quite worthless. Jolly attempted to prove Ware's retraction and disprove his confession. He managed neither. The one thing which he did prove was that the Appeal Court had been utterly wrong to wash its hands of the matter. Under its jurisdiction fundamental questions would have been properly answered. Evidence would have been given about the bloodstains on Ware's raincoat; the question of Ware's knowledge of the location of Edward Macdonald's shop would have been closely scrutinised; other details would have been examined with a fine toothcomb. Had Ware retracted his confession in the witness box and substituted the story which he later gave to Jolly, then Rowland's Counsel would have been on hand to examine him about it.

But would Ware have retracted his confession? It is worth recalling that neither Burke nor Hinchcliffe were present at his interview with Jolly. Instead a man of obviously limited intelligence and a history of mental illness, was left to fend for himself in the presence of a top K.C. and two high ranking police officers. Yet as Jolly admits:

> *'After persisting at first in maintaining that his former statements as to the murder were correct, Ware admitted that they were false, saying "I'd better turn it in".'*

We are not told how long Ware persisted with his confession, or the precise reason why he decided to 'turn it in'. But there are some clear hints in the retraction:

> *'My health has not been too good since the outbreak of the war and I really do feel I want some treatment.'*

This may imply that Jolly brought up the subject to Ware's wretched mental history and played upon it, holding out the promise of psychiatric treatment if he jumped through the right hoops. If this was the case then it apparently did not occur to Jolly that Ware was unbalanced enough to have murdered Balchin.

Ware made four statements in all; three comprising his confession and the fourth in which he retracted that confession. Of the three confessional statements only the first two were strictly in his own words. The third, to quote Jolly, 'consisted of replies to questions put to him by Mr Hinchcliffe, Rowland's solicitor.' Ware's answers were recorded by Hinchcliffe who clearly applied his own grammar and punctuation to them. Of Ware's retraction, Jolly states:

> *'A statement in writing was then taken from him... and written down by Inspector Hannam.'*

The implication here is that Hannam was recording Ware's own words. But consider the following extract:

> *'...I didn't realise the serious consequences it might entail had the confession been believed.'*

Phraseology such as 'serious consequences', and words like 'entail' do not conform to the use of English which Ware displayed in his opening two statements. The first of these was very brief and to the point. The second was much longer and tells a good deal more about his standard of literacy than the first. To put it bluntly Ware's usage of the English language in that second statement was wincingly crude. But the whole tone and tenor of his retraction was on a much higher plane. Either Ware's grasp of the language improved beyond all recognition in a remarkably short period of time, or the retraction was not in his own words. In fact it is even on a much higher level than the question and answer session taken down by Hinchcliffe and abounds with words such as 'magnified', 'spectacular', 'tableaux', 'depicting', 'gratuity', and articulate phrases and sentences like 'snatched him from the gallows', and 'From the conversation I judged that both women were married and aged about 35 to 40'. In short, there is a suggestion that words were put into Ware's mouth.

Now of course none of this proves, beyond doubt, that Ware was guilty. But for the moment let us leave that particular issue and concentrate on how the Jolly report relates to Walter Rowland.

The real point at issue is whether Ware's confession would have altered the verdict of the jury. The jury themselves could not answer this question; the Appeal Court ran away from it, and Jolly, with neither the time nor the inclination to examine it properly, sought refuge behind a fetid attempt to prove Ware's retraction. The Appeal Court mistakenly said that it would have been usurping the function of a jury; Jolly did usurp that function. He also set himself up as Ware's defence Counsel, and donned the ermine robes of a phantom trial Judge. His report is a strange "Alice in Wonderland" affair in which he places Ware on trial; defends him without the hindrance of a prosecution; vaults onto the bench to sum up in his favour, and then finally does a quick shuffle across to the jury box when he finds him not guilty. Perhaps the kindest way of explaining Jolly's conduct would be to compare him with a Mathematics Professor who misreads the question in front of him, tackles it by using the wrong formulae, and ends up with a thoroughly warped answer. My own view is somewhat less tolerant. I believe that the question of Rowland's innocence was entirely subordinated to preserving the fiction of judicial infallibility. Setting Rowland free would have been an admission of error. The performance of the judicial system and of the Police would have been called sharply into question. Armed with the knowledge of just how close the state had come to putting an innocent man to death, the anti-capital punishment lobby would have had a field day.

Now an additional factor creeps into the reckoning; one which no doubt lurked just below the surface of Jolly's mind throughout the inquiry. Pardoning Rowland would have created a highly complex and potentially damaging situation. A crime demands a culprit. If Rowland was not the guilty party then someone else would have to pay the price; Ware for instance. But Ware could not simply be shunted into the death cell in direct substitution for Rowland. There would first have to be a trial. What if Ware retracted his confession and the jury believed him? The conventionally minded would then have questioned the wisdom of Rowland's pardon, to say nothing of the competence of Mr John Catterall Jolly, K.C. On the other hand, if Ware retracted his confession and the jury did not believe him, the conviction would still be open to grave doubts. Much of the evidence used to convict Rowland would have been called in Ware's defence, thereby giving rise to such doubts. Some people would have seen it as an attempt to railroad an innocent man to the gallows. Moreover, then, as now, the jury system had its critics, and they would have capitalised on the fact that twenty-four different jurors had split evenly down the middle when assessing the reliability of witnesses who had testified against Rowland, but for Ware.

There was one way of avoiding these problems without disproving Ware's confession; advise the Home Secretary that his story could neither be proved or disproved, and recommend that Rowland's sentence be commuted to life imprisonment. But even this puerile attempt at compromise would have been pregnant with difficulties. Press and Public, applying their own rationale to the situation, would have argued that if there was nothing in Ware's confession then there was no reason for Rowland not to hang; if on the other hand there was something in it then Rowland should receive the benefit of the doubt. Cries of 'cover up' and 'evasion' would have been heard everywhere.

The whole situation was fraught with danger. Looking at it, Jolly must have seen legal bogeymen waiting to spring out at him from every nook and cranny. The only way of steering a path through them was to induce Ware to retract his confession and then attempt to put together a case to support the retraction.

Faced with the choice of either leaving Rowland to his fate or of plunging into cold and complex waters in which he had no wish to tread, Jolly opted to take the easiest and safest way out. Ultimately, it is fair to say of him that he dipped his hands into the muddied waters of the case and then dried them on the rope around Rowland's neck.

February 26th. The measured tread of the Prison Governor as he makes his way to the death cell. Prison Governors have placed on record their abhorrence at having to tell a man that he must hang; the psychological scars remained for life. The Governor of Strangeways that day had not one but two onerous pieces of information to impart. One was that the inquiry had found against Rowland; the other was that he would not be reprieved.

After hearing the news a crushed and bitter Rowland sat down and wrote the letter which I quoted from earlier. Nothing in life became Walter Rowland as the leaving of it. Through its incompetence the legal system had martyred a child killer and anti-social misfit. I hold no brief for Walter Rowland as a man. I believe he was a worthless lump of humanity. But I believe he was innocent of murdering Olive Balchin and should not have hanged. I also believe that the poor prostitute victim of this ugly crime deserved better than that an innocent man should pay for it whilst her real killer went free.

Rowland wrote these words in his last letter:—

> '...you have my sacred word at this time when I am too near death's door, that I am an innocent man.'

A few hours later he was dead.

(10)

After Rowland's execution David Ware went to hell fast as the saying goes. His mental affliction grew worse, and following his release from prison he wandered pathetically from one mental home to the next; a thoroughly substandard human being whose only real connection with the World was that he happened to exist in it.

Finally, on the afternoon of July 10th, 1951, the remaining cords of his sanity snapped completely. He bought a hammer from a hardware shop in Bristol and shortly afterwards launched a murderous attack on a woman named Adeleine Fuidge. He later surrendered himself to the Police saying that he had killed a woman and that he kept on having the urge to hit women over the head. Fortunately, his attack on Mrs Fuidge was not fatal. Charged with attempted murder, Ware was found to be unfit to plead. He was then committed to Broadmoor. In 1954 he ended his life by hanging himself. Appropriately enough the date was April 1st: All Fool's Day!

The attack on Adeleine Fuidge was an exact replica of the murder of Olive Balchin. It could almost be described as an action replay! Ware admitted a compulsion towards hitting women over the head. Later he hanged himself, an action which could be interpreted as a belated atonement for the Balchin murder. What do these facts suggest? Do they amount to conclusive evidence that it was Ware, and not Rowland, who slew Olive Balchin?

In legal terms, the real importance of Ware's behaviour lies in the fact that no reasonable jury could have convicted Rowland if they had known that a mentally disturbed man would later make a full, highly credible, confession to the crime and then try to commit an identical murder.

Strictly speaking, it is not really necessary to go any further. But let us examine the evidence against Ware and see where it takes us.

David Ware was mentally ill. That is beyond doubt. In 1943 he was diagnosed as a manic depressive. I am not competent to give a psychiatric assessment of this condition but manic depressives do suffer from violent mood swings. In Ware's case this is borne out by his criminal history. Save for the attempted blackmail, which was ongoing when he was arrested, his crimes were invariably followed by his giving himself up. His confession to the murder of Olive Balchin fits this pattern exactly.

Ware was clearly suffering from an extreme form of depression. He was unable to support or succour his family; unable to work at a job, put down roots, create or maintain relationships; unable even to bear arms in His Majesty's forces at a time when manpower was at an absolute premium and even child murderers were being released for service. According to Jolly, he did however develop a morbid interest in murder which harnessed to his illness, his lack of any career focus or regular sexual outlet, can only be viewed as a highly dangerous development. Ware admitted, after the attack on Mrs Fuidge, that he felt compelled to hit women over the head.

The attack on Adeleine Fuidge exactly mirrored the Balchin murder. Ware bought a hammer from a hardware shop and went to a place called "The Downs". There he accosted Mrs Fuidge who was sitting on a park bench. After a while he suggested that they go for a walk. Then he got her to sit down beside him on some grass. At this point the words of his confession to the Balchin murder rustle uneasily in the mind:—

> *'I... suggested moving further inside [the bombsite] where we could not be seen.'*

Once they were seated he launched a maniacal assault on Mrs Fuidge. One thing, and one thing only saved her life: the hammer head flew off after the first blow. Even so he continued to rain blows on her head until he was satisfied she was dead. Then he ran away. Three days later he gave himself up to the Police.

That is the psychological evidence against Ware. It is evidence both of a dangerous and deteriorating condition and a system of murder allied to that condition.

Now we look at the circumstantial evidence. It is for you to decide but in my own view it is of the most powerful that could be adduced against an accused man.

Ware provided a complete description of the locale of Edward Macdonald's shop. He gave a description of Macdonald himself; he said that the hammer was on sale in the window along with other second hand items, exactly as Macdonald testified. He fitted the shopkeeper's description of the purchaser and repeated the conversation which Macdonald said he had had with the man.

The time at which the hammer was purchased dovetailed with Ware picking Balchin up in Piccadilly twenty minutes later. Balchin was not seen in her usual haunts that night. Nobody has disputed the existence of the cinema, or of the route which Ware says he and Balchin took to Deansgate.

Ware's description of the murder was entirely in accordance with the evidence. The injuries were to the right side of her head and she had tried to protect herself and lost a fingernail. She was found next to a wall and blood had spurted, exactly as the Pathologist said. Ware said that it spurted on to his raincoat and there was blood on the front of the coat and both the sleeves. Remember here also the evidence in the Beron case which I quoted earlier. Blood would have been expected to run down the murder weapon and drop on to the assailant's sleeve. Afterwards Ware had attempted to remove the blood on the sleeves.

Ware said that afterwards he ran to Salford station. There he caught a bus to Piccadilly and then another to Stockport. Despite Jolly's attempts, the time at which Ware arrived at Richards lodging house could not be ascertained except that it was after eleven.

Most of these details could not be gleaned from the Press. Only the murderer could know them. Even those that were available from other sources could only be obtained by making a nonsense of Ware's retraction.

That then is the factual case against David Ware. You do not need the base machinations of a John Catterall Jolly in order to decide it. Simply look at it logically, simply and fairly.

I will interpose a third possibility and say that on the evidence overall it is not entirely absurd that the murderer was not Rowland or Ware, but a third party. If so then that would be a bizarre situation, but perhaps no more outlandish than the Evans-Christie case which was more suited to detective fiction than real life.

But personally I think it wholly unlikely. It really boils down to Rowland or Ware. I will not recap, but think for yourselves. Do you think there is any real evidence against Rowland, and if so, does it override the strength of the defence case which he put forward? Or do you find the case against Ware, provided by his own testimony and that of his mental state, consistent and cogent? My own view is that Ware was undoubtedly the guilty party.

The innocence of John Dickman and Walter Rowland is subordinate to the issue of the system which tried and executed them. This book has looked at that system in operation. It is for you now to decide for yourselves whether you think that system is adequate. It is, after all, a system which operates in your name.

EPILOGUE. LESSONS LEARNED?

Five years later Walter Rowland's execution, two young Mancunians, Edward Devlin and Alfred Burns, were convicted of the murder of a woman in Liverpool.

After the trial a fifteen year old girl came forward to say that one of the leading prosecution witnesses, a girlfriend of Devlin's, had told her that her evidence against Devlin had been a pack of lies: that the real killer was another of her boyfriends.

The case went to the Appeal Court where Devlin sought to introduce the girl's story into evidence. As with Rowland, the senior Appeal Judge was Lord Goddard, the Lord Chief Justice, and once again he refused to hear the fresh evidence, saying:

> *'If necessary that matter can be submitted to those whose duty it is to advise the Crown in these matters. It is not a matter which this court can go into.'*

The Home Secretary, Sir David Maxwell-Fyfe, duly instructed Denis Gerrard Q.C. (later a High Court Judge) to investigate the Devlin/Burns case. Gerrard was ordered to:

> '*...consider any further relevant information laid before him and to report whether, in his opinion, the result of his investigation affords any reasonable grounds for thinking that there has been or may have been a miscarriage of justice.*'

Gerrard carried out his inquiries and reported that:

> '*There has been no miscarriage of justice.*'

This despite the fact that Devlin's girlfriend admitted making the remark to the fifteen year old. Her excuse was that it was a lie. Gerrard dismissed the matter with the astonishing comment:

> '*Her motives for making the untrue statements are a matter for speculation orly.*'

It was precisely this matter of speculation that he had been asked to investigate!

Devlin and Burns were executed on April 25th, 1952.

Despite Gerrard's conclusion, the case does seem to have struck a cord of anxiety in Lord Goddard's mind. Initiating a debate to introduce a retrial facility for criminal cases into English law, he said:

> '*There was no power to order a new trial, but what is in fact a new trial took place without oath, without counsel and in private.*'

Implicit in these words is a belated admission that the Appeal Court treated not only Devlin and Burns but also Walter Rowland very shabbily.

APPENDIX ONE
Charles Bolton?

Leslie Hale recounts the following story in his book "Hanged in Error".

Whilst Rowland's trial was in progress, a Manchester lodging house keeper approached the defence and told them that on the night of Friday, October 18th he had let a room to a man of medium height who had a pale face, dark well greased hair, and was dressed in a fawn raincoat and a blue suit.

At 7:50 on the morning of Sunday, October 20th, as Olive Balchin's as yet undiscovered body was lying on the bombsite, the man arrived at the lodging house dirty, dishevelled and upset. He told the landlord:

'I have almost committed a murder.'

Presumably some time after October 23rd (Hale is not clear when), the lodger also claimed to have been in the Queen's Cafe on the night of the murder, and to have seen the man with the two women.

The lodger came forward. He proved that he was not involved in the murder, but stuck to his story about the cafe. The man, he said, was not Rowland.

It may well be that the mysterious lodger was the unsatisfactory defence witness Charles Bolton. If so, then it is hardly surprising that nobody attached any credence to his evidence.

APPENDIX TWO
Reports after Jolly

To the best of my knowledge the Jolly inquiry was the first of its kind in a murder case. Ronald True[*] was the subject of an inquiry whilst he occupied the death cell, but that was to determine sanity, not culpability.

However, the Jolly report appears to have set something of a precedent, a highly unfortunate and unhealthy one whose progeny has been sickly and undistinguished.

The Gerrard inquiry into the convictions of Devlin and Burns has already been examined. Hot on its heels came the infamous Scott Henderson report on the Timothy Evans case. To recap briefly: Evans was charged with strangling his wife and daughter. Tried for the murder of the child, he was convicted and

---

[*]   Convicted in 1922 of the murder of a prostitute.

hanged. At his trial he accused his neighbour, John Christie, of the murders. Three years later Christie was exposed as a mass murderer who had strangled several women in an identical fashion to Evans' wife and daughter. Before his execution Christie confessed to the murder of Mrs Evans. At that point the Home Secretary, Sir David Maxwell-Fyfe, commissioned John Scott Henderson Q.C. to report on whether Evans had been wrongly hanged. Incredibly, Scott Henderson decided that he had not been! Doubtless he took the view that clearing the name of one rather pathetic little man, three years dead, was not worth the risk of damaging public confidence in the judicial system. Equally there can be no real doubt that Maxwell-Fyfe shared this opinion.

But in fact they were making an error of fantastic proportions.

Opponents of capital punishment believed they had a genuine *cause célèbre* in Timothy Evans. In reality they did not. Evans' conviction was a freak accident, unlikely to be repeated in a thousand years. On the evidence before them his jury could not have brought in any other verdict. Evans was not so much a victim of a miscarriage of justice as a bizarre and unique set of circumstances. It is fair to say that his execution was really an act of capricious fate. Clearing him, which would have been sensible and popular, entailed no danger of seriously denting the credibility of British Justice. Quite the contrary.

Instead, Maxwell-Fyfe and Scott Henderson served up a document which bordered on idiocy. A large segment of the community was outraged. Articulate opinion condemned the report as at best an insult; at worst a cover-up. The campaign to abolish capital punishment was given its first real martyr — courtesy of one of its leading defenders!*

Criticising Scott Henderson became something of a popular literary blood sport. The report was also a Godsend to tub thumping politicians. Finally, successive Home Secretaries wearied of scraping it up off the floor of the Commons and in 1966 a public inquiry was set up under Justice Daniel Brabin.

Brabin decided that on the balance of probabilities Evans was innocent of murdering his child, but guilty of slaying his wife. Eventually this conclusion led to his being awarded a posthumous free pardon. But in fact Brabin's conclusions were mind boggling; his report deficient in logic and intellectually dishonest. He spent much of his time shoring up Scott Henderson's long discredited findings, in the process quarrelling with point after point which favoured Evans. When at the very end of the report, Brabin concluded that Evans had not murdered his daughter he was therefore forced to indulge in reasoning which was specious and unconvincing. Nevertheless, it was sufficient to dump the red hot political potato of Evans' innocence back into the lap of the Home Secretary. As an exercise in fence sitting it was worthy of a Talleyrand: as an objective inquiry it failed utterly.

---

*   Maxwell-Fyfe

Six years after Parliament voted to abolish capital punishment, Lewis Hawser Q.C. presented his findings on the case of James Hanratty. Hanratty was a young burglar who had been executed in 1962 for the murder of a research scientist. The evidence against him at his trial was highly tenuous, even contradictory, and he put forward a strong defence. Unfortunately it was marred by a lie which he retracted during the trial. Had he told the truth beforehand then it seems certain that he would have tipped the balance in his favour. Some of the evidence on his behalf which emerged after the trial was particularly impressive.

However, just like a stuck gramophone needle, Hawser went the way of Jolly, Gerrard, Scott Henderson and Brabin in deciding that justice had not miscarried. Home Secretary Roy Jenkins praised him publicly as a Counsel of the highest repute. Nobody would quarrel with that. Nor would anyone question his integrity. Where he is open to legitimate criticism is that he did not do a particularly good job. Even the best of Generals fight bad battles: Napoleon at Waterloo, Wellington at Fuentes de Onoro, Grant at Cold Harbour and so on. Advocates, even of the highest calibre, are no different.

The most recent English report is the Fisher report on the convictions of Colin Lattimore, Ronald Leighton and Ahmet Salih. They were convicted in 1972 of being concerned in the death of a transvestite named Maxwell Confait. Lattimore, an educationally sub-normal, was found guilty of manslaughter, Leighton, a borderline ESN, of murder, and Salih of arson. Lattimore and Leighton were also convicted of arson (setting fire to Confait's room after his death).

In 1975 the cases of all three were referred back to the Court of Appeal. After a week-long hearing the Court decided that the convictions had to be set aside. Shortly afterwards the Home Secretary asked Sir Henry Fisher, a retired High Court Judge, to lead an inquiry into the case. In October, 1977 Fisher produced his findings: Lattimore, he thought, was probably guilty of arson but had not been involved in the death of Confait: Leighton and Salih, he decided, were probably guilty of arson, and were also probably connected with the killing.

The main evidence against Lattimore, Leighton and Salih were confessions which they had made to the police, confessions which it was now alleged were false and had been extracted from them by improper means. Fisher concluded that Lattimore's confession to arson had been true, but that he had falsely confessed to being involved in Confait's death at the behest of Leighton and Salih! Meanwhile, said the Judge, Leighton and Salih's confessions had been true, except in so far as they had been falsified to include Lattimore! If this sounds like double-dutch then it is because it is double-dutch!

Happily, we now know that Lattimore, Leighton and Salih were innocent. A few years later a man arrested for other offences made a statement to the effect that he had been present when Confait had been killed and named the man whom he said was responsible. This man was duly questioned. No charges were actually preferred, but the police announced that they were perfectly satisfied that one of the two men had killed Maxwell Confait. Lattimore, Leighton and Salih were then compensated as victims of a miscarriage of justice. Their compensations owe absolutely nothing to a report which produced only gobbledegook.

Finally, there is the Hunter report on the case of Patrick Meehan, a Glaswegian who was convicted of the murder of a woman in Ayr in 1969. Meehan was given a free pardon in 1976 following confessions by two other men. Lord Hunter, a Scottish Judge, was then asked to inquire into the case. In 1981 he produced a mammoth report which ran to three hefty volumes of evidence and a further volume of exhibits. In the main the Hunter report is exhaustive, authoritative, and highly objective, but Hunter chose to ruminate at length on the highly controversial notion that the murder could have involved more than two men, thus implying that Meehan could have been connected with it after all.

Hunter was right to speculate. His brief was to make a complete inquiry into all aspects of the case. However, he left the unfortunate impression of believing in his multiple killers theory. In advancing it as a serious possibility he opened up an avenue down which nobody, not the police, not the prosecution in two trials, nor the Scottish Office, had ever wandered previously, and he produced little or no evidence to support his meandering stroll. In the end, albeit unintentionally, he threw dust in the eyes of his Employers and tarnished Meehan's pardon. His report redounds with the expression 'clear and convincing evidence', and it is the very lack of this in support of his speculation which is worrying. He was right to examine the issue, but in my opinion, wrong to suggest that there might be substance to it without more tangible support.

The questions which this series of reports raises are simple ones: is there any merit in such a system of examining these issues, and if not, then is it not time we replaced them with something better?

APPENDIX THREE

Innocent?

The exact number of men and women wrongly hanged in Britain this Century will never be known.

Nobody can say with certainty whether somebody is innocent. We can only go by personal opinion. Below I list the names of twenty-three people (excluding Dickman and Rowland) about whose guilt I have a doubt, some stronger than others.

Herbert Bennett 1901

Hawley Crippen 1910*

Frederick Seddon 1912

Louis Mackay a.k.a. John Williams 1912

Louis Voisin 1918

Edward Black 1922

Edith Thompson 1923

Edward Rowlands 1923

Norman Thorne 1925

Alfred Rouse 1931

William Podmore 1930

Frederick Parker 1934

Charlotte Bryant 1936

Robert Hoolhouse 1938

Timothy Evans 1950

Alfred Moore 1951

Alfred Burns 1952

Edward Devlin 1952

Derek Bentley 1953

Alfred Whiteway 1953

Jack May 1960*

George Riley 1961

James Hanratty 1962

* In the cases of Crippen and May the question is whether it was murder or manslaughter.

SELECT BIBLIOGRAPHY

Brabin, Sir Daniel, *The Case of Timothy John Evans*, H.M.S.O., 1966

Bresler, Fenton, *Scales of Justice*, Weidenfeld & Nicholsen

Cecil, Henry, *Trial of Walter Graham Rowland*, David & Charles, 1975

Coleridge, Lord, *This for Remembrance*, Fisher Unwin, 1925

Fisher, Sir Henry, *Inquiry into the Death of Maxwell Confait*, H.M.S.O., 1977

Foot, Paul, *Who Killed Hanratty*, Jonathan Cape, 1971

Hale, Leslie, *Hanged in Error*, Penguin, 1961

Hastings, Sir Patrick, *Cases in Court*, William Heinemann, 1949

Hawser, Lewis, *The Case of James Hanratty*, H.M.S.O., 1975

Hollis, Paget & Silverman, *Hanged and Innocent?*, Gollancz, 1953

Hunter, Lord, *Inquiry into the Murder of Mrs Rachel Ross*, H.M.S.O., 1981

Jessel, David, *Trial and Error*, Headline, 1994

Koestler, Arthur, *Reflections on Hanging*, Gollancz, 1956

O'Brien, Sean, *Bloody Ambassadors*, Poolbeg, 1993

Rowan-Hamilton, Sidney, *Trial of J.A. Dickman*, William Hodge, 1926

Taylor, Bernard, *Perfect Murder*, Grafton Books, 1987

Watson, Eric, *Trials of Adolf Beck*, William Hodge, 1924

Whittington-Egan, Richard, *The Ordeal of Philip Yale Drew*, Harrap, 1972

Woffinden, Bob, *Miscarriages of Justice*, Hodder & Stoughton, 1987

Woodruff, Douglas, *The Tichborne Claimant*, Hollis & Carter, 1957

Yallop, David A., *To Encourage the Others*, W.H. Allen, 1971